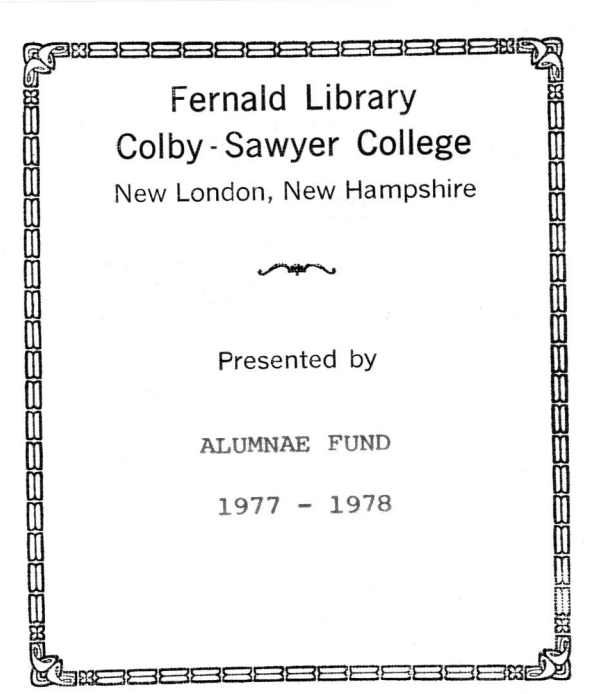

THE FAUVES

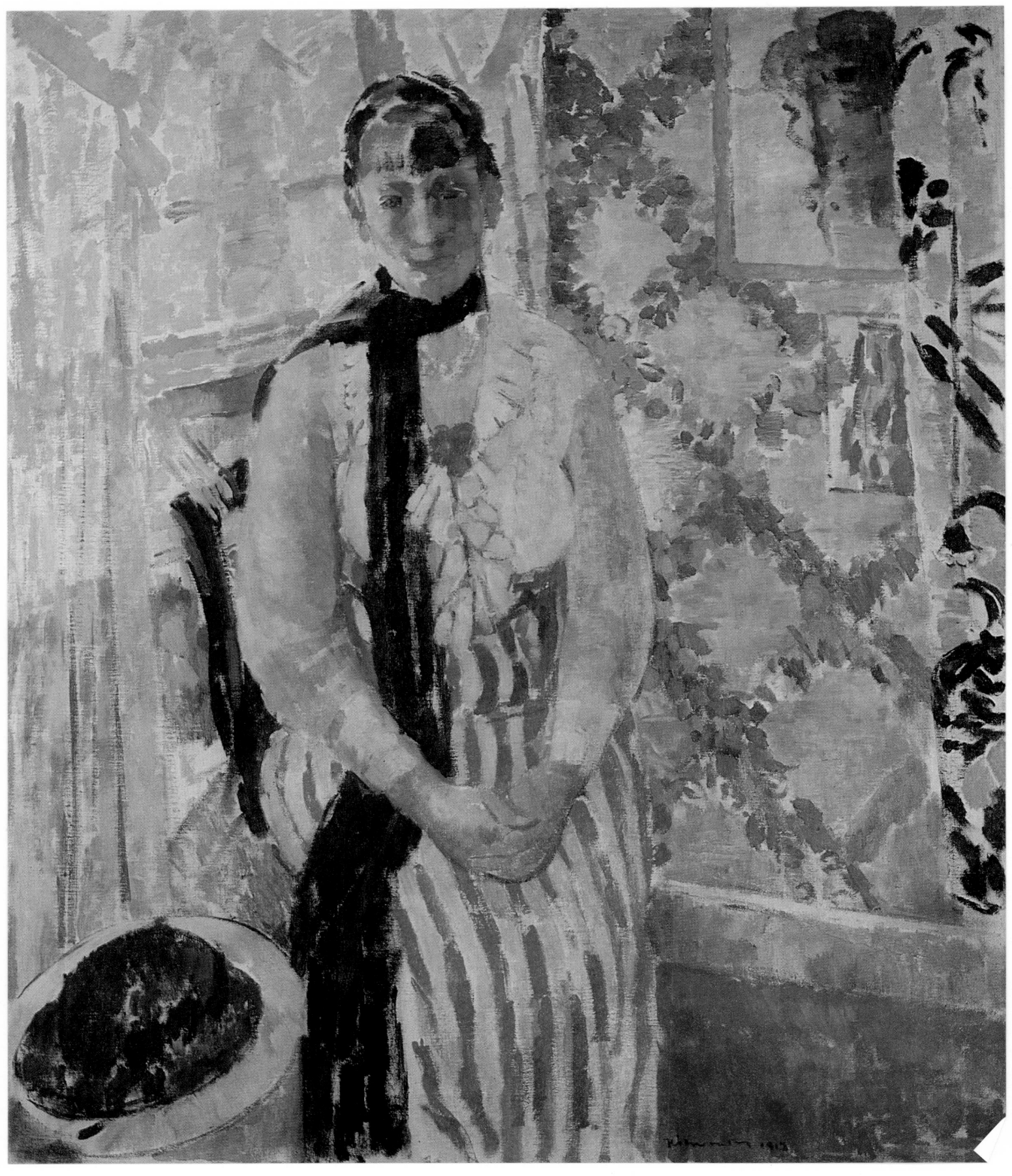

THE
FAUVES

Gaston Diehl

HARRY N. ABRAMS, INC., *Publishers*, NEW YORK

Nai Y. Chang, *Vice-President, Design and Production*
John L. Hochmann, *Executive Editor*
Margaret L. Kaplan, *Managing Editor*
Barbara Lyons, *Director, Photo Department, Rights and Reproductions*
Robin Fox, *Designer*

Library of Congress Cataloging in Publication Data

Diehl, Gaston.
    The fauves.

    (Library of great art movements)
    Bibliography: p.
    1. Fauvism—History.   2. Painting, Modern—20th
Century.   I. Title.
ND196.F3D5313   759.06   72-5650
ISBN 0-8109-0114-5

Library of Congress Catalogue Card Number: 72-5650
Published by Harry N. Abrams, Incorporated, New York, 1975
Printed and bound in Japan

CONTENTS

COLORPLATES

ACKNOWLEDGMENTS

I wish to express my warm gratitude to all those who have so generously assisted me in my research:

foreign cultural attachés and advisers in Paris: Gheorghe Baltac (Rumania), H. Bugge-Mahrt (Norway), Guy C. Buysse (Belgium), Sadi de Gorter (Netherlands), Frédéric Dubois and Charles Hummel (Switzerland), Marat Kharazian (U.S.S.R.), Lorenz von Numers (Finland), Gabor Pap (Hungary), Professor Giovanni della Pozza (Italy).

abroad: P. A. Ade, Director of the Haus der Kunst, Munich; Katarina Ambrozic, Curator of the National Museum, Belgrade; M. Bafcop, archivist-curator of the Musée-Centre Culturel, Mechelen; Barbu Brezianu, Director of Research at the Art History Institute, Bucharest; Mme Chartrain-Hebbelinck, Musée d'Art Moderne, Brussels; Dr. G. Händler, Director of the Wilhelm-Lehmbruck-Museum der Stadt, Duisburg; Luc Hasaerts, Brussels; Jiri Kotalik, Director of the National Gallery, Prague; Myron Laskin, Jr., and Joanna Marsden, The National Gallery of Canada, Ottawa; Marija Pusic, Curator of the Museum of Modern Art, Belgrade; Franco Russoli, Curator of the Brera Gallery, Milan; Dr. Laszlo Tarr, Editor-in-chief of the Corvina Press, Budapest; Gabriel White, The Arts Council of Great Britain, London; René Cheval and René Hombourger of the French Cultural Services in Germany.

artists: Béla Czóbel, Sonia Delaunay-Terk; also Mmes Camoin and Larionov.

collectors: B. J. Fize, R. Stanley Johnson, David and Samuel Josefowitz, Claude Laurens, Pierre Lévy, Mme Lucie Martinais-Manguin, Raymond Nacenta, Georges Pillement, Jacques Pignet, Dr. Jean Valtat, Georg Waechter Memorial Foundation.

curators: Jean Adhémar, Chief Curator, Print Room, Bibliothèque Nationale, Paris; Pierre Berjole, Curator, Musée de l'Annonciade, Saint-Tropez; Victor Beyer, Curator, Musée des Beaux-Arts, Strasbourg; Danielle Giraudy, Curator, Musée Cantini, Marseilles; Michel Hoog, Curator, Musée National d'Art Moderne, Paris; Mme Latour, Curator, Musées de Marseille; Mlle Martin-Mery, Curator, Musées de Bordeaux; Mlle Popovitch, Curator, Musées de Rouen; Claude Souviron, Curator, Musée des Beaux-Arts, Nantes; Mme G. Testanière, Curator, Nouveau Musée des Beaux-Arts, Le Havre.

art galleries: Galerie Charpentier, Galerie Maeght, Galerie de Paris, Galerie Denise Valtat.

THE FAUVES

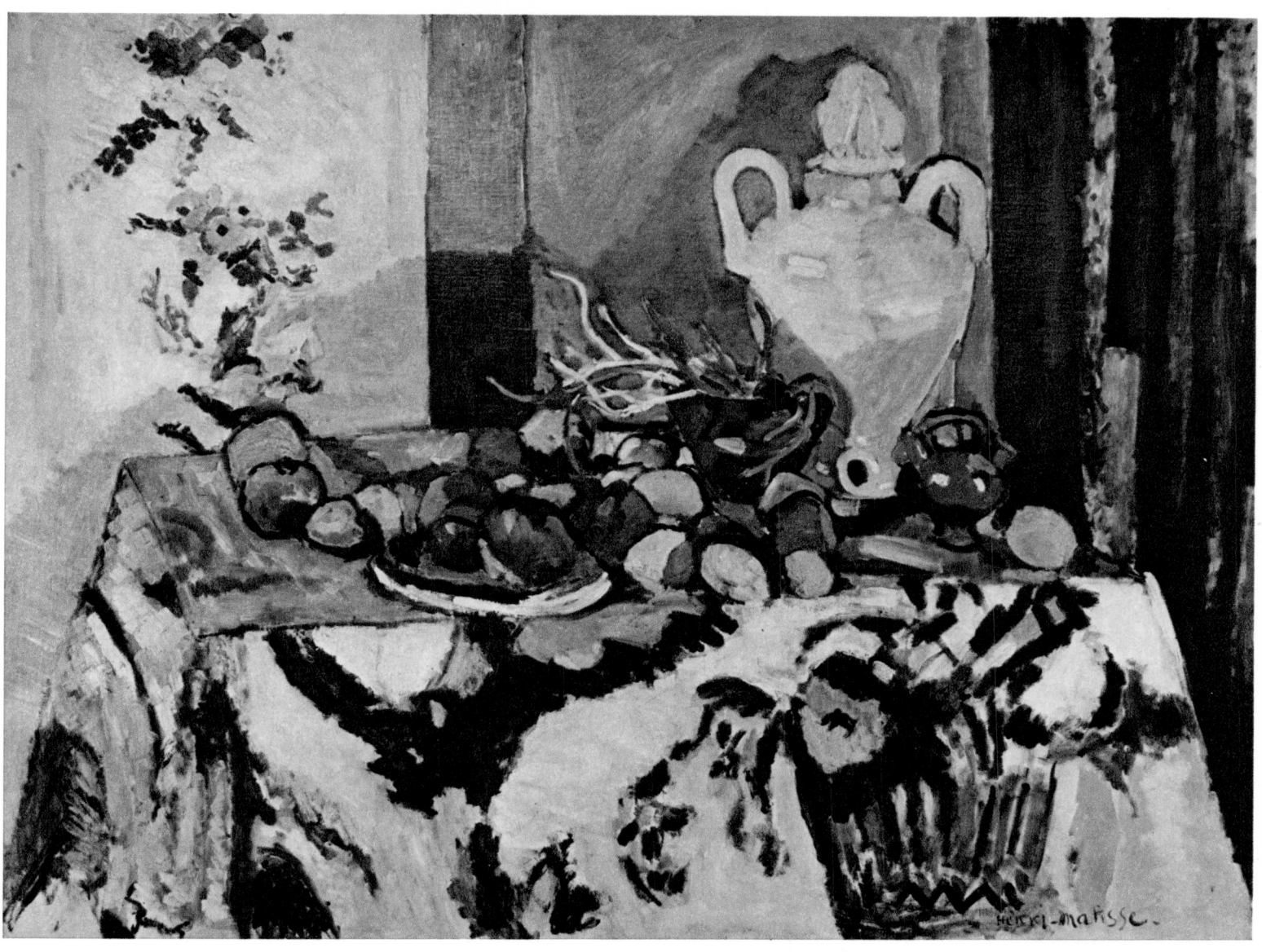

1. Henri Matisse. BLUE STILL LIFE. 1907. Oil on canvas, 35 × 45 3/4″. © *The Barnes Foundation, Merion, Pa.*

A DEFINITION

Seen in itself, at the moment it happened, the event may seem rather insignificant, one more anecdotal incident destined for oblivion.

At the 1905 Salon d'Automne, held in the recently opened Grand Palais, a few young artists who have already gained recognition—Marquet, Manguin, Camoin—together with such newcomers as Derain, Vlaminck, Van Dongen—find their works assembled in one room around those of Matisse, considered to be the leader of the group. The striking unity of the canvases, with their heightened colors, creates a sensation and announces the birth of a new school. The public, however, bursts out laughing and thinks it is having its leg pulled. The worthy bourgeois of the day, it is true, are in the habit of going to the Salon des Indépendants and the Salon d'Automne to exchange jokes and sarcastic remarks about the new artists. The press follows suit, and a page of *L'Illustration* of November 4 reproduces several pictures in order to hold them up to ridicule, including in its condemnation such other painters as Valtat and Rouault, whose works are exhibited in the neighboring rooms.

Who could have taken these artists seriously in the middle of *la belle époque*, in a heedless and continually festive capital, where the newspapers were more concerned with the exploits of the queens of *tout Paris*—Caroline Otéro, Emilienne d'Alençon, Liane de Pougy, or Cléo de Mérode—than with the Kaiser's visit to Tangier or the promulgation of the law on the separation of Church and State? Even

and discussed feature of these exhibitions. Art galleries and collectors, particularly from abroad, take a growing interest, with the result that the Fauves finally obtain a certain recognition from the public and press despite the objections and reservations still being voiced even by such critics as Vauxcelles or Malpel, who stand by them and believe in their future.

Everything seems to revert to normal, however, by 1908. There is a general sigh of relief, but a short-lived one, since a new pictorial adventure has begun in the privacy of the studios—Cubism, which soon replaces Fauvism at the Kahnweiler Gallery. In the *Gil Blas* of March 20, Vauxcelles sadly remarks of the Salon des Indépendants: "Alas! The heroic period is over. Where are the days when the Independents, with their violent excesses, provoked the Homeric mirth of the bourgeoisie and the press? It's really sad." Yet he is the first to congratulate Friesz, still exhibiting among the Fauves, for having abandoned the path along which "he has been straying for the last two or three years," and for finally escaping "from his abstractions" to "join the true French tradition."

At the Salon d'Automne of the same year, the Fauve heresy seems to have subsided, with many of its adherents choosing to compromise or give up the struggle. The group has disappeared once and for all. Its former members are now scattered at random in the different rooms. Matisse finds himself in near isolation, presenting an impressive array of works and defining shortly thereafter—in *La Grande Revue* of December 25—the aesthetic principles that govern his art, it being understood that these principles, which he has every intention of following, are not binding on anyone but himself.

And so, scarcely born and after only three short years of development, Fauvism is ingloriously liquidated. Abandoned or disowned by most of its members, the group is totally disbanded. Nor was there any reason to believe at the time that the incident was not irrevocably closed.

If we ignore the future of these artists—and it is in fact better to forget what we know about their development, their changes of direction, the successes and failures that await them—their association seems fortuitous, destined to be short-lived, and their school all the more ephemeral, not to say artificial.

Unlike their predecessors the Impressionists and the Nabis, they never constituted a truly organized group in the Salons nor in the few galleries where their works were assembled as friendship and circumstances dictated. They did not hold common meetings, nor did they publish a manifesto like their German colleagues, who at the same time were founding Die Brücke.

Hence the rather hasty conclusion reached by certain critics and historians who refuse to admit the existence of a group and still less of a movement. In their eyes, Fauvism remains a simple fit of growing pains, a youthful elation

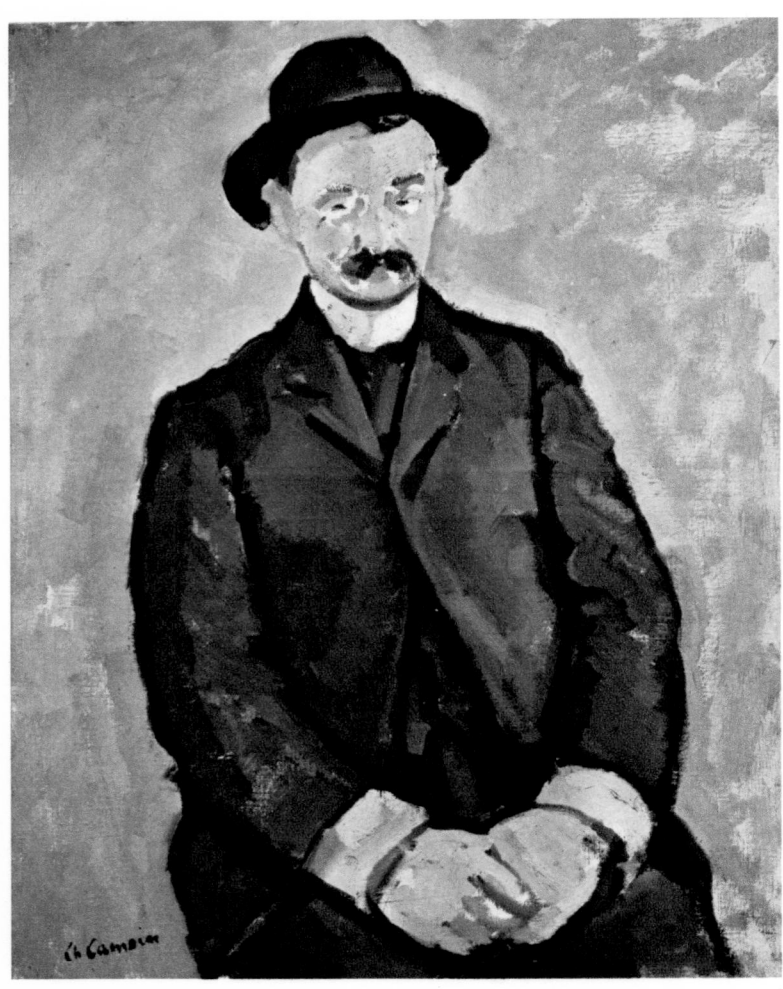

2. Charles Camoin. PORTRAIT OF ALBERT MARQUET. C. 1904. Oil on canvas, 36 1/4 × 28 3/4".
Musée National d'Art Moderne, Paris

the critic Louis Vauxcelles, a friend and defender of these artists, is disconcerted by their latest works and cannot resist making a witticism at their expense by dubbing them *fauves* (wild beasts) in his review in the October 17 issue of *Gil Blas*.

This ironical nickname will stick to them, whether they like it or not, for the rest of their careers. Yet under this flag their rather chance existence as a group, which they themselves never formally acknowledge, gains them notoriety and numbers, attracting such new recruits as Friesz, Dufy, and later Braque. In 1906 and 1907, at the Salon d'Automne and at the Salon des Indépendants as well, the "Fauves' den," as it is derisively called, tends to become the center of attraction and prestige, the most anticipated that seized certain artists, spreading from one to another, until the inevitable moment when each had proved his powers sufficiently to be able to oppose the others.

No one can deny that the course of the history of art, particularly at the beginning of the twentieth century, is almost entirely governed by these strong personalities, who stand out against their period and indeed give it a new face. At rare intervals, however, there arise moments of convergence, of symbiosis, when the efforts of these artists combine and harmonize. The bold impulse that they generate becomes further strengthened and heightened, thereby attracting a wide following.

Fauvism fully deserves its exceptional place in the history of art, because it in fact constituted this unexpected crossroads, this influential meeting place, this privileged stage, and imparted to the period an unprecedented common impulse that corresponded to the diffused aspirations of the time. The movement represented a crucial involvement, a culminating phase for a whole generation. Matisse, his friends, his pupils or followers, and even succeeding generations, all constantly drew upon it as from a fountain of youth, making it "the inexhaustible source of limitless beginnings," to borrow Jean Cassou's excellent phrase. One might also quote the definition proposed by the same author in 1960: "In the final analysis, Fauvism must be considered not as a school, but as the moment when, in its continual progress from style to style, a fundamental tendency in the art of painting reached a high point of dazzling intensity."

This moment, which had such a deep influence on art and artists, is thus far more important than a brief and summary account would at first suggest. To establish its real significance beyond mere appearances, the Fauvist phenomenon must be investigated in detail and studied from the three following standpoints:

—its true position within the period and the diverse interpretations of that period that it provides;

—its actual development, bearing in mind the long gestation that had already brought these artists close to one another well before the birth of the movement in 1905;

—its unexpected, and so far seldom mentioned, continuation through the immediate or distant repercussions that it provoked in France as well as abroad.

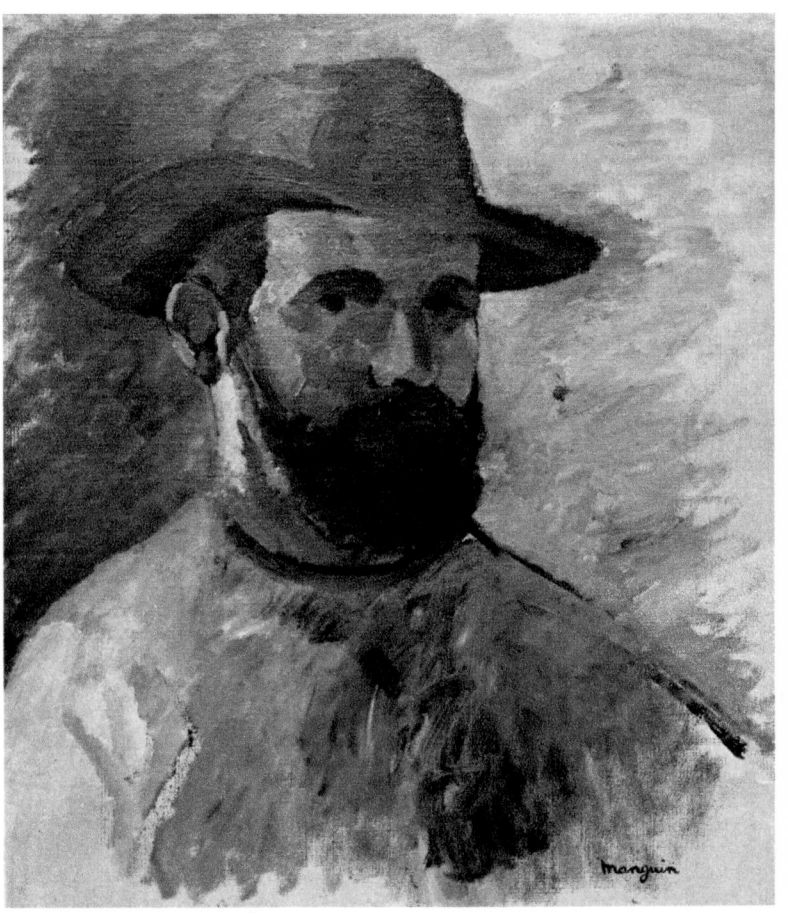

3. Henri Manguin. SELF-PORTRAIT. 1905.
Oil on canvas, 21 5/8 × 18 1/8".
Collection Mme Lucile Martinais-Manguin, Paris

IN RAPPORT WITH THE TIMES

A false picture, stemming from a Parisian bourgeois tradition of the beginning of the century, long fostered the belief that most modern artists lived on the fringes of society, totally cut off and even ostracized. A persistent and overpublicized legend had grown up about the widening gulf supposedly being formed between artists and society, and both parties had moreover ended by believing it themselves. The supporters of an obsolete academicism had welcomed it because it conveniently justified their systematic neglect of most of the Impressionists and of the great innovators who had died young, such as Seurat and Van Gogh. The artists, for their part, were quite prepared to take this opportunity to play the role of misunderstood outcasts from a society they despised.

Yet on the aesthetic level there were a number of indications of the deep changes in taste that were taking place. At the Universal Exposition of 1900, the centennial exhibition of French art could not refuse to admit the Impressionists. For some years now the Nabis had enjoyed an

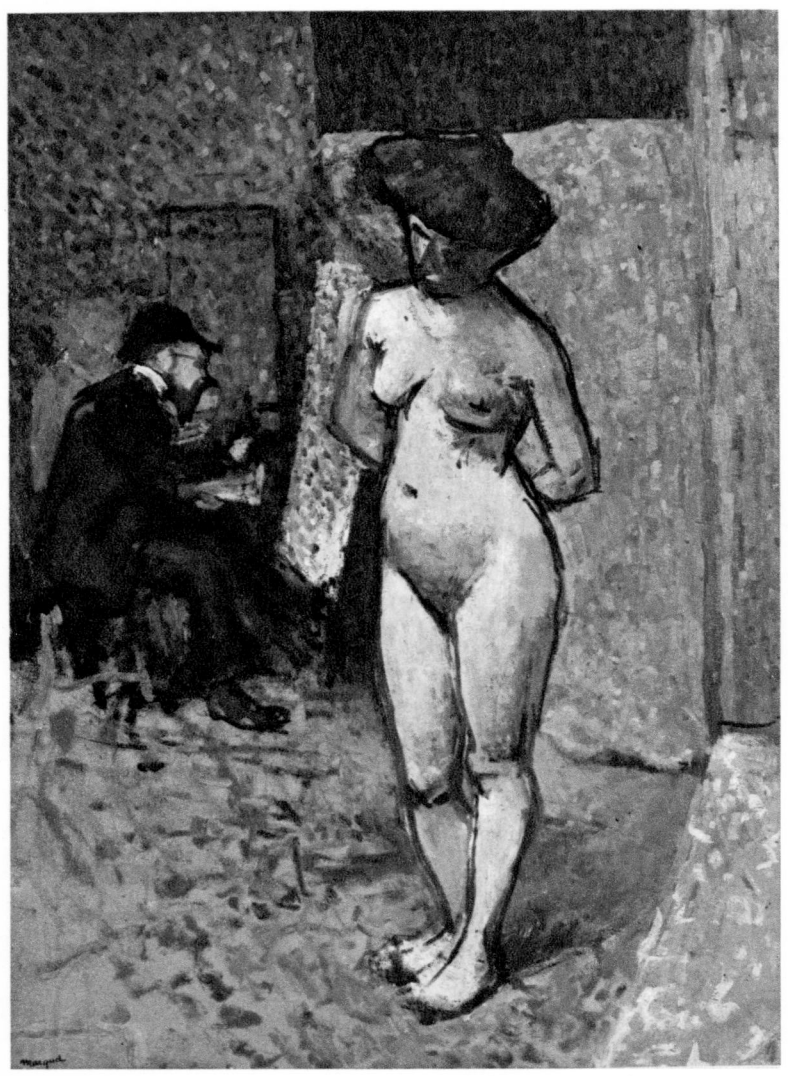

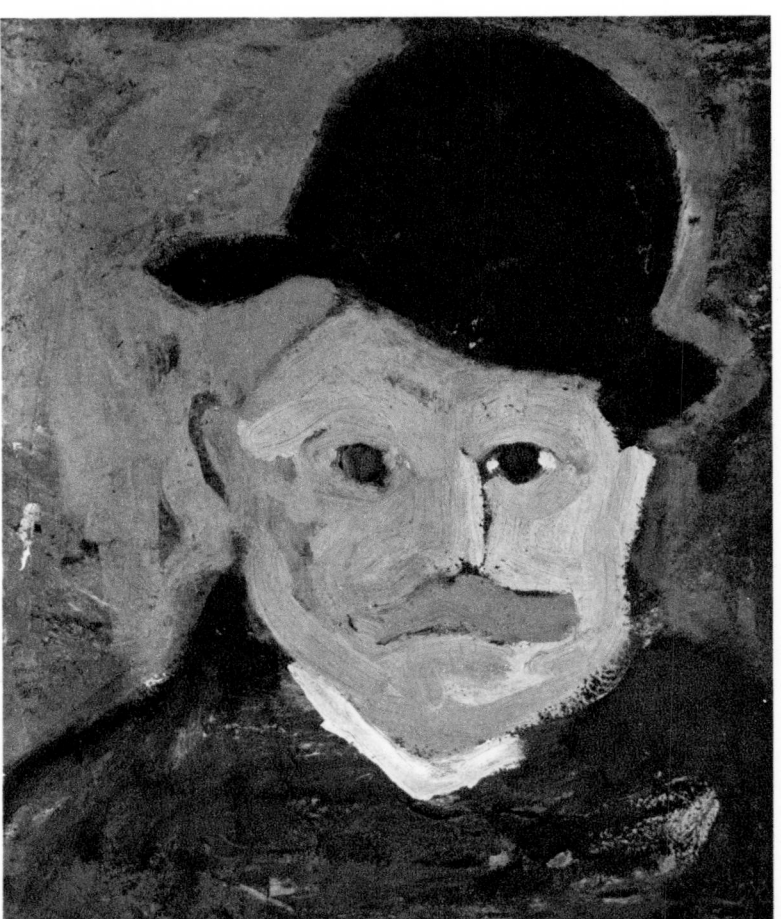

5. André Derain. PORTRAIT OF VLAMINCK. 1905.
Oil on canvas, 16 1/8 × 13″.
Private collection, Paris

4. Albert Marquet.
MATISSE PAINTING A NUDE IN MANGUIN'S STUDIO. 1904–5.
Oil on canvas, 39 3/8 × 28 3/4″.
• *Musée National d'Art Moderne, Paris*

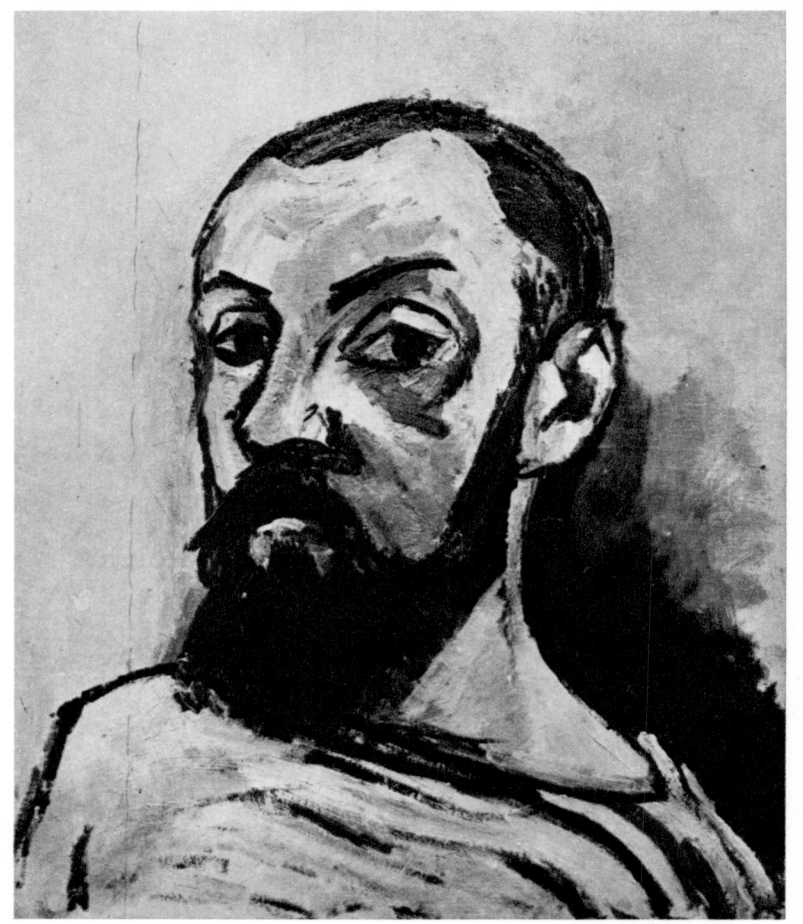

6. Henri Matisse. SELF-PORTRAIT. 1906.
Oil on canvas, 21 5/8 × 18 1/8″.
Statens Museum for Kunst, Copenhagen

enviable position in the art world. Before long, posthumous recognition and respect for the initiators of modern art were to become widespread. Although the official Salon kept a part of its clientele and the support of the State and press, its position was nonetheless weakened both by the extension of the Salon des Indépendants, which attracted large numbers of exhibitors, and by the creation in 1903 of the Salon d'Automne, which received a favorable reception from the critics. The simultaneous increase in the number of art periodicals and galleries, and above all the international exchanges stimulated by the Salon d'Automne and by the foreign visitors who were beginning to flock to Paris, show that what was happening instead was a sudden broadening of understanding between the public and the artists, an effort at greater rapport.

A rapidly changing society was in fact discovering new needs, new objects of inquiry, a future rich in promise for which writers and artists were intuitively the spokesmen. Only a small part of this society, all the more vocal because it felt itself to be swimming against the tide, clung to the past and fought to preserve its outdated notions.

Although they opposed this overly conservative bourgeoisie, the masters of tomorrow, as their friends confidently called them, had no wish to escape the influence of the time by withdrawing into isolation. Indeed, they developed the most vital elements of the period and gave expression to its primary aspirations. For, as the late Pierre Francastel declared: "Man continues to create the imaginary space in which artists project a fascinating interpretation of his convictions and habits. Plastic space inevitably changes according to our common ascendancy over the external world; inevitably it reflects both our mathematical conception of the physical laws of matter and those values of sentiment that we should like to see triumph."

A survey of the most salient aspects of the period will show in what manner they provided the inspiration and setting for the works of the Fauves.

A spirit of such unshakable optimism was ushered in by the new century, despite its trials and crises, that it came to be known to posterity by the enviable name of *la belle époque*.

The premises were favorable. The Universal Exposition of 1900 was a great success, attracting many sovereigns and foreign visitors and bringing together East and West as the Exposition of 1889 had tried to do before. Although the pompous appearance of the monuments that it left behind —the Grand Palais, Petit Palais, and the Pont Alexandre III—reveals the self-confidence and prosperity of the time, their smiling composure remains highly conventional. The smile becomes more equivocal, more acid, in the growing number of satirical papers such as *Le Rire* and *L'Assiette au beurre*, which enjoyed unprecedented popularity.

Although they did not set themselves up as reformers or judges of society, our artists occasionally earned their living by contributing to these papers and are thus closely associated with the mixed and often contradictory trends that were beginning to emerge. In a confused way they express by turns the appetite for pleasure, the return to nature and even to the elemental, the critical examination and questioning of all accepted ideas, the determined pursuit of nonconformity, the feeling of brotherhood, the prevailing dynamism of the time—in other words, all the dominant elements of the period that we are considering.

There was a growing opposition to *fin-de-siècle* tastes, condemned as decadent, to Symbolism or Intimism with their refinements and affectations, confined atmosphere, and anxious or malevolent esotericism. As early as 1897, in *Les Nourritures terrestres*, André Gide glorified the Dionysiac spirit: "Pleasure! Let me repeat this word constantly; let it be a synonym of *well-being* and even, quite simply, of *being*." He extols the intensity of the moment, the beauty of light, gardens, and open windows; he sings the charms of the Maghreb regions and the desert; he ends with this proud and fervent profession of faith that will, along with the rest, be scrupulously followed by the Fauves: "Cleave only to those things in yourself which you feel exist nowhere outside yourself, and make of yourself, impatiently or patiently, the most unique of beings."

At the same time Saint-Georges de Bouhélier is publishing his *Chants de la vie ardente* (1902) and Verhaeren *Les Forces tumultueuses*. Colette, with Willy's help, begins the *Claudine* series, which is to celebrate man's ties with nature and animals, while Péguy, in the *Cahiers de la quinzaine*, examines the writer's mission in society. At Créteil, on the outskirts of Paris, the Abbaye group with Georges Duhamel, Charles Vildrac, Raymond Arcos, and Georges Chennevière assembles in a kind of commune, from 1904 to 1906, under the leadership of Jules Romains. In the name of the doctrine of Unanimism that he launches with his friends, Romains urges poets and men of letters to become the chief instruments in the soul's conquest of the universe, in man's exploration of reality, which he himself describes in impassioned terms: "My body is the tremor of the city. . . ."

Thus, among writers and more particularly within this last group, which was to recognize its affinities with the Fauve painters and constantly support their efforts, a marked change of attitude was strongly manifested in a thirst for life, an interest in everyday themes, the need for liberation and the external expression of instinctive forces, communion with nature and the masses, an imperative revision of values.

Philosophers and aestheticians were concerned with similar questions. From Freud to Croce, from Durkheim to Lévy-Brühl, they turned to the study of motivations and the deeper impulses, to the psychology of the individual and the community, and to the relations between them in order to evolve an increased mutual understanding.

It is interesting to note that this search for the foundations of society, pursued by philosophy throughout the millenniums, brings about an actual return to sources and origins in other areas, often casting doubt on long accepted values. Classical and traditional concepts were being breached on all sides by Evans's excavations at Knossos, which brought to light the archaic civilizations; by the rehabilitation of the French Primitives at the 1904 exhibition; by the growing interest in folklore, popular art, prehistory, and, before long, in the arts of so-called savages. In France and Germany, ethnographical museums began to attract artists. At the same time Strzygowski, in his *Orient ou Rome*, raises the question of making a choice, while Courajod in his lectures at the Ecole du Louvre, and Riegl in his writings both stress the importance of the art of primitive peoples.

A virulent anti-conformism spreads to all levels of a society which is undergoing rapid economic and industrial changes and rebelling against the teachings and inherited fetters of the past, including the now bitterly opposed tenets of religion. The desire for emancipation and conquest asserts itself triumphantly throughout the world. Despite unrest, the anarchist plots and increasing strikes, the recourse to violence urged by Georges Sorel, the series of wars in the Far East, the bloody insurrections in Saint Petersburg and Moscow, and the continual risk of conflict in Europe, an atmosphere of optimism persists. Everyone trusts in the future. Socialism partially imposes its views and succeeds in unifying itself. The Dreyfus case is at last reviewed. Above all, thanks to the fraternal élan that grips artists and writers from Steinlein to Romain Rolland, Péguy, and Gorky, the people recover their sense of strength and dignity.

In reality, human hopes are now focused predominantly on the machine, whose astonishing advances are daily accelerating the tempo of life. Its feverish round revolution-

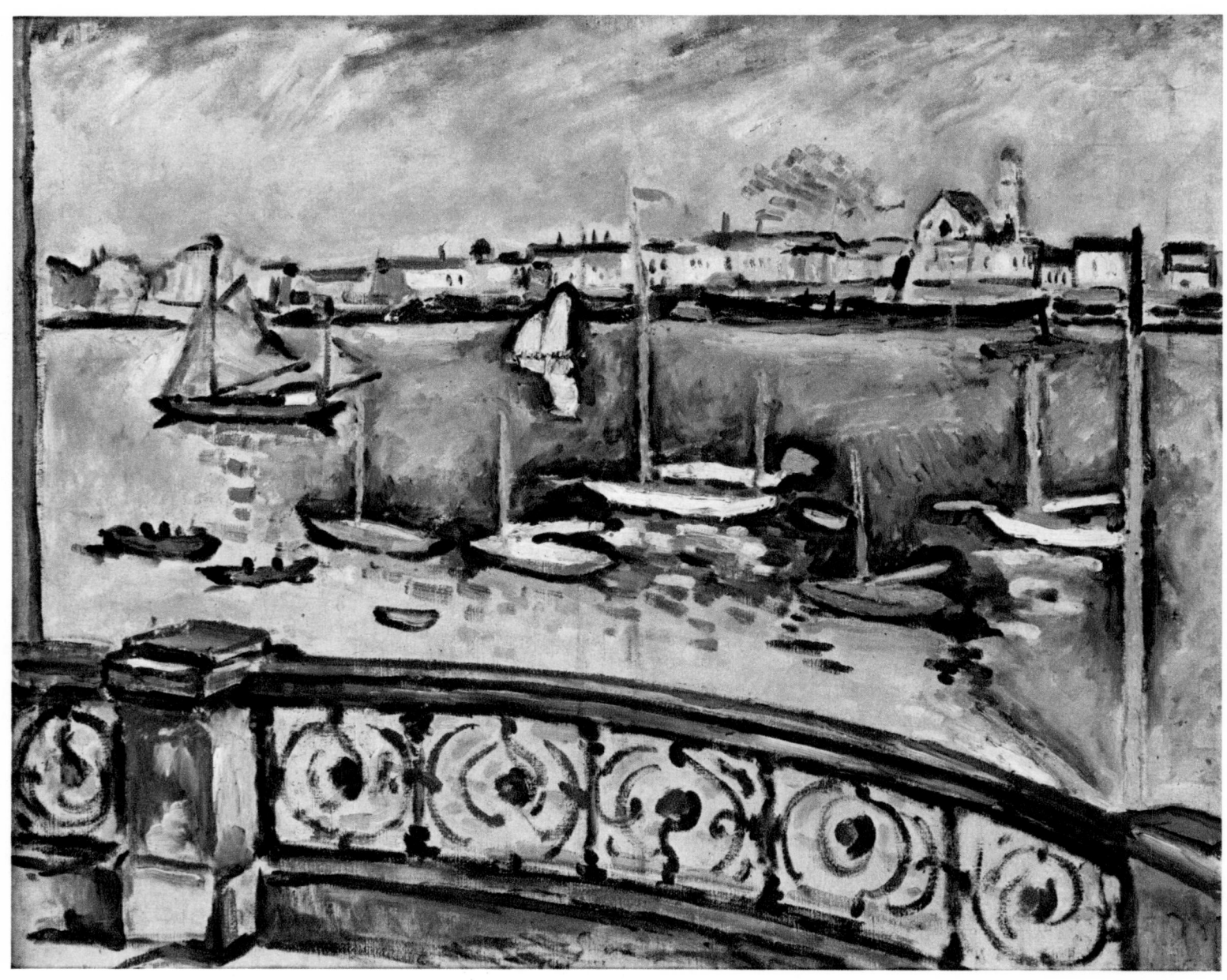

7. Georges Braque. LE PORT D'ANVERS (ANTWERP HARBOR). 1906. Oil on canvas, 19 5/8 × 24″.
The National Gallery of Canada, Ottawa

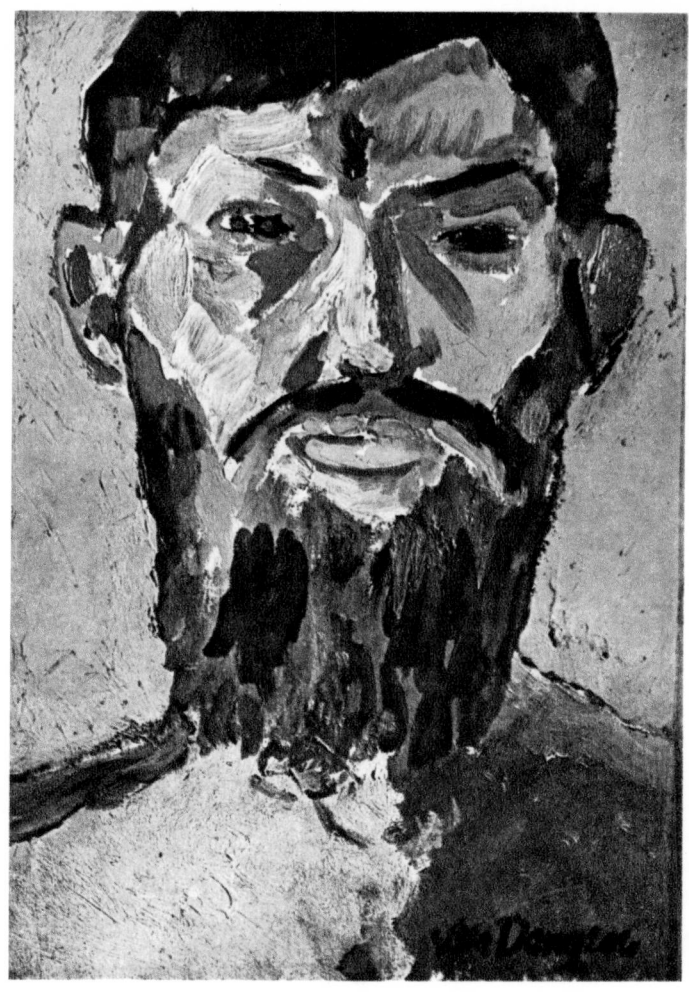

8. Kees van Dongen. SELF-PORTRAIT. 1905.
Oil on canvas, 21 5/8 × 15".
Private collection, Monaco

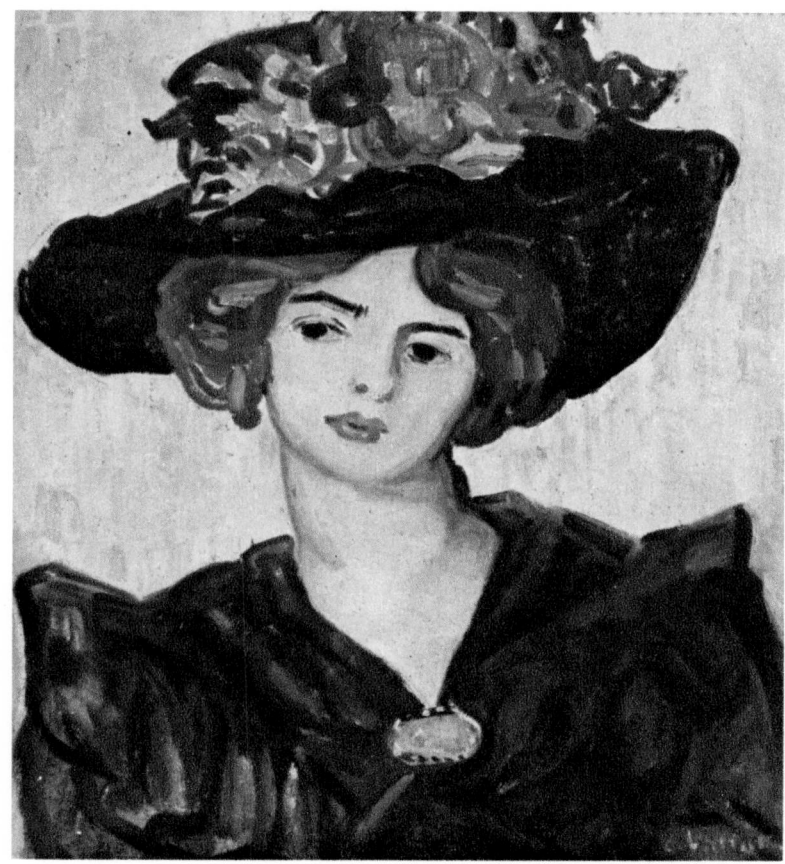

10. Louis Valtat. WOMAN WITH A HAT. 1900.
Oil on canvas, 25 5/8 × 18 1/8".
Private collection, Paris

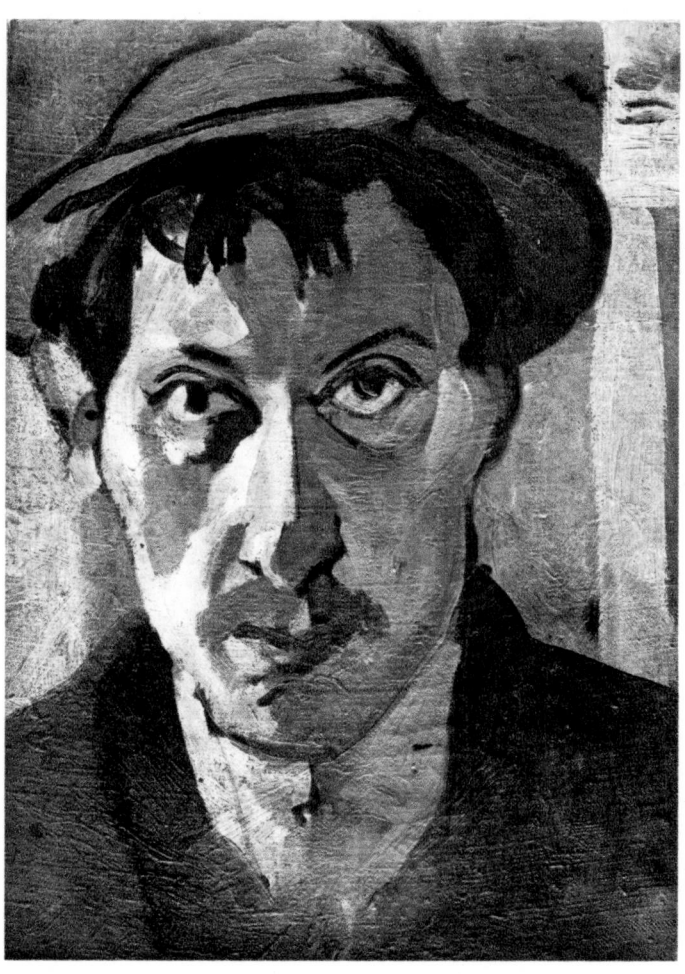

9. André Derain. SELF-PORTRAIT. 1904–5.
Oil on canvas, 13 5/8 × 9 1/2".
Private collection, Paris

izes Paris successively with the *Métro* in 1900, the Salon de l'Auto in 1901, the first buses in 1906, and the Salon de l'Aéronautique in 1908.

Enthralled by the power of this pervasive dynamism, our artists spontaneously decide to appropriate its effects in order to sublimate them. They make it the coordinating element for all the needs of the moment, all the problems that arise. By the same token, they use it as an individual means of protection, an instrument of liberation from the constraints of an increasingly rational organization of society.

They thus become the heralds and spokesmen of this jubilant, vital impulse, to which they give the necessary breadth and animation. Around them caricaturists and poster artists employ the same bright and even violent colors, the same vigorous and incisive lines, thereby preparing the public for a visual re-awakening that the painters will not fail to exploit.

The Three Ages of Fauvism

PRELUDE

At the start of nearly every movement there is a rallying point, a place where young students come into contact with each other, work together, and become friends. Thus, for preceding generations the Académie Suisse and the Atelier Gleyre had served as a meeting place for the future Impressionists, as did the Académie Julian for the Nabis. It may seem surprising that the Ecole des Beaux-Arts in Paris— sunk as it then was in mediocrity and reputedly a bastion of the worst academicism—should have played a similar role for some of the future Fauve painters, even to the point of exerting a lasting influence on them. To refurbish its tarnished reputation and to attract a younger generation indifferent to academic honors and the Prix de Rome required the providential presence of Gustave Moreau, one of the leading representatives of Symbolism and a liberal spirit who succeeded his friend Elie Delaunay as professor there at the age of sixty-six.

In the studio that he directed from January, 1892, until his death in April, 1898, he tried, with a rare eclecticism and a complete disregard for Salon fashions, to encourage his students in a thorough study of the old masters, whose works he urged them to copy in the Louvre, at the same time drawing their attention to such outstanding contemporaries as Cézanne, Degas, and Toulouse-Lautrec, and in the end leaving each free to follow his own temperament. His exhortations, couched in striking formulas, were to have lasting echoes: "The evocation of thought through arabesques and plastic means, such is my aim"—"The contained and measured work in its burning passion . . ."— "Nature in itself is nothing! It merely gives the artist an occasion to express himself. Art is the unflagging pursuit through plastic means of expression and inner feeling"— "One must think color, one must have it in the imagination."

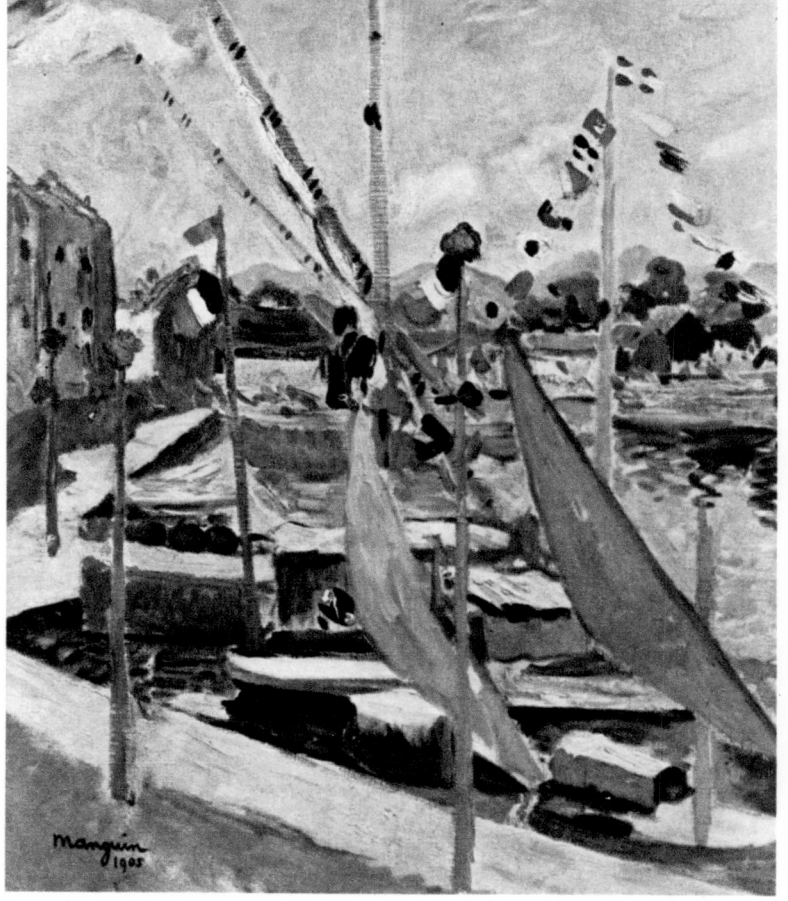

11. Henri Manguin.
THE FOURTEENTH OF JULY AT SAINT-TROPEZ. 1905.
Oil on canvas, 24 × 19 5/8".
Collection Mme Lucile Martinais-Manguin, Paris

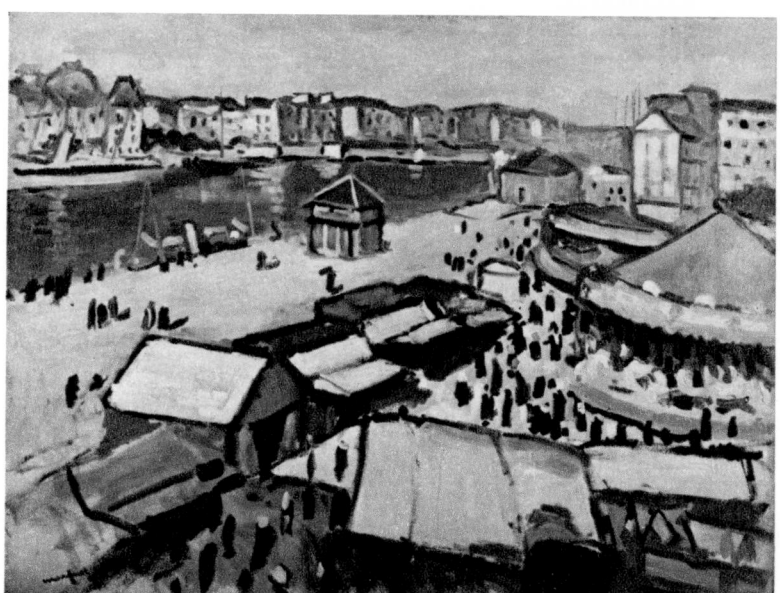

12. Albert Marquet. CARNIVAL AT LE HAVRE. 1906.
Oil on canvas, 25 5/8 × 31 7/8".
Musée des Beaux-Arts, Bordeaux

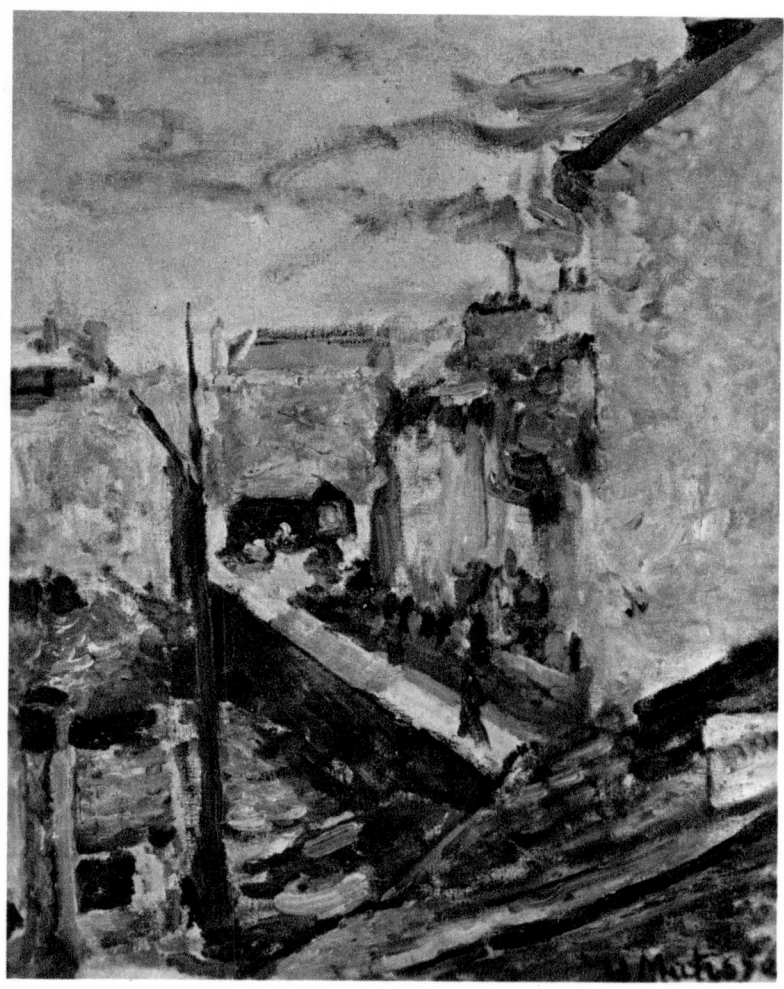

13. Henri Matisse. VIEW FROM BELLE-ÎLE. C. 1897.
Oil on canvas, 18 1/8 × 15".
Musée des Beaux-Arts, Bordeaux

Although he rarely showed his seductively manneristic canvases and still less his sketches and watercolors, executed with amazing freedom in a bold, splashing technique, he nevertheless attracted a following through his feeling for lavish colors and rich textures, his incisive draftsmanship, his taste for a fabulous East, his strong idealism, vast culture, and refinement. The encouragement, affection, and understanding that he lavished on his most gifted pupils explain his stimulating influence and the enthusiasm he inspired. As Roger Marx wrote in 1896: "The fires of insurrection have been lit in the very heart of the Ecole des Beaux-Arts; all the rebels against routine, all those who wish to develop in their own individual way, have gathered under the shield of Gustave Moreau."

Apart from his run-of-the-mill pupils (numbering more than eighty at the time of his death), a small nucleus consisting of former students or friends who had become almost disciples had emerged and met from time to time. It included Desvallières, Piot (admirer and self-appointed historiographer of Delacroix), and Rouault; such older habitués as Lehmann, the Belgian Evenepoel, Milcendeau, and Bussy; the newcomers who flocked in after 1895, Matisse and Marquet (who had met at the Ecole des Arts Décoratifs), Flandrin, Prat, Manguin, Linaret, the Rumanian Pallady; and the last recruits, Rouveyre and Camoin. A deep sense of comradeship united most of these young artists, all about the same age, who had generally worked and had their first exhibitions together in 1896 at the Salon de la Société Nationale des Beaux-Arts, in 1901 at the Salon des Indépendants, and in 1903 at the Salon d'Automne. The fact that in 1905 Vauxcelles could still recall "that cohort, cultivated to the point of Byzantinism, that formed around Moreau" shows how relatively united

their group remained over the years and through its various transformations.

Matisse, slightly older than the others, quickly assumed leadership. As early as 1896, during a summer stay at Belle-Ile and under the guidance of a friend of the Impressionists, the Australian painter John Russell, who offered him two drawings by Van Gogh, he discovered with a rapture that by his own admission astonished him "the brilliance of pure color" in a small seascape. The following year he repeated the experiment. His teacher could hardly disapprove of this trend, already being followed by Evenepoel and still more by Linaret. Aided by his new passion for Japanese textiles and by the advice of Pissarro, whom he had gone to consult together with Manguin, he completes his emancipation in solitude under the radiant sky of Corsica, where he spends the beginning of 1898. His disappointments at the Nationale, Moreau's death, and his quarrels with Cormon, who bars him from his studio, lead him to break definitively with the Ecole. Soon after, he draws Marquet into a brief Pointillist experiment, as can be seen from the latter's *Nu fauve* in the Bordeaux Museum. Before long the two friends, working together freely at Arcueil and the Luxembourg, and accompanied in the succeeding years by Manguin, Camoin, and a few others, embark on what has been properly called "Pre-Fauvism" because of its joyful lyricism, its spirited, brilliantly colored brushwork, which the sun of Toulouse was to heighten still further in Matisse's paintings of 1899. Matisse was by now so firmly set on his course that on his return from the South of France and despite his limited means—his second child had just been born—he decided to buy two small canvases that he had seen briefly at Vollard's, a Cézanne and a Gauguin, and these were to serve him from then on as models.

The budding group that was later to be christened the Fauves acquired additional followers in 1898 in a second establishment attended by Matisse.

Anxious to work more from the human figure—he now took up sculpture and followed evening classes in the Rue Etienne Marcel—Matisse, wishing to avail himself of a live model and engrossed as always by the play of values, enrolled in a small private academy recently opened by a certain Camillo in the Rue de Rennes, where Eugène Carrière was a teacher. Cordiality and mutual respect grew up between the self-styled student and the kindly old teacher, who refrained from commenting on Matisse's powerfully expressive nudes, their bold ultramarine volumes heightened by the violently contrasting oranges and pinks that satisfied Matisse's new passion for constructing his pictures exclusively with color. The results, which Matisse justified by extolling Cézanne, soon earned him a following among his comrades, most of them his juniors: Biette, Laprade, Derain, Chabaud, the Norwegian Karsten, and Migonney, who was shortly joined by his friend Jean Puy. In Puy's words, the group found in him "the inspiring element that arouses one's spirit." He communicated his enthusiasm to everybody, "the flame of his passion propelled them toward the goal to which they ardently aspired." It was from their ranks that he was to recruit some of his new and most faithful associates, notably Puy and Derain. When the school closed its doors, they continued to meet occasionally at Biette's, but more often in Manguin's new studio in the Rue Boursault.

Although he did not remain aloof, Marquet rarely went to the Rue de Rennes. With Camoin, who soon left to do his military service, he preferred to mix with the crowd and make sketches from life. For a part of the year 1900, however, he earned his living by working daily with Matisse in the studio of the decorator Jambon. Sometimes the two friends would spend an evening in a cabaret—the sketches they made were shown at the Indépendants in 1901. That year Marquet spent the summer in Normandy with Manguin.

Thus, through these shared interests, these frequent meetings, which must surely have promoted an enthusiastic exchange of ideas, ever closer ties are forged among them. One after another they join the Indépendants—Manguin in 1902, Camoin and Puy in 1903, and so on, as well as the Salon d'Automne, where in 1904 Camoin and Manguin are reunited with Matisse and Marquet, who had already been invited in 1903. They form an even tighter group in the small gallery opened by Berthe Weill in December, 1901, in the Rue Victor Massé, where she judiciously alternates the works of young painters with those of the celebrated draftsmen of the period: Abel Faivre, Cappiello, Sem, Willette, Léandre, Forain, Chéret, Steinlein, Helleu, and such of their followers as Rouveyre and Villon. Beginning in February, 1902, she shows Marquet, Matisse, and his neighbors from the Quai Saint-Michel—Flandrin and Mme Marval. She also welcomes Girieud, Maillol, and Milcen-

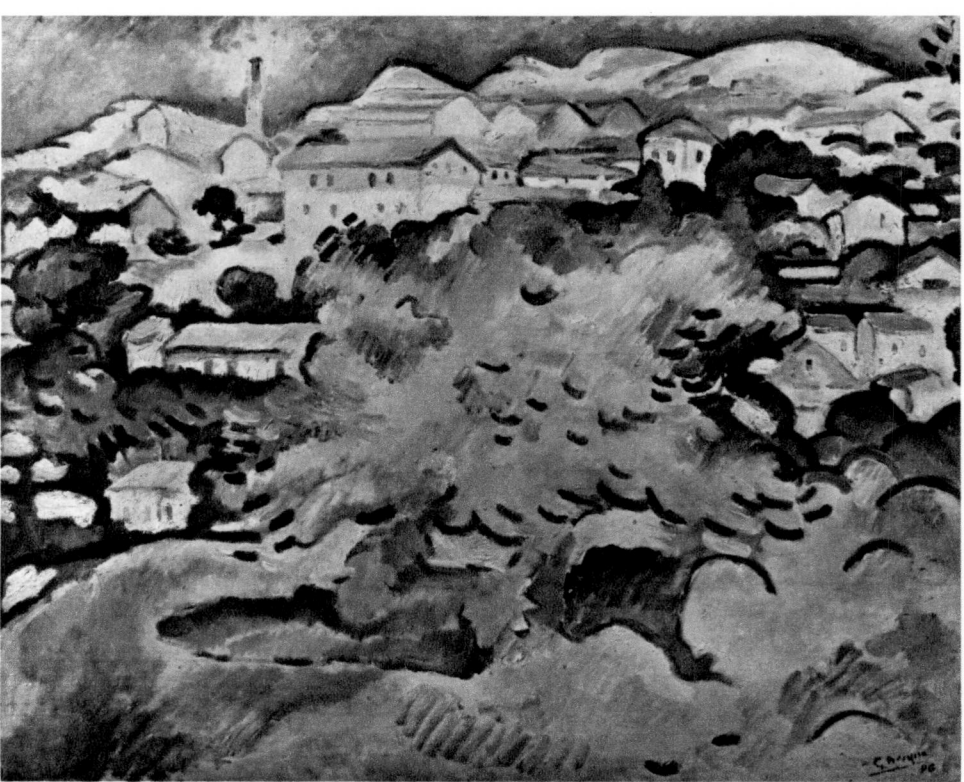

14. Georges Braque.
LANDSCAPE AT L'ESTAQUE. 1906.
Oil on canvas, 23 5/8 × 28 1/4".
Private collection, Paris

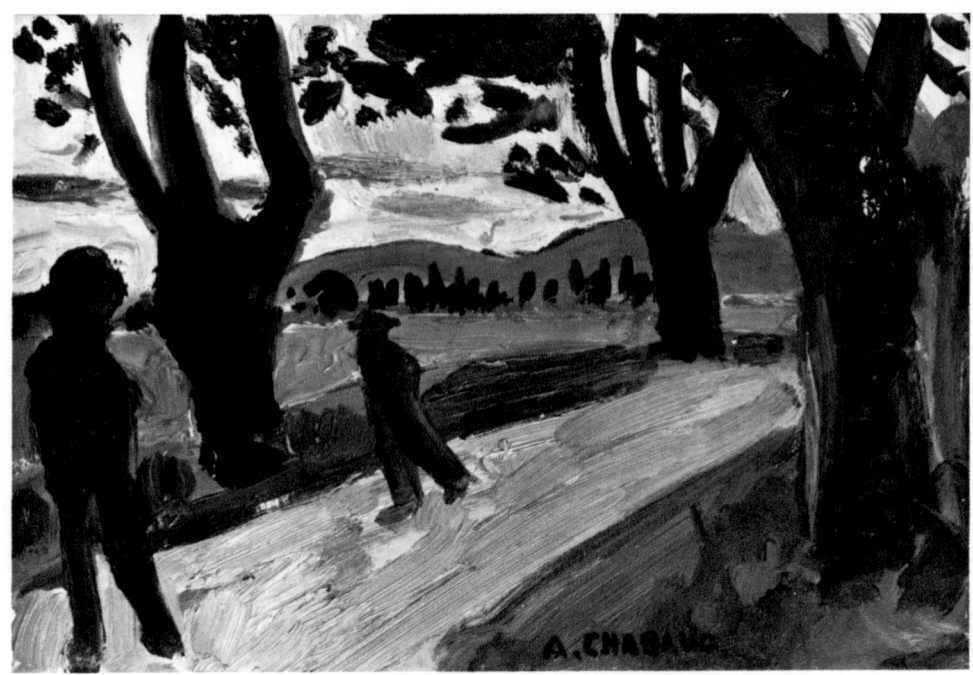

15. Auguste Chabaud.
TWO PASSERS-BY ON THE ROAD. C. 1905.
Oil on canvas, 9 1/2 × 13".
Private collection, Paris

deau, and becomes an early promoter of Picasso and Dufy. She holds a series of fragmentary showings, but it is only in April, 1904, that the group finally appears in a well-defined form, consisting of Camoin, Manguin, Marquet, Matisse, and Puy, to be immediately noticed by the critic Roger Marx, who stresses their "common desire for significance, which they strive to achieve through plastic means carried to the highest point of power and seductiveness." They finally have the satisfaction of seeing their patient efforts rewarded, since collectors now begin to show an interest in their works. In June Vollard organizes in his gallery a show of forty-six paintings by Matisse, and the State, as Michel Hoog records, buys works by Camoin, Marquet, and Matisse at the Salon d'Automne in 1904 and also at the Indépendants in 1905.

An outside circumstance helped to accelerate these developments. Invited to spend the summer of 1904 at Saint-Tropez with Signac and his Neo-Impressionist friends, Matisse was converted to their pictorial doctrine, which on his return he made a sincere effort to apply, particularly in his important work *Luxe, calme et volupté* (colorplate p. 79) executed during the winter and exhibited at the Indépendants in 1905, where its severity and rich harmonies caused a sensation. Under its influence, and no doubt still more under that of the great Seurat retrospective held that year at the Indépendants, several of Matisse's friends hastened in their turn to Saint-Tropez. As the critic Vauxcelles wrote: "In the spring of 1905 there was a valiant little colony of artists painting and conversing in this enchanted land—Signac, Cross, Manguin, Camoin, Marquet."

The new vogue spread rapidly. Even such painters as Van Dongen and Vlaminck, who up to now had remained slightly aloof, did not hesitate to use gay, kaleidoscopic splashes of color in most of the works that they exhibited —Vlaminck for the first time—at the Indépendants in 1905. From different backgrounds and living somewhat on the margins of the group, Van Dongen in the Impasse Girardon in Montmartre and Vlaminck in Chatou—where after June, 1900, he had close ties with Derain—they are typical representatives of a northern atavism that draws its resources primarily from the force of instinct, in the manner of Van Gogh, who became Vlaminck's "god" when he was first revealed to him in 1901 at the Bernheim Gallery and later the same year at the Indépendants. Despite their definite vocation, their course had so far remained rather uncertain, although for his show at Vollard's in November, 1904, Van Dongen had been able to muster a hundred or so paintings that still showed restraint, as well as a few dynamically explosive watercolors.

The stage was therefore set when in 1905 the protagonists assembled at the Salon des Indépendants in a sort of dress rehearsal before their impending historical debut. Even Derain was present, returning from his three years of military service to take up painting with Vlaminck again on the banks of the Seine, in the makeshift studio that they shared on the Ile de Chatou not far from the Fournaise restaurant, that favorite haunt of the Impressionists.

Vauxcelles is so well aware of what the artists are preparing half secretly in their studios or in their minds that some time before the opening of the Indépendants he announces "the audacities and extravagances . . . of some passionate young artists . . . who honor Cézanne as one of their masters, or rather one of their initiators, on a par with Gauguin, Van Gogh, and Monet. . . ." In his review, published March 23 in *Gil Blas* on the eve of the Salon opening, he criticizes Matisse's incursion into Pointillism while nevertheless recognizing his talent and the impor-

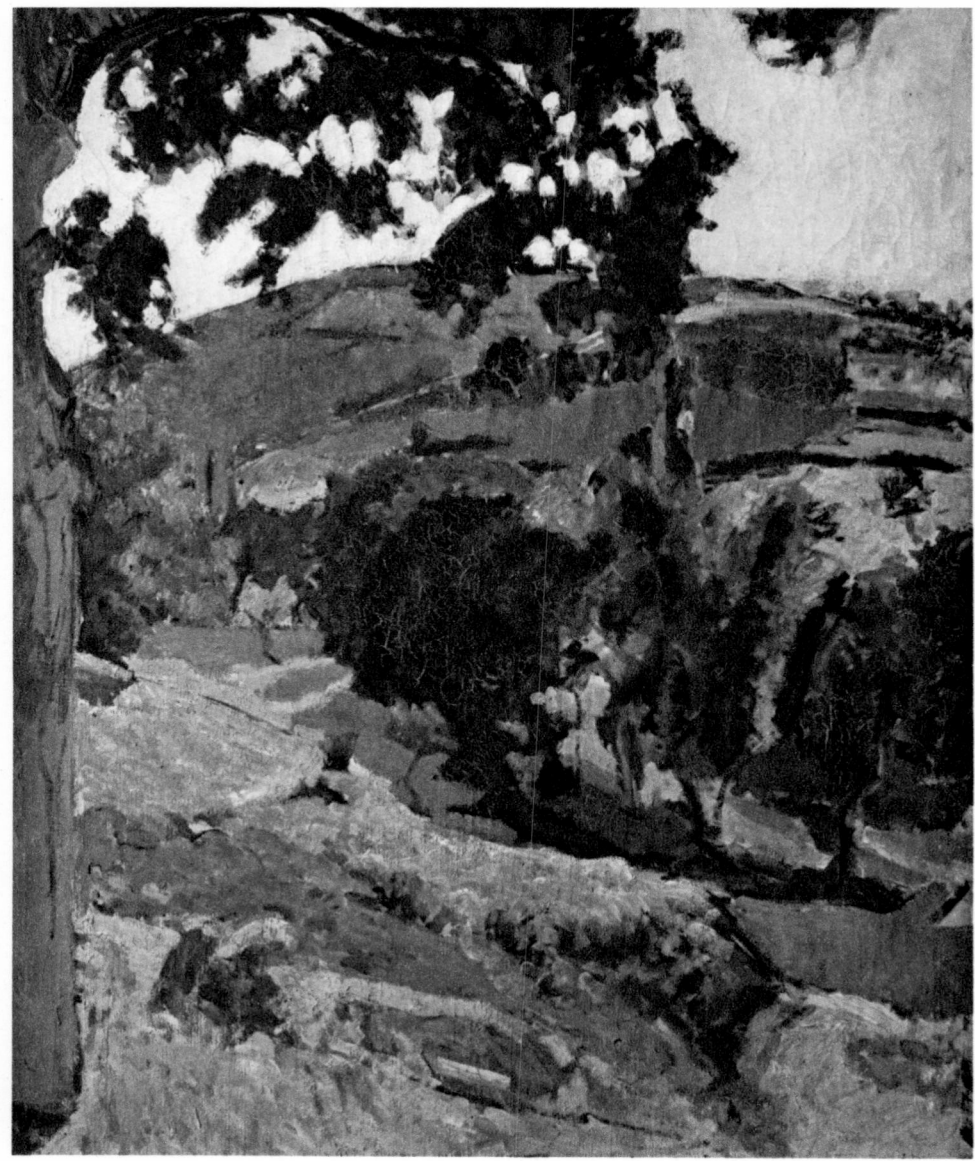

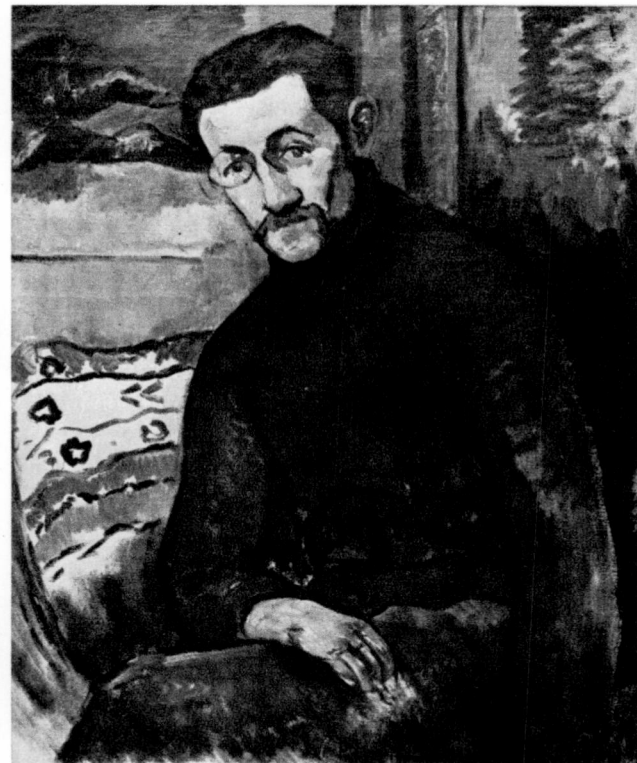

17. Henri Manguin. PORTRAIT OF JEAN PUY. 1905.
Oil on canvas, 31 7/8 × 25 5/8″.
Collection Mme Lucile Martinais-Manguin, Paris

16. Jean Puy. LANDSCAPE. 1904. Oil on canvas, 37 × 29 1/2″.
Musée des Beaux-Arts, Rouen

tance of his role: "This young painter . . . assumes, whether or not he wishes to, the position of head of the school; his friends Manguin, Camoin . . . Puy, impressed by his vigor, sometimes give a brutal turn to their senior's direct energy."

There can be no doubt that this Salon, considered "tumultuous" even by its champion Vauxcelles, met with the usual antagonism from the public and press. Yet this was followed by a certain shift of opinion in its favor. The newspaper *Le Temps* notes the conciliatory attitude of the new Director of Fine Arts, Dujardin-Beaumetz: "He had declared himself determined to encourage young artists. He is scrupulously keeping his promise. . . . He has opened a number of those exhibitions . . . which the Administration of the Fine Arts . . . made it its strict duty to ignore. Yesterday, for example . . . he was studying with obvious interest the Salon des Indépendants, which today is a center for the works of young artists." For the first time, in fact, the State was to make purchases at this Salon, buying twenty-three works.

Berthe Weill makes a similar observation in her mem-

oirs: "The Salon des Indépendants will certainly start a progressive movement toward *young painting;* the interesting Seurat and Van Gogh retrospectives can effectively silence the most recalcitrant. . . . The artists are very enthusiastic."

It remained for Matisse, however, to take the final step in the course of the summer and give a decisive turn to this converging movement. During the several months that he spent in the little port of Collioure, he was led to modify his ideas fundamentally under the combined influence of the warm Mediterranean sky and the strong contrasts in color of the Catalan landscape, the encouragement given by Maillol, the stimulating company of Derain, who had come to join him, and above all his delighted contemplation of the many Gauguin masterpieces kept by Daniel de Monfreid in his house at Saint-Clément. Gradually abandoning the dilutions of Pointillism, he imparts a new vigor to his touch, carrying color to its saturation point and adopting broad flat areas and bold outlines in a series of paintings—including *Open Window, Collioure* (colorplate p. 81)—which he was to continue on his return to Paris with *Wo-*

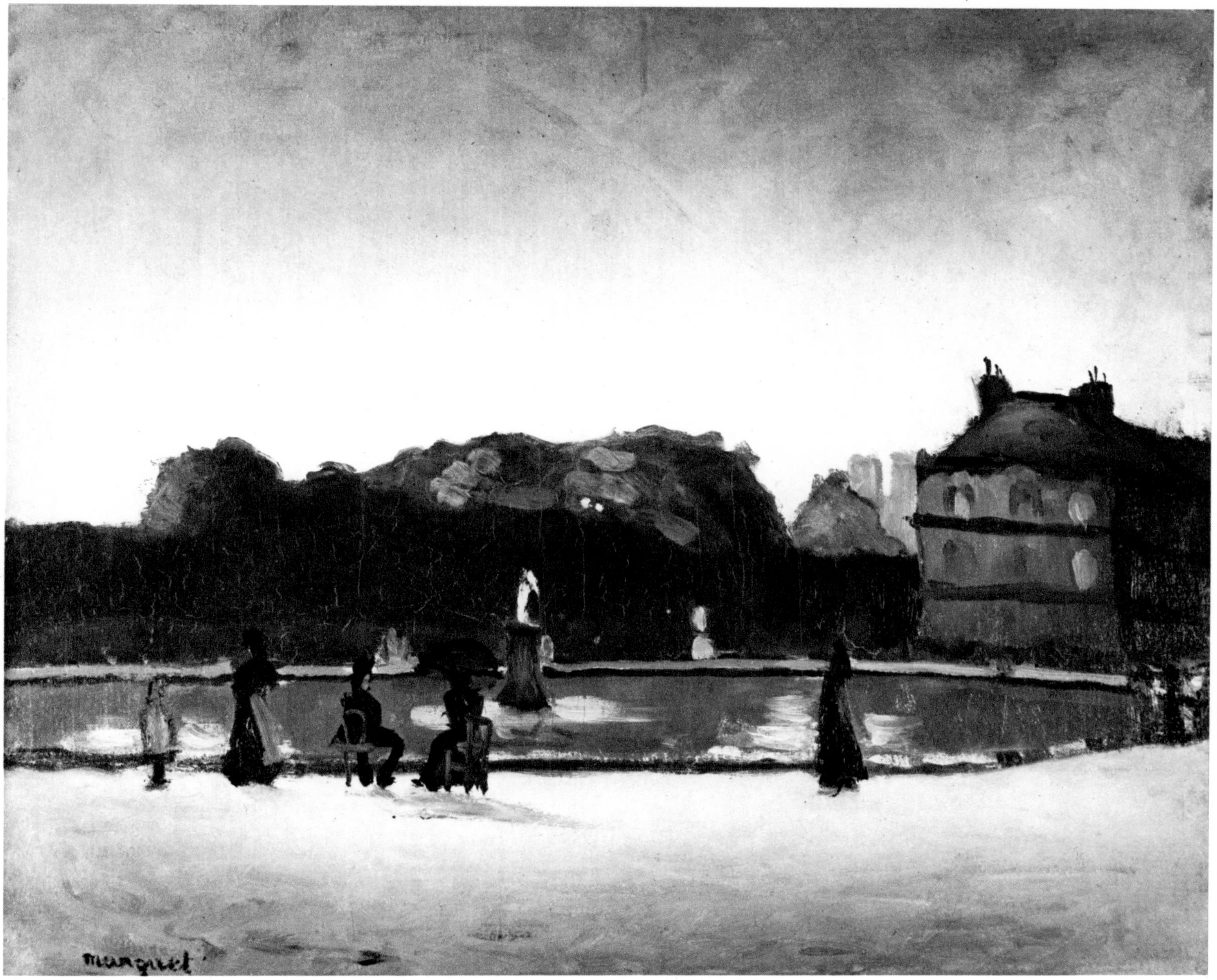

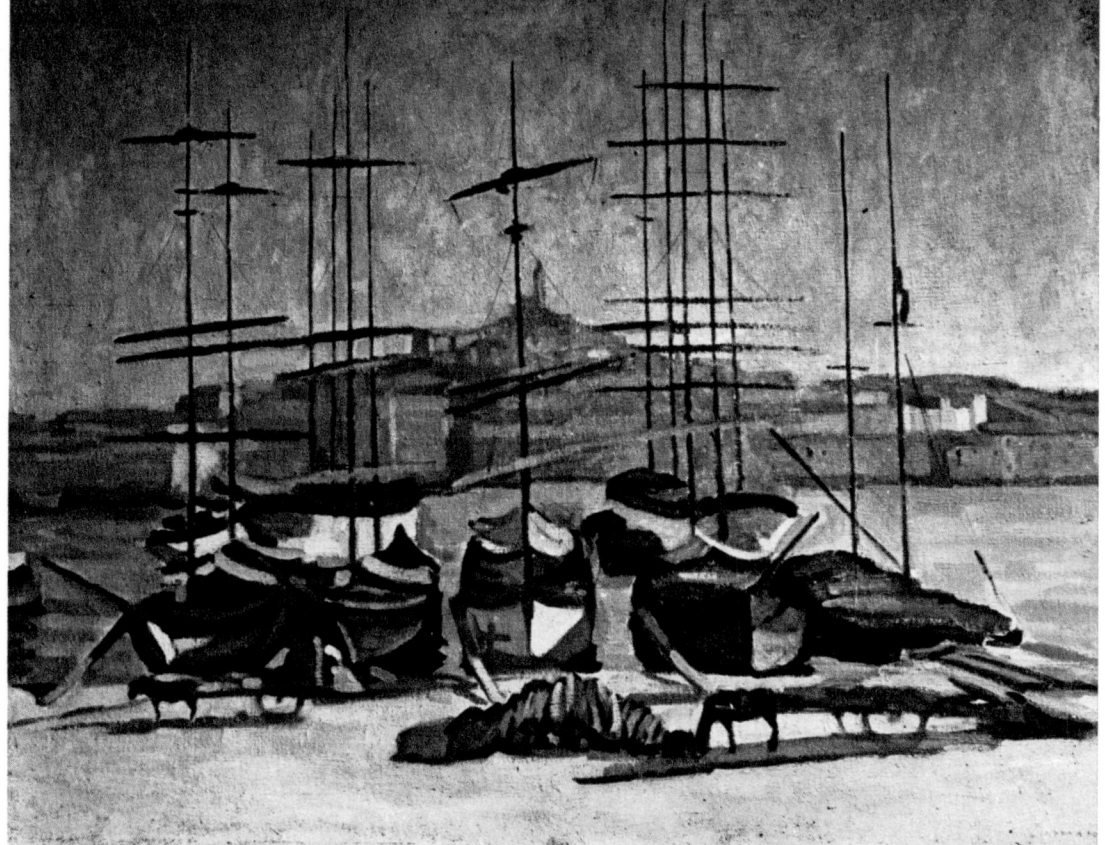

18. Albert Marquet.
THE LUXEMBOURG GARDENS. 1902.
Oil on canvas, 18 1/8 × 21 5/8″.
Musée des Beaux-Arts,
Bordeaux

19. Charles Camoin.
PORT OF MARSEILLES. 1904.
Oil on canvas, 23 5/8 × 31 7/8″.
Nouveau Musée des Beaux-Arts,
Le Havre.
Gift of Auguste Marande, 1936

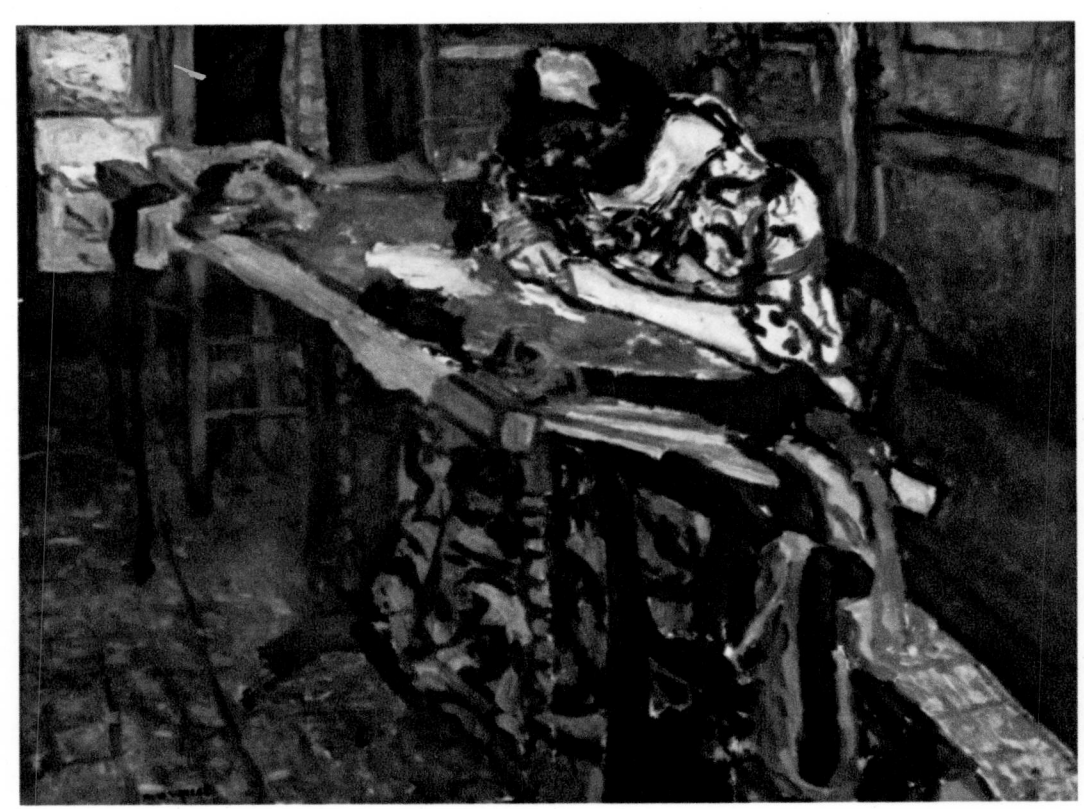

20. Albert Marquet.
MADAME MATISSE
DOING NEEDLEWORK. 1905.
Oil on canvas, 25 5/8 × 31 7/8″.
Private collection, Paris

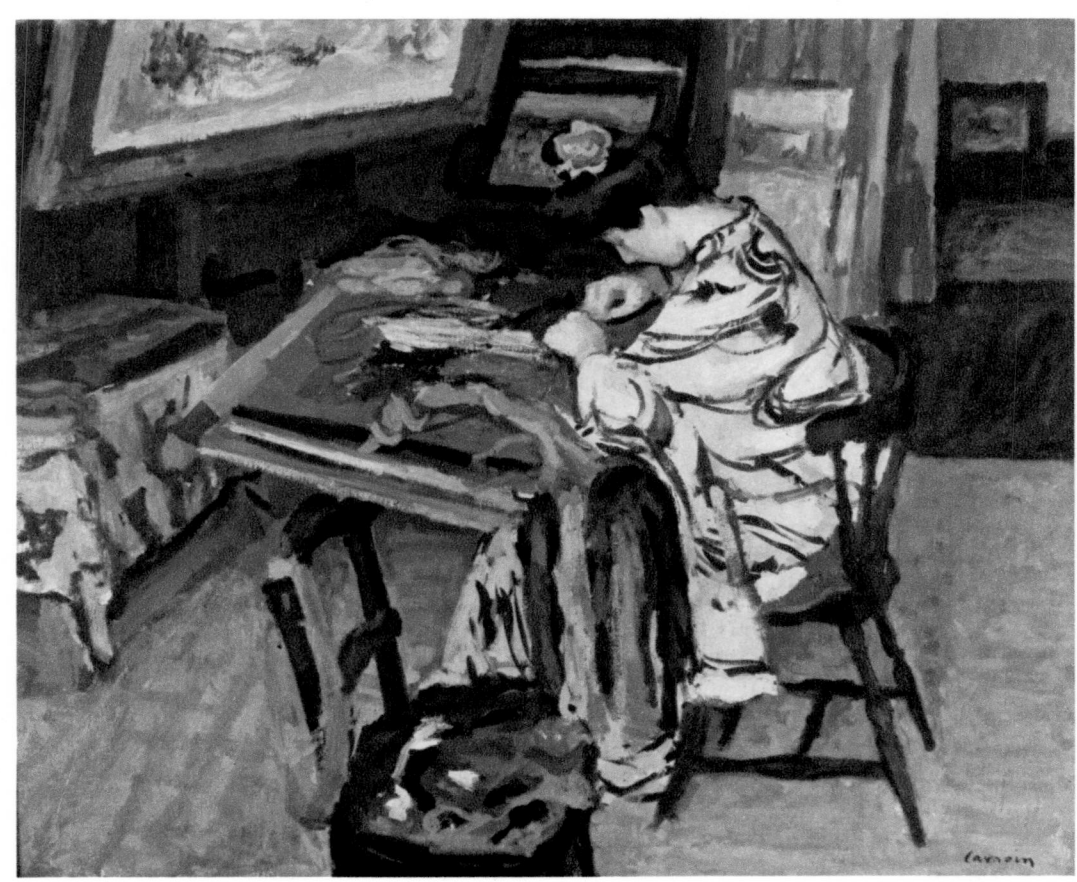

21. Charles Camoin.
MADAME MATISSE
DOING NEEDLEWORK. 1905.
Oil on canvas, 25 5/8 × 31 7/8″.
Musée des Beaux-Arts, Strasbourg

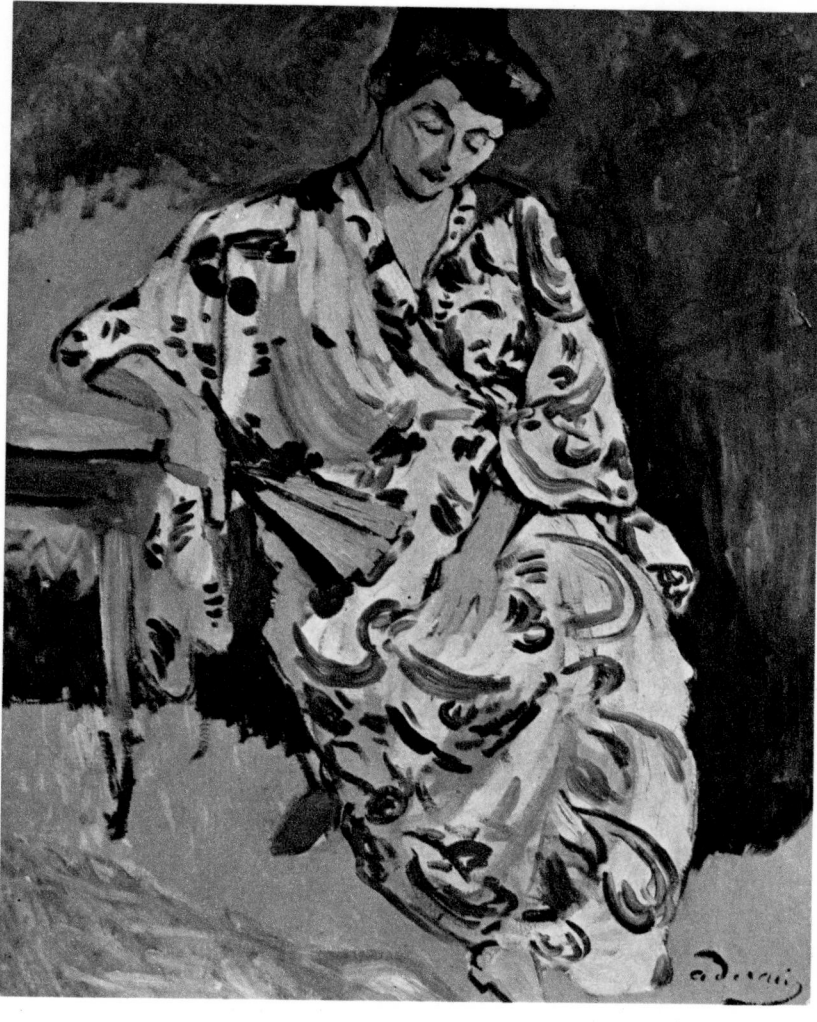

22. André Derain. WOMAN WITH SHAWL. 1905.
Oil on canvas, 31 1/2 × 25 5/8".
Collection B. J. Fize, Paris

man with a Hat (colorplate p. 83) and *Portrait with a Green Line* (Royal Museum of Fine Arts, Copenhagen), and some of which were to be exhibited at the Salon d'Automne in 1905. Derain, likewise intoxicated with light and in the grip of an elation that banished hesitation, followed suit to the best of his ability.

It would appear that this need to intensify brushwork and transform color was sufficiently felt by everyone, for when they met in October—those from Collioure, those from Saint-Tropez, and the rest—all showed a more or less similar development. Room VII at the Salon d'Automne had been reserved for them, one of the main central rooms, and here the works of Matisse, Derain, Vlaminck, Czóbel, Girieud, Manguin, Marquet, Camoin, and Van Dongen were hung side by side. But the public and the press inevitably connected them with the rather similar works scattered in the neighboring rooms: those of Puy in Room III; of Valtat, whose experiments had preceded those of his companions, in Room XV; even of Rouault in Room XVI, Marinot, and others. Vauxcelles is the first to be struck by this violently expressed unanimity, and he describes Room VII as the "room of the daring extremists," whose merits he appreciates and whose progress he stresses. His article in *Gil Blas*, however, begins by denouncing the "decorative simplifications of Gauguin that haunt young brains to the point of obsession," and he cannot resist a final quip in mentioning the sculptures by Marque exhibited in the center of the room: "The candor of these busts is surprising in the midst of such an orgy of pure tones: Donatello among the *fauves*."

The joke immediately made the rounds of Paris and spread abroad. Informed people realized that an event of capital importance had just taken place. They discovered that a whole generation, after years of struggle, was triumphantly asserting itself.

MATURITY

Certainly no one was more surprised than the Fauves themselves, both by the scandal that they had unintentionally caused and their sudden and long-awaited success with dealers and collectors.

At the end of October Berthe Weill opened a group show of her faithful exhibitors, who now included Derain and Vlaminck. As she remarked: "The group, with these additions, has suddenly become much sought after; the Fauves are beginning to domesticate the connoisseurs." She also takes note of the interest shown by Guillaume Apollinaire.

There was a similar group show a little later at the Prath & Magnier Gallery, of which Léon Rosenthal wrote: "There is a gathering of avant-garde painters, masters of the intense touch and bold colors, the heroes of the Salon d'Automne, Manguin, Marquet, Matisse, Camoin, Van Dongen, Girieud. . . . Perhaps the time has come to . . . extol the harmony of pure tones and the glory of undiluted color. . . ."

Vollard, who had long had a contract with Valtat, immediately signed up Derain and Puy, and the following year Vlaminck.

Druet for his part had taken on Marquet, and in November, 1905, he held a Van Dongen show in the gallery he had opened at the beginning of the year. In March, 1906, he mounted a large exhibition for Matisse, whose works were beginning to be highly esteemed by French, American, and, before long, Russian collectors.

The Salon des Indépendants of 1906 confirms the general triumph. At the sight of the 5,552 works assembled, Vauxcelles exclaims: "Today the battle is won." Apropos of Room VI, which he calls the "Salon Carré of the young school," he does not hesitate to declare: "It contains a collection of artists several of whom will achieve fame and fortune . . . Marquet . . . Manguin . . . Puy . . . Vlaminck . . . Van Dongen . . . and Munch," whom he judiciously includes in the movement that was so indebted to him.

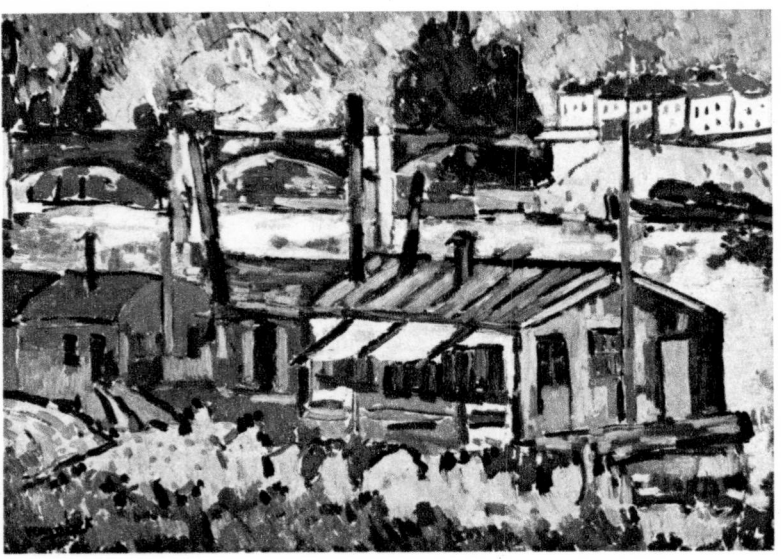

23. Maurice de Vlaminck. THE BRIDGE AT CHATOU. 1905–6.
Oil on canvas.
Musée de l'Annonciade, Saint-Tropez

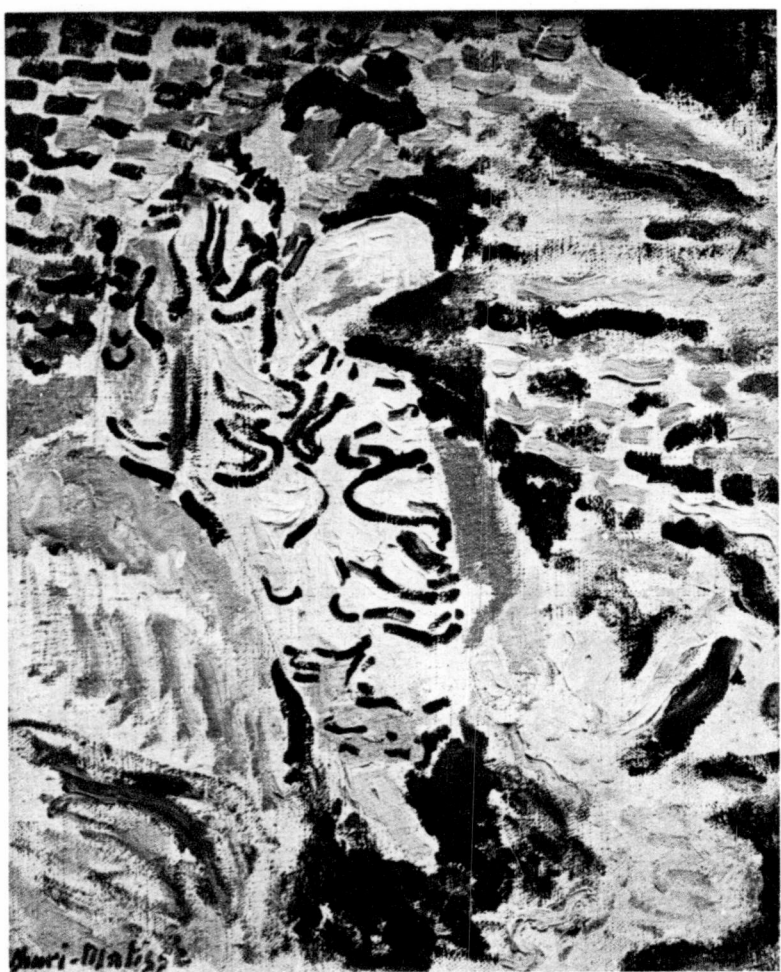

24. Henri Matisse.
MADAME MATISSE OR THE JAPANESE WOMAN
AT THE SEASHORE. 1905.
Oil on canvas.
Collection Philip Lilienthal, San Francisco

The center of attention, however, is one vast canvas by Matisse, *Joy of Life* (fig. 25), which has been placed in Room VI along with the paintings of Derain and Czóbel. The stir penetrates to the heart of the Salon committee, and extends as far as Montmartre. Rejected by many, including Vauxcelles, who nevertheless concedes that it "conveys a feeling of refreshing joy," this flamboyant profession of faith, with its powerful and orchestrated rhythms in which Matisse acknowledges his particular debts to Gauguin and foreshadows his own whole future development, puts the seal on his prestige as leader. His following was soon to be enlarged by three friends from Le Havre—Friesz, Dufy, and Braque—already well represented at the Salon, the first two as early as 1903. Friesz was later to work beside Matisse when the latter installed himself in the deconsecrated convent of the Sacred Heart on the Boulevard des Invalides; during the summer of 1906, he accompanies Braque to Antwerp. Dufy, an admirer of Matisse and an old friend of Marquet, was to spend the summer painting the same scenes with the latter at Trouville, Sainte-Adresse, and Le Havre, as his friends had done the year before, taking Mme Matisse along as a model.

Scattered in different places, Matisse at Biskra and then again at Collioure, Derain at L'Estaque between two visits to London, Manguin at Saint-Tropez, where he chose to spend a large part of the year, Camoin at Marseilles, Vlaminck faithful to the banks of the Seine, Van Dongen living in the Bateau Lavoir, they nevertheless all prepare enthusiastically for the opening of the new season in October, which, as they know, will be a decisive occasion for them.

In the hostile opinion of the critic Camille Mauclair, published in *Art et décoration*, the organizers of the Salon d'Automne had been careful this time not to "appear to present as the most interesting and the most worthy of critical attention, as they did last year . . . those dozen or so artists . . . with their pretentious, ignorant, and clownish works. . . ." They had been confined to a single room in order that they "no longer bring discredit on the talent of their more serious and sincere colleagues."

With the exception of Puy, faithful to Cézanne, in Room VI, Valtat, whose painting was nonetheless considered violent, in Room XVI, and Braque, who had not submitted anything, all the Fauves were indeed assembled in Room III. The effect was all the more striking because the important Gauguin retrospective of 227 works was on display almost next door. The Fauves, united and almost fully represented, here reach their peak. For once Vauxcelles has nothing but unreserved praise for "this blinding room where pure colors sing at the top of their lungs," as he describes the "fireworks" set off by these *enfants terribles de la maison.*" The collection as a whole struck him as "gay, young, ardent," and all found some favor in his eyes: Matisse, Manguin, Marquet, Derain, Vlaminck,

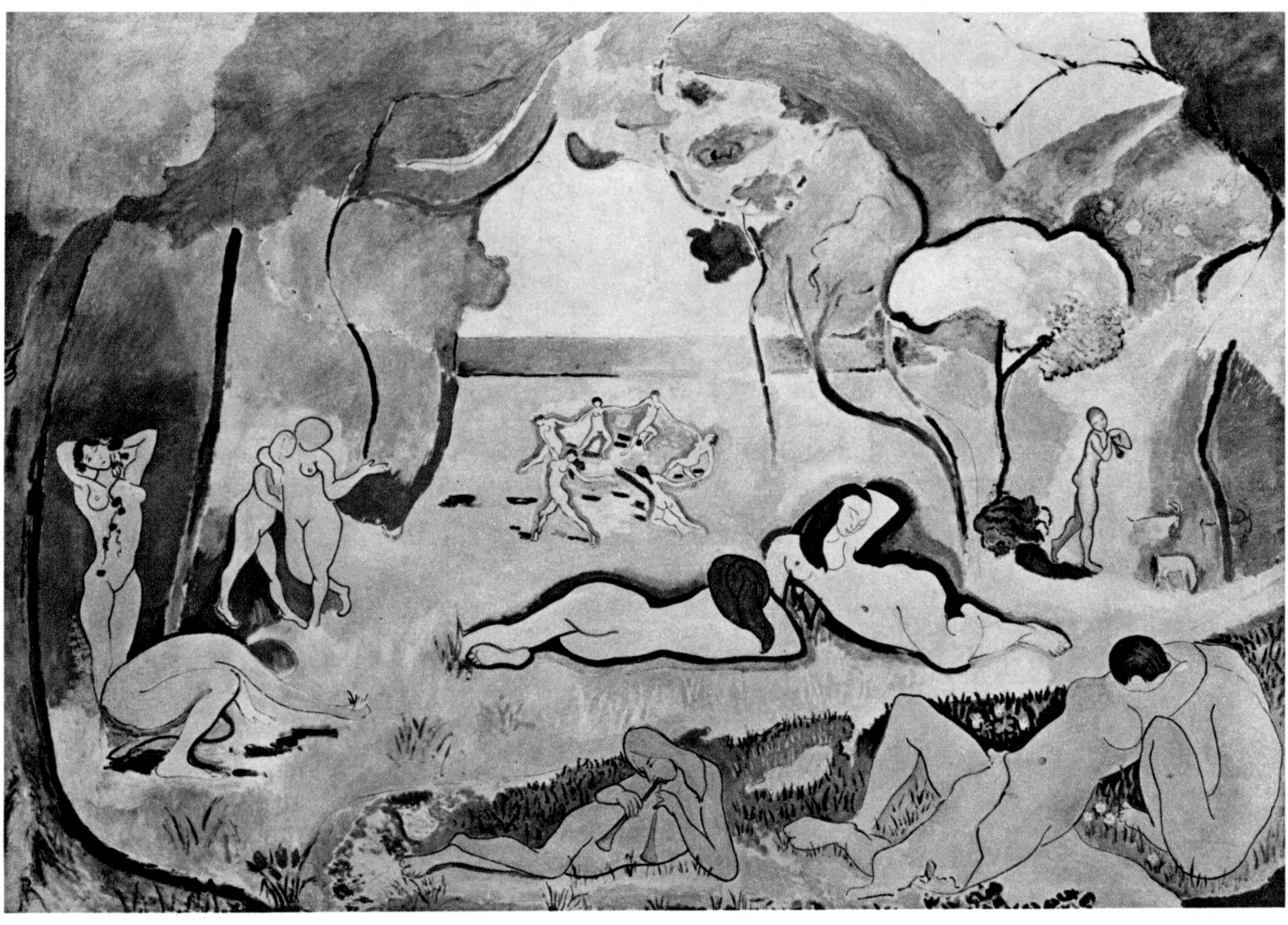

25. Henri Matisse. JOY OF LIFE. 1906–7. Oil on canvas, 68 1/2 × 93 3/4″. © *The Barnes Foundation, Merion, Pa.*

Czóbel, Van Dongen, Girieud, and Friesz, whom he congratulates on having "deliberately enrolled under this banner." Only Dufy was not mentioned, but the critic Paul Jamot, in *Gazette des beaux-arts*, points out his contribution to the group and "the liveliness of his renderings of sunlit crowds." Dufy, moreover, was having a large show at Berthe Weill's. She had decided to hold two annual exhibitions of the Fauve group, in March and November.

The year 1907 was to be for all the Fauves the year of their greatest development and the crowning of their success both in the Salons and the galleries, which vied with each other for the honor of exhibiting their works: Marquet and later Friesz at the Druet Gallery, Camoin and Van Dongen in Kahnweiler's shop in the Rue Vignon, which also bought from Derain and Friesz. The Blot Gallery organized a group show. The writer Elie Faure had been urging them for some time to collaborate in the decoration of the charity hospital, but unfortunately the project came to nothing.

And they remain the center of interest, the essential element in every discussion, despite the fact that they are split up in the Salons, divided alphabetically at the Indépendants, and dispersed also at the Salon d'Automne, Marquet in Room XV, Valtat in Room XVI, Manguin and Camoin placed with Duchamp-Villon in Room XVII, while the main body of the group, in which Braque is now finally included after the Indépendants, is assembled in Room XVIII.

Having championed them so far, Vauxcelles begins to be uneasy at the growing audience they attract, the authority they acquire, and the example that they set. In his review in *Gil Blas* on March 20, 1907, he passes to the attack with an ironical classification: "Matisse Fauve-in-chief, Derain deputy Fauve-in-chief, Friesz and Dufy adjutant Fauves, Girieud the irresolute Fauve . . . Czóbel the boorish Fauve, Bereny the apprentice Fauve, Delaunay the Fauvelet." He accuses Dujardin-Beaumetz, the Director of Fine Arts, of having "tried to domesticate the Fauves by giving them official recognition." He openly protests that "a movement that I consider dangerous (despite the strong sympathy

27

that I feel for its leaders) is forming among a small group of young artists. A chapel has been set up where two imperious priests, Derain and Matisse, officiate; a small band of innocent catechumens has there received baptism. The dogma consists in an uncertain schematism, which in the name of some obscure pictorial abstraction bans all relief and volume. I find little to attract me in this new religion."

In September he rejoices that the Salon d'Automne has ceased "to favor only the Fauves" by scattering them in different rooms, and attacks Matisse for "his uncouthness as a draftsman . . . his disregard for form," accusing him of "being a theoretician rather than a painter." He also blames the "highly gifted" Friesz for "having thrown himself headlong into the abyss," and suspects Vlaminck of wanting to "defect." In *Gazette des beaux-arts*, André Pératté discusses the "painters of today and tomorrow who declare themselves followers of Gauguin and Cézanne." While congratulating Manguin and Camoin for having "abandoned arbitrary distortions in favor of classical simplicity," he is inclined to show indulgence toward what he calls "the excesses of the rabid Cézannists, of whom Matisse is the standard bearer," and praises André Métthey for having enlisted the collaboration of the group for his experiments in painted ceramics, exhibited at the same Salon d'Automne.

What is the situation at the end of this year in which Fauvism has definitively taken shape, attracted widespread general attention, and gained a strong influence in France as well as abroad?

Vauxcelles's fears are far from unjustified. In two years

a new pictorial language has been introduced and propagated, and now acquires for many artists the force of law and habit. Based on spontaneous transposition and the exaltation of direct emotion, on the possibilities of expression through color contrasts, linear elements, rhythm and surface combinations, this language above all seeks intensity, impact, cursiveness, and simplification. This conception necessarily implies abandoning traditional conventions regarding subject and object, relief, chiaroscuro, and effects of perspective; it requires a complete transformation of one's notions of space and time. In reality it confines painting to an experiment in two dimensions, but one where the bold equivalents of light, the orchestration of color values, the plastic organization of the composition all combine to satisfy the needs of expression and to recreate depth and space in other dimensions that suggest a continuous unfolding in time. Accentuated and harmonized by the economy of means used, the pure intensity of the moment is deepened and prolonged in a joyous outburst, in radiant delight.

No preconceived system prevails, however, among these artists; no method is dogmatically applied. The artists remain highly individualistic despite their common practice of treating the same subject, and their experiments run parallel. If in the beginning pure color had often played a decisive role as a dynamic factor and catalyzer, its use in flat areas, broad expanses, bold brushstrokes, and light washes remains extremely diversified, and as early as 1906 Matisse and Derain venture to use half-tones, shades of gray and ocher. They also exploit the resources of drafts-

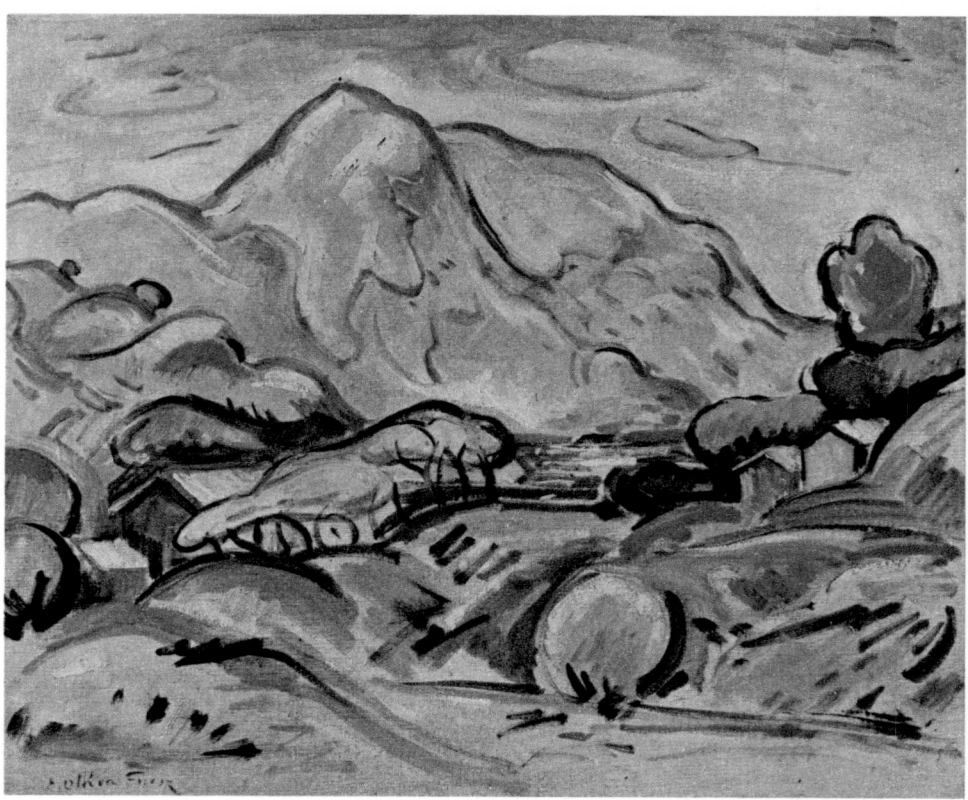

26. Othon Friesz. LANDSCAPE. 1906.
Oil on canvas, 13 × 16 1/8".
Private collection, Switzerland

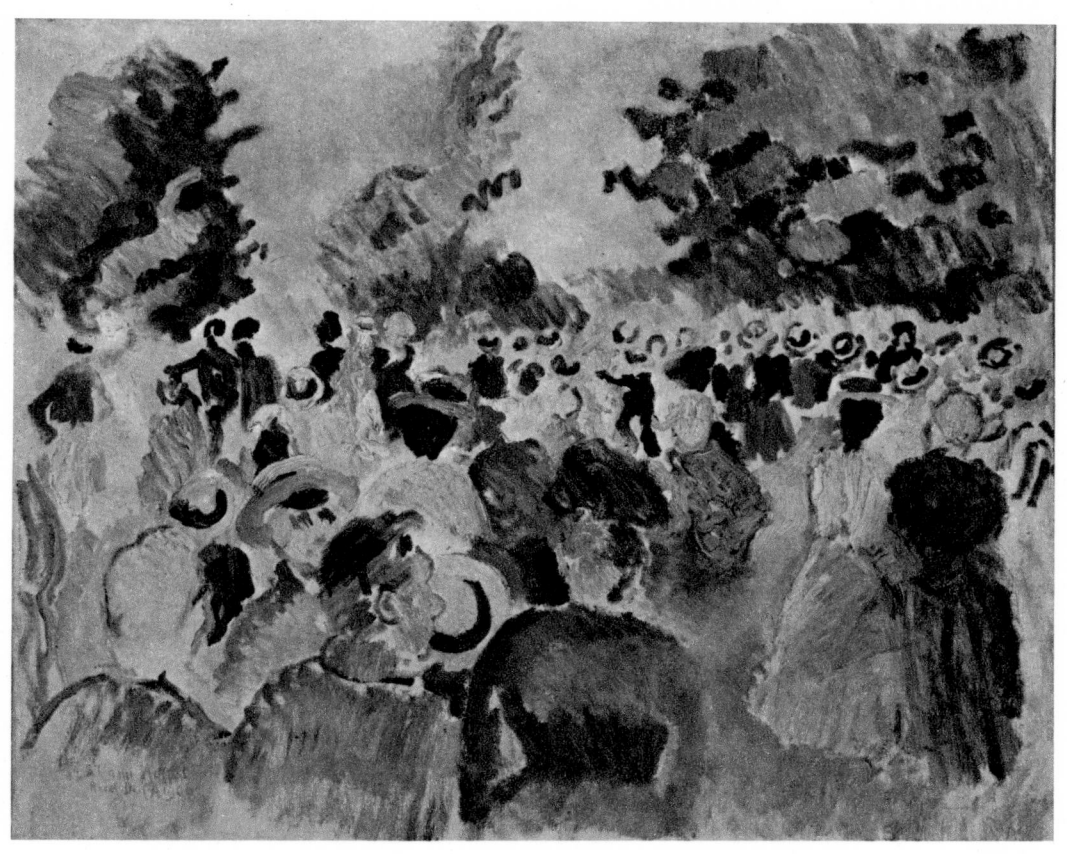

27. Raoul Dufy. COUNTRY FESTIVAL. 1906.
Oil on canvas, 18 1/8 × 21 5/8″.
Private collection, Paris

28. André Derain. L'ESTAQUE. 1906.
Oil on canvas, 50 3/8 × 76 3/4″.
Private collection, Paris

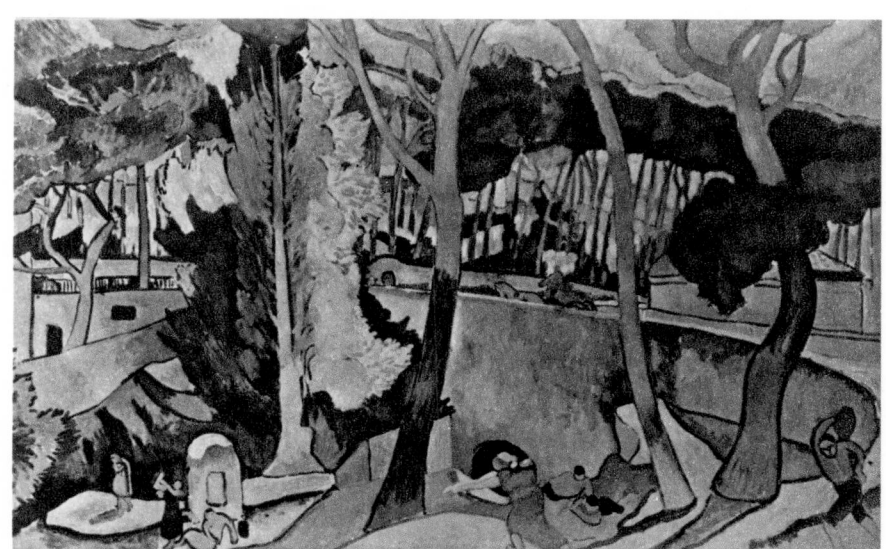

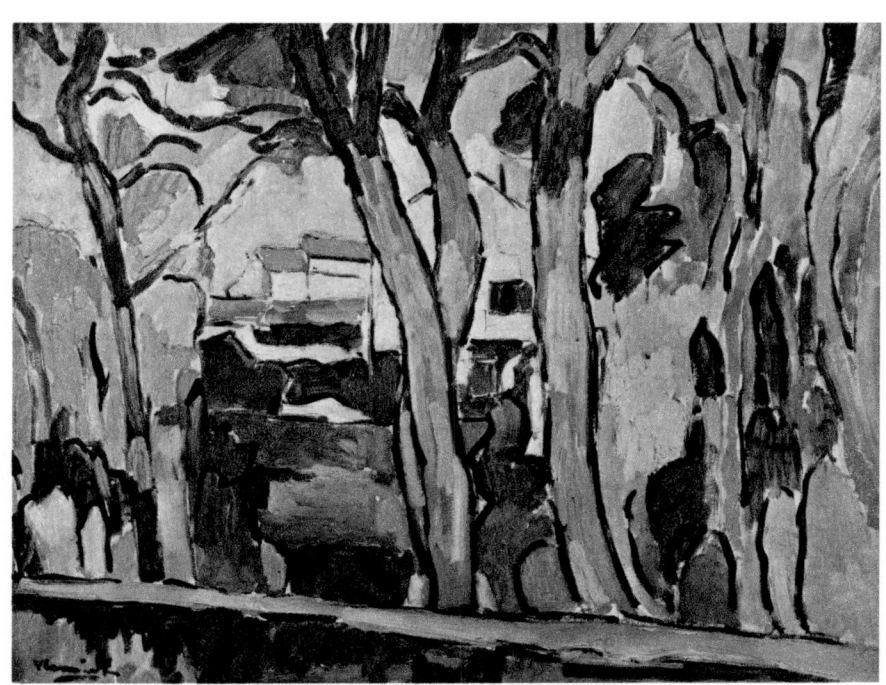

29. Maurice de Vlaminck. THE RED TREES. 1906.
Oil on canvas, 25 5/8 × 31 7/8″.
Musée National d'Art Moderne, Paris

manship in an infinite variety of ways: marked contours, arabesques, allusive or decorative symbols, and subjective distortions.

Before long each painter reveals his particular commitment: Valtat an eloquent fervor, Marquet concision, Vlaminck and Van Dongen the violence of impulse, Camoin and Puy a desire for moderation, Czóbel an expansive lyricism, Friesz a tendency to the baroque, Dufy a vibrant exuberance, Braque a refined taste, Derain and Matisse the need for order. In *La Phalange* of December, 1907, Apollinaire gives an extraordinarily penetrating analysis of Matisse's work, isolating first of all his typically French artistic qualities: "his forceful simplicity and gentle lucidity." He praises him for "confidently following his triumphant instinct," and clearly discerns that "the nature of his art is to be reasonable." Finally, he affirms that if Matisse has "assumed the stature and confident pride that distinguish him," it is because, while pursuing his interest in the art of every race, he has remained faithful to the European heritage.

This judgment may seem overly subtle and irrelevant, but is actually quite just, and no doubt explains why, in the years that followed, Fauvism, particularly in the person of Matisse, continued to exert such a powerful attraction and undiminished authority throughout Europe, while in its country of origin its disappearance was soon to be officially recorded.

DENOUEMENT

As we have already seen, the story of the Fauves draws to a rapid close during the year 1908. The final act seems to play itself out unbeknown to the protagonists, which only shows that they feel free to develop as they like, unhindered by doctrines. They continue moreover to meet, work together, and participate in the same shows.

In 1907, Marquet, Camoin, and Friesz had gone together to London, and Braque and Friesz had spent the summer at La Ciotat—in 1908, Derain and Vlaminck paint side by side at Les Martigues during the summer, while Friesz and Dufy travel to Munich. The following year, Manguin and Marquet visit Naples, and Matisse and Marquet go to Munich with Purrmann. They all gather once more at the biannual show at Berthe Weill's, who at Matisse's request holds a Czóbel exhibition in 1908, while Bernheim-Jeune shows the work of Van Dongen. The provinces have begun to take an interest in Fauvism, which occupies the limelight at Le Havre in June, 1908, at the Cercle de l'Art Moderne, in a general presentation introduced by Apollinaire, and again in Toulouse, where Charles Malpel organizes successive exhibitions on the premises of *Le Télégramme* and *L'Union artistique*.

The group, however, was already on the point of dis-

banding. Several, like Marquet, Camoin, and particularly Puy, have grown tired of the prolonged tension, and for some time have shown a desire to escape from this state of paroxysm, which clearly does not suit them, in order to return to more traditional painting. Several others, headed by Friesz and soon to be followed by Derain, Dufy, and even Vlaminck—not to mention Braque, now frankly in opposition—seem to have lost their confidence, and in their indecision take their inspiration from Cézanne.

This spectacular resurgence of the old Aix master after his death in 1906 is readily explainable. His prestige and influence had grown steadily among the new generation, according to the conclusions of the inquiry conducted in its midst and published in *Le Mercure de France* by Charles Morice, himself more a partisan of Gauguin. The articles published after Cézanne's death, and the twin retrospectives in 1907 at the Bernheim Gallery and at the Salon d'Automne, revealed to everybody the importance of his work, which had so far remained rather inaccessible. Bathers and still lifes immediately came back into fashion, and Matisse was not afraid to go along by paying homage to the artist whom he always called "the god of painting."

For many this was to be the occasion to put themselves in order, to resist the magic of pure color, now branded dangerous and a dead end, and to undergo a cure of austerity and constructive discipline. Thus the ground was prepared for Cubism. Almost a year before its public appearance on the scene at the Braque exhibition at Kahnweiler's in November, 1908, Cubism had revealed itself forcefully in Picasso's *Demoiselles d'Avignon*. It had been widely discussed in the studios and especially in the Stein drawing room in the Rue de Fleurus, where Picasso and Matisse amicably but firmly confronted each other.

A new page is being turned. As we have seen, Vauxcelles is so well aware of this that, at the time of the 1908 Indépendants, he ridicules "the schematizers . . . who want to create an abstract art," and faced with Braque's canvases he admits: "I am completely out of my depth. This is Kanaka art, willfully and aggressively unintelligible." The whole of this Salon, despite its array of 6,700 works, disappoints him and sounds the death knell of many hopes. The excitement of the previous years is spent. The public lacks curiosity and the artists enthusiasm. For the first time Matisse has submitted nothing, nor has Derain, and their friends have dispersed in all directions. In Room VII, which Vauxcelles still calls "the Fauves' den" by way of final farewell, he notes that all except Van Dongen have "fled." He no longer thinks to use the expression, except to recall a vanished past, in mentioning the Salon d'Automne of the same year.

No more special rooms, no more group aspirations— the divergences grow more marked, and everyone again falls into line. The whole movement has broken up or disappeared. Ironically enough, the organizers have tried to

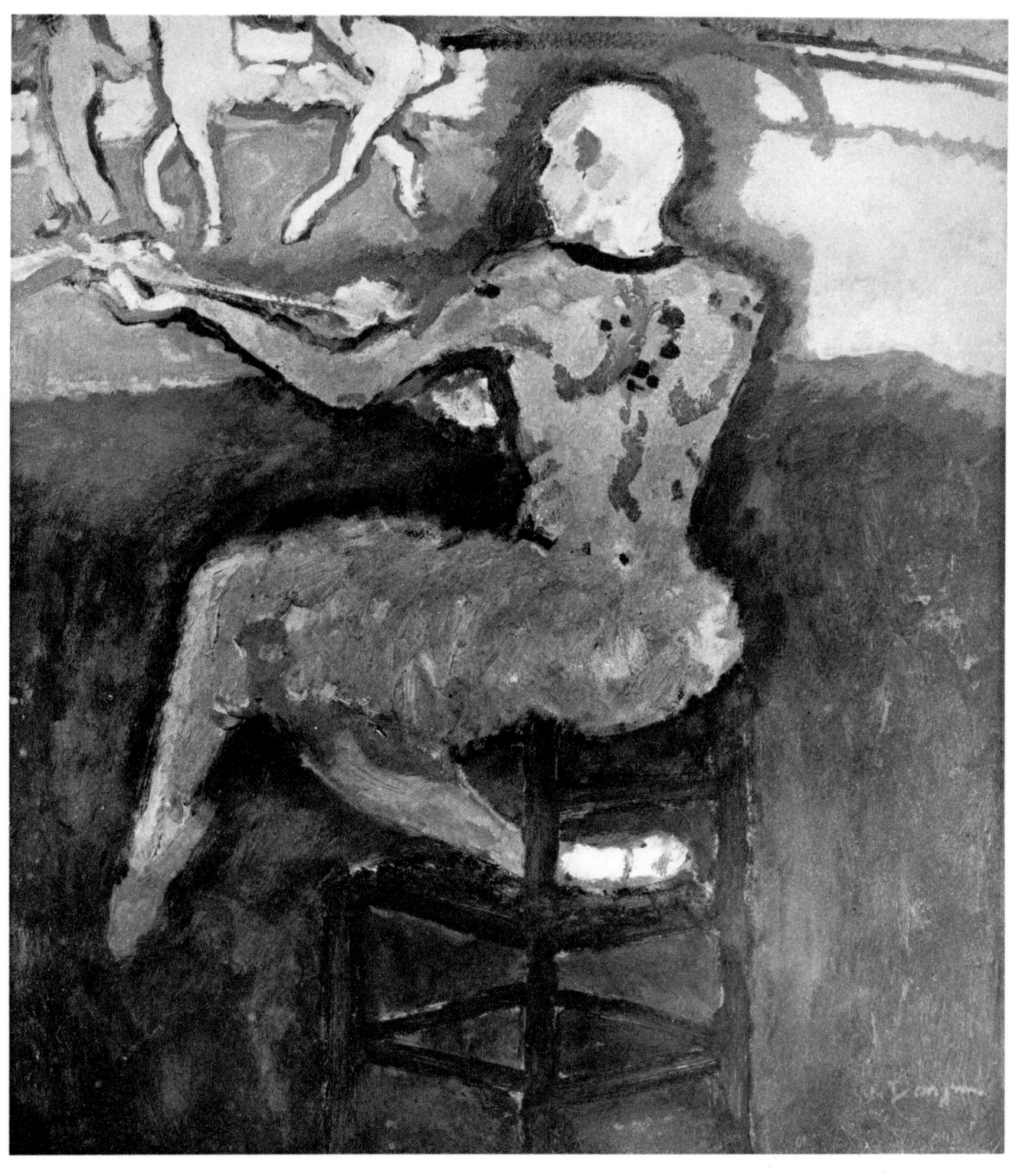

30. Kees van Dongen. THE CLOWN. 1906. Oil on panel, 29 1/8 × 23 5/8″.
Collection Mme Lucile Martinais-Manguin, Paris

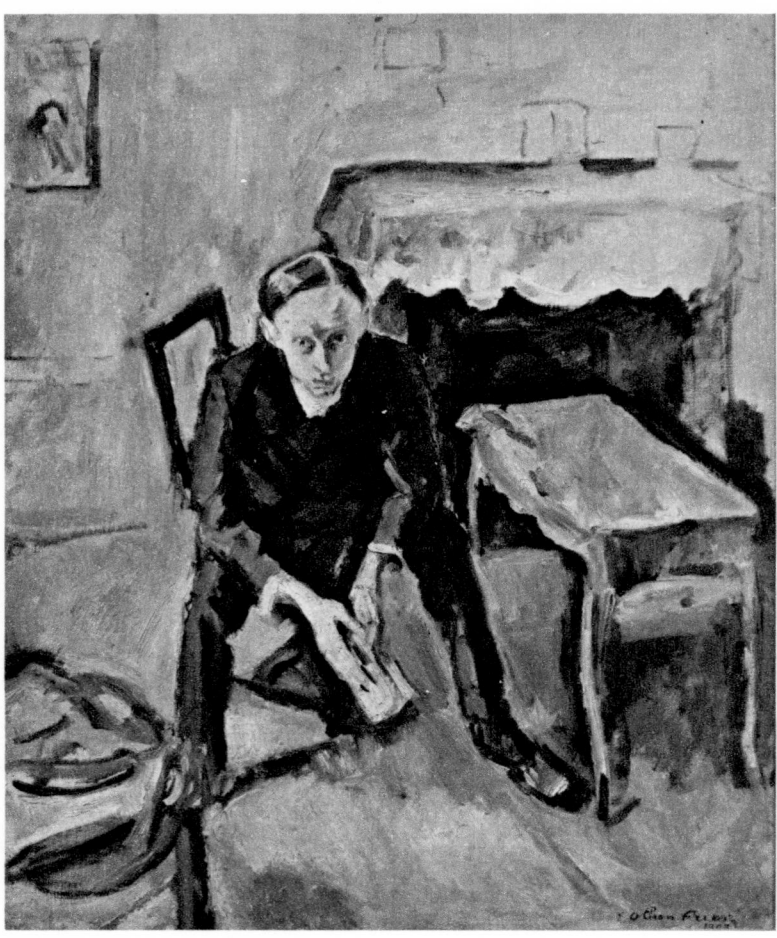

31. Othon Friesz. PORTRAIT OF FERNAND FLEURET. C. 1907.
Oil on canvas, 28 3/4 × 23 5/8".
Musée National d'Art Moderne, Paris

make strange juxtapositions, as Vauxcelles observes: the Cézannian austerity of Derain's bathers and cypresses beside a society portraitist in Room XII, or Vallotton in Room XVI opposite Matisse accompanied by Van Dongen and Camoin. The dispersal is complete. Manguin hangs in Room III, Puy and Vlaminck in Room VI, Friesz and Valtat in Room XVII. Braque and Dufy are absent and Marquet is represented only by drawings.

Fragmented and divided, Fauvism is now nothing but a vanishing ghost. The critics, however, continue out of habit to group together friends who are now separated by the Salon organizers or by their individual tendencies. In *Gazette des beaux-arts* Pierre Hepp concludes his article by declaring that a "family resemblance" still exists among Matisse, Friesz, Derain, Vlaminck, and Van Dongen, who "all have fire," and stresses that this "blaze of hope warms the Salon d'Automne and creates a center of energy there."

Malpel writes similarly about the Indépendants of 1909, that "Van Dongen, Matisse, Valtat, Friesz, Marquet, Dufy, Manguin reign here." Yet their works, which meet with increasing opposition, are scattered as usual throughout the relatively empty rooms—there were only 1,700 entries!—and beside them hang those of such painters as Léger, Metzinger, Herbin, and Lhote, who within two years, as their official successors, will constitute the Cubist group.

Life and Survival of the Myth

With the more accurate perception that comes with time, we are today in a better position to evaluate a phenomenon that so far has hardly been taken into account, no doubt because it was found too difficult to explain. Just when the Fauve group, seemingly moribund, is breaking up and disappearing as such from the Salons, it recovers its strength elsewhere, gaining in France, and still more abroad, an immense range of influence scarcely to be compared with what preceded or followed it.

There are various reasons for this reversal. First of all, Fauvism, at the time of its appearance, aroused a lively interest in Parisian circles, many artists taking up its cause even if later they rejected it completely. Secondly, Matisse rapidly established a personal reputation which enabled him, through his work, his writings, and especially his Academy, to exert an influence that soon spread beyond the confines of France.

Finally, it would seem that there was a general need connected with the period, since regardless of whether Fauve paintings are present or not—it hardly matters—an identical current develops within a relatively short space of time in almost all European countries, thus confirming the existence of the Dionysiac myth forged by the Fauves.

IN FRANCE

Among the original nucleus of artists who gave birth to the movement and were represented in the rooms set aside for the Fauves, many familiar names, closely connected with the discussions and reviews of the time, deserve at least to be mentioned—Linaret, who died prematurely; Biette and Milcendeau, who have since been forgotten; Girieud, who, after a promising start, unfortunately took another path.

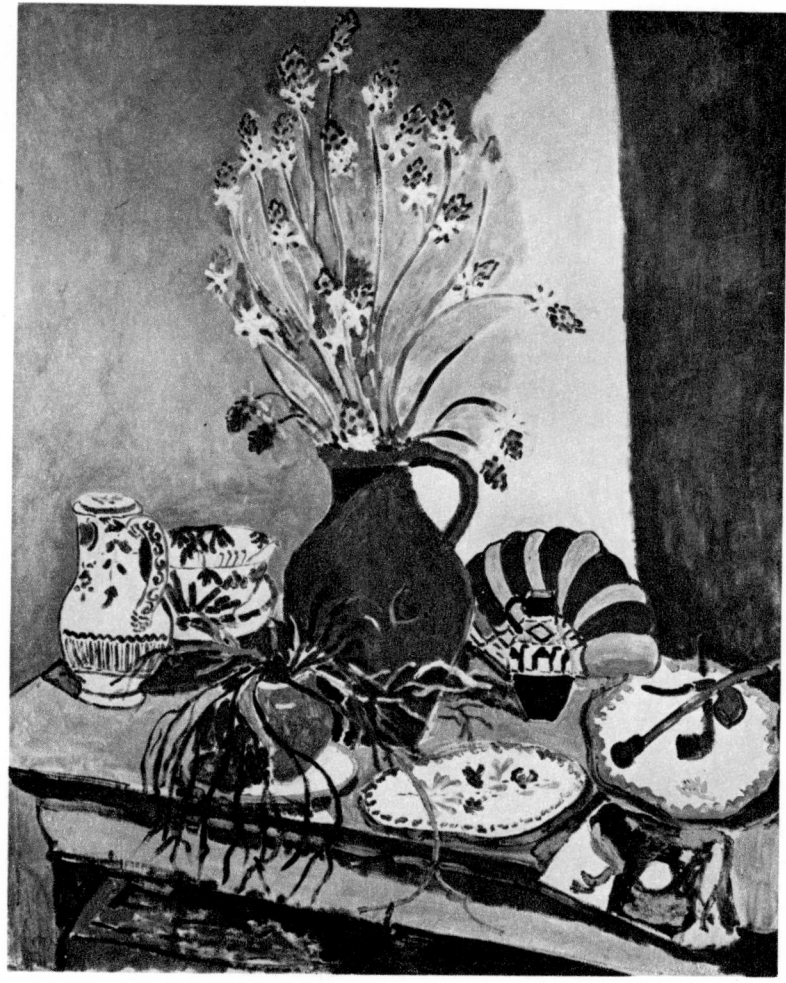

32. Henri Matisse. L'ASPHODÈLE. 1907.
Oil on canvas, 45 7/8 × 35".
Museum Folkwang, Essen

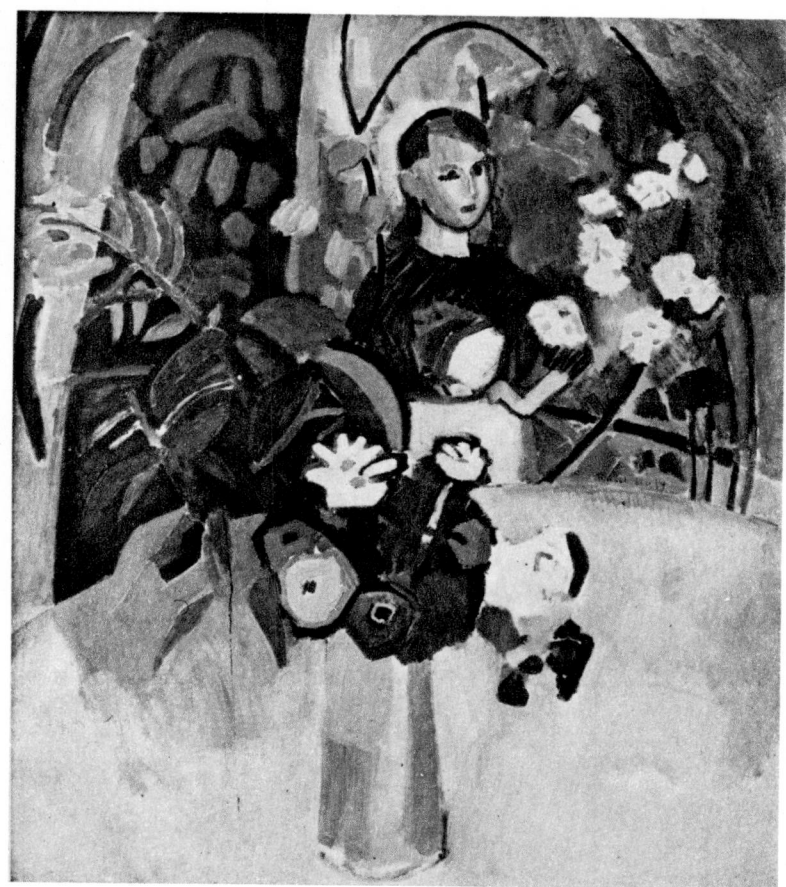

33. Maurice de Vlaminck. STILL LIFE. 1907.
Oil on canvas, 28 3/4 × 23 5/8".
Staatsgalerie, Stuttgart

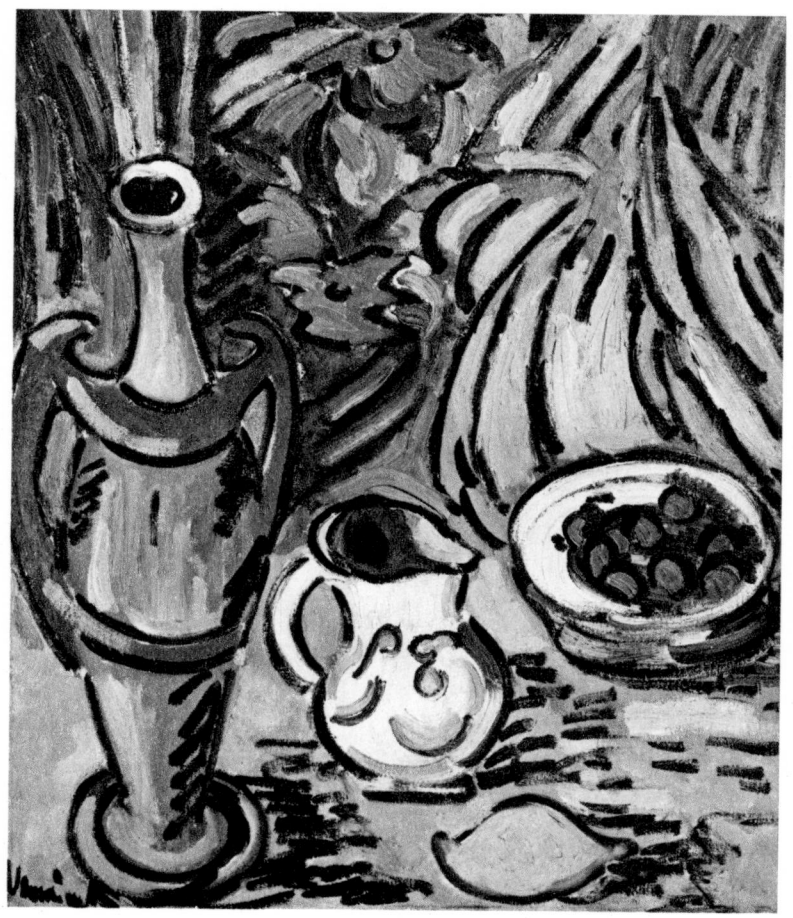

34. Raoul Dufy. JEANNE AMONG THE FLOWERS. 1907.
Oil on canvas, 35 3/8 × 30 1/4".
Nouveau Musée des Beaux-Arts, Le Havre.
Gift of Mme Dufy, 1963

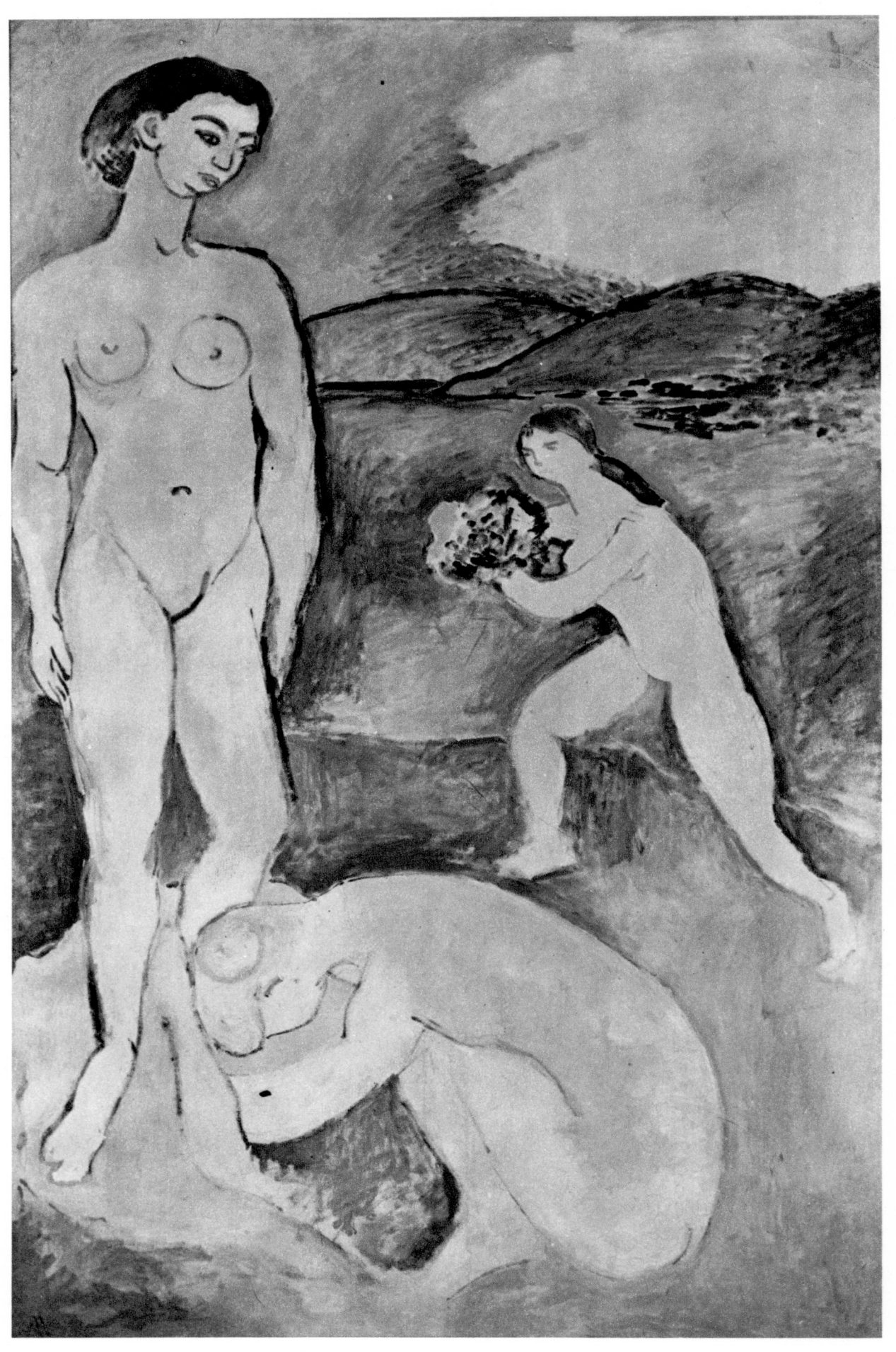

35. Henri Matisse. LE LUXE. 1906. Oil on canvas, 82 5/8 × 54 3/8". *Musée National d'Art Moderne, Paris*

The group grew so fast, however, that it is difficult to establish its exact membership. Its ranks swelled particularly between 1906 and 1907, when it reached its peak. Vauxcelles, as we have seen, ironically notes the presence of Delaunay and Bereny at the time of the Salon des Indépendants in 1907; in the same year Michel Puy remarks that "Metzinger, Le Fauconnier, Perlrott, all of them characterized by their brilliant colors, have joined the ranks." The names of many other French painters should be added, as well as those of foreign artists who were flocking to Paris. A number of future Cubists—Picasso was not among the first to make the experiment—passed in varying degrees through the intermediary stage of Fauvism. They included Villon and still more his brother Marcel Duchamp, who was closely associated with Kupka and likewise painted a number of highly expressive portraits. The same is true of Pascin, and above all of Modigliani, whose works were to hang in the Salons beside those of the Fauves.

An increasingly important group called Les Dômiers, from which Matisse was later to recruit his pupils, had formed in Montparnasse in 1905. Most of them habitually spent their days at the Café du Dôme (hence their name), had studied in Munich, and showed a lively interest in the new trends. They include Germans and Hungarians, among them Rudolf Levy, Eugen Spiro, Czóbel, Purrmann, such other friends of Pascin's as William Howard, the Americans Maurice Sterne and Max Weber, and the future critic Wilhelm Uhde, who at the time exhibited Fauve canvases in his small gallery next to the closely allied paintings of Sonia Terk. Nearly all of them embraced the current fashion and had the distinction of taking part in the Salon d'Automne as early as 1906 or 1907.

Apart from this throng of foreigners who lived in Paris for a number of years and often became deeply involved in the prevailing trend, others gave the movement temporary but nonetheless effective support. Such is the case with Kandinsky and Jawlensky, who since 1904 had regularly sent works from Munich to the Salon d'Automne, but without attracting much attention. Finally Kandinsky, wishing to enter further into the Paris milieu, settles for a year in the Rue de Binelles in Sèvres with Gabriele Münter. Here he works intensely, and the results that he exhibits in such profusion at the Salon d'Automne of 1906 (twenty pieces: paintings, woodcuts, various handicrafts made in collaboration with Gabriele), and in smaller numbers at the Indépendants of 1907, already mark a very interesting development that will assume a more definite form soon after at Murnau and will finally earn him a favorable reception at the Paris Salons, to which he remains faithful even after moving away.

Munch was similarly faithful to the Indépendants from a distance, despite the unjust scorn in which he was held by the French press. His *Garçons baignants*, to use the title in the 1904 catalogue, brilliantly anticipates his future development. Another distant contributor to the Indépendants was Cuno Amiet, who ended by joining the movement.

Two Americans then living in Paris, Patrick Henry Bruce and Alfred Maurer, exhibited regularly at the Salon d'Automne. They soon became closely associated with Fauvism, and when Matisse opened his Academy, Bruce was the *massier*, the pupil charged to collect the subscriptions and pay the expenses of the studio.

In the spring of 1908, at the instigation of his friends Sarah Stein and Purrmann, whom he had met at the Rue de Fleurus, Matisse agreed to advise a small group of artists who met in his studio in a secularized convent in the Rue de Sèvres. Later obliged to move, he took larger quarters at 35 Boulevard des Invalides, in another former convent, that of the Sacred Heart. The news of the instruction he was prepared to give soon spread, and, with the arrival of

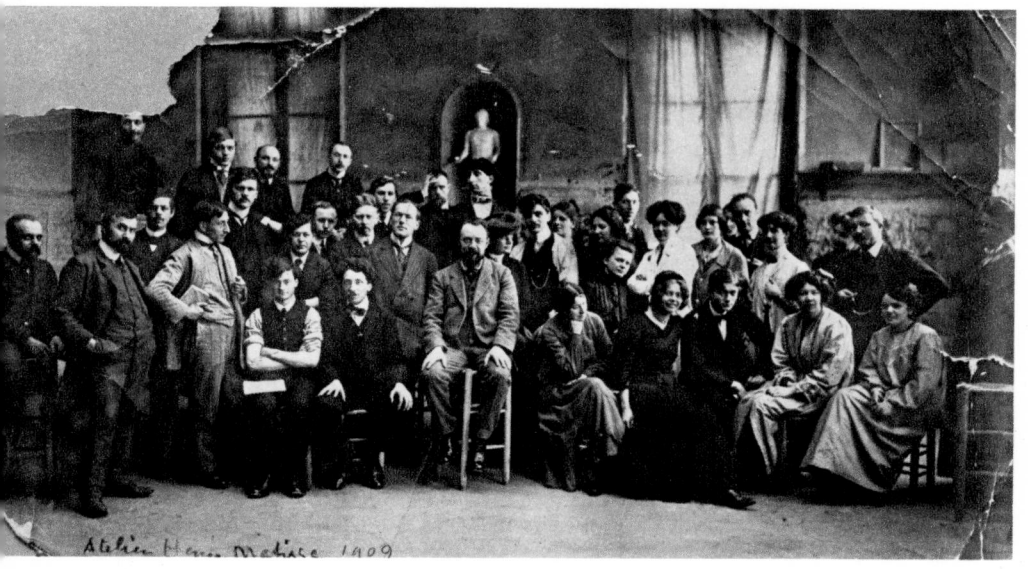

36. Matisse's Studio in 1909

1. Straube, 2. Perlrott-Csaba,
3. Purrmann, 4. Dubreuil, 5. Rosam,
6. Guindet, 7. Revold, 8. Levy,
9. Matisse, 10. Grünewald,
11. Vollmoeller-Purrmann, 12. Wassilief,
13. Sörensen, 14. Jolin, 15. Palme,
16. Hjerten-Grünewald

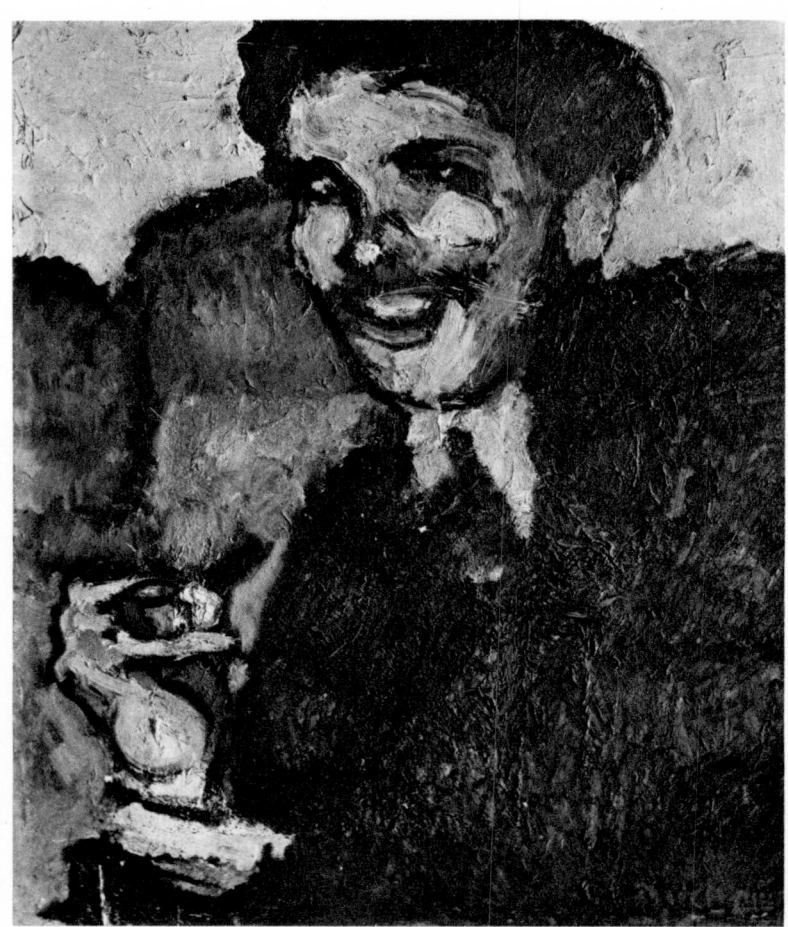

38. Marcel Duchamp. PORTRAIT OF DOCTOR TRIBOUT. 1910.
Oil on canvas, 21 5/8 × 17 3/4″.
Musée des Beaux-Arts, Rouen

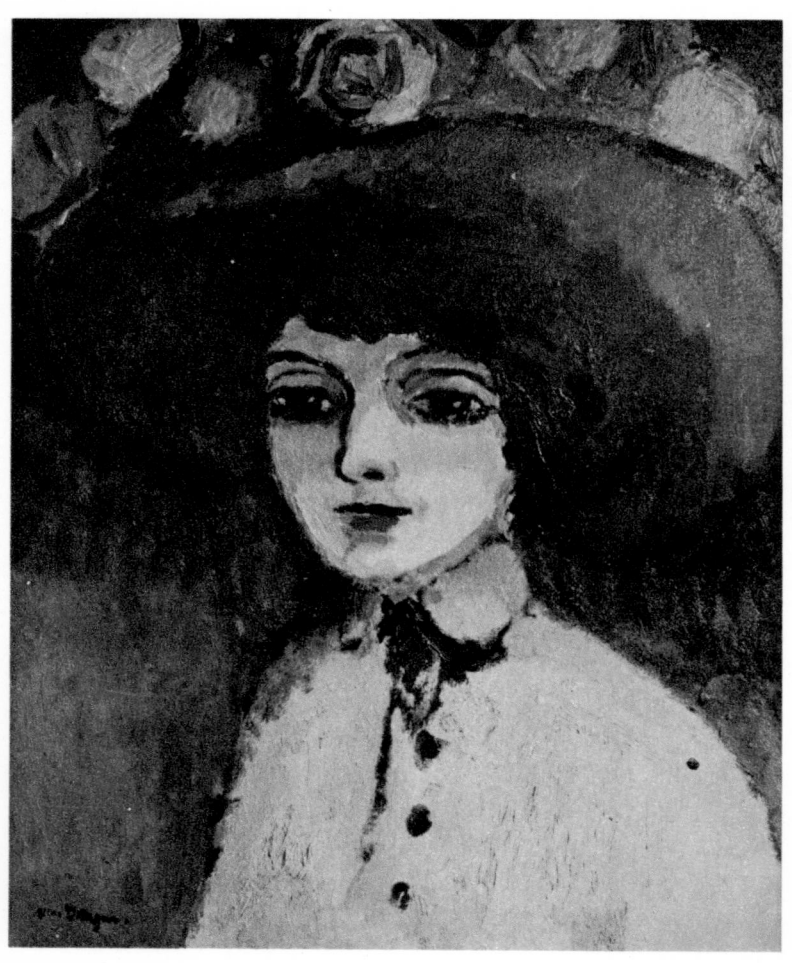

37. Kees van Dongen.
PARISIAN FROM MONTMARTRE. C. 1907.
Oil on canvas, 25 5/8 × 21 1/4″.
Nouveau Musée des Beaux-Arts, Le Havre.
Gift of Auguste Marande, 1936

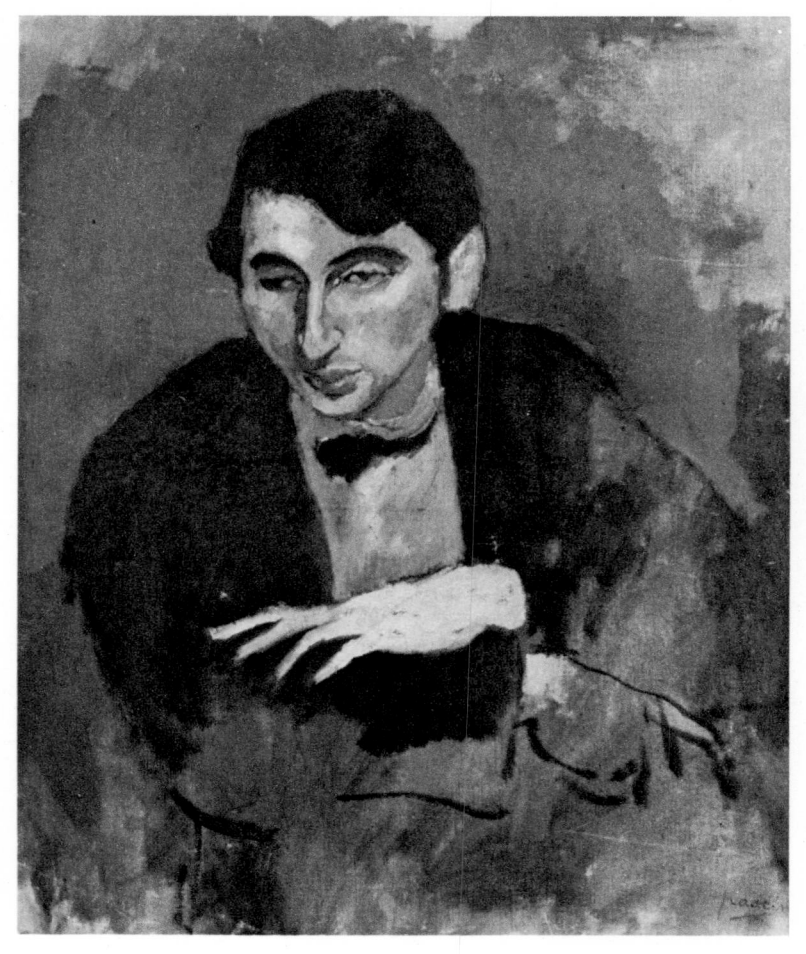

39. Jules Pascin. PORTRAIT OF ISAAC GRÜNEWALD. 1911.
Oil on canvas, 25 5/8 × 21 1/4″.
Collection Lucy Krogh, Paris

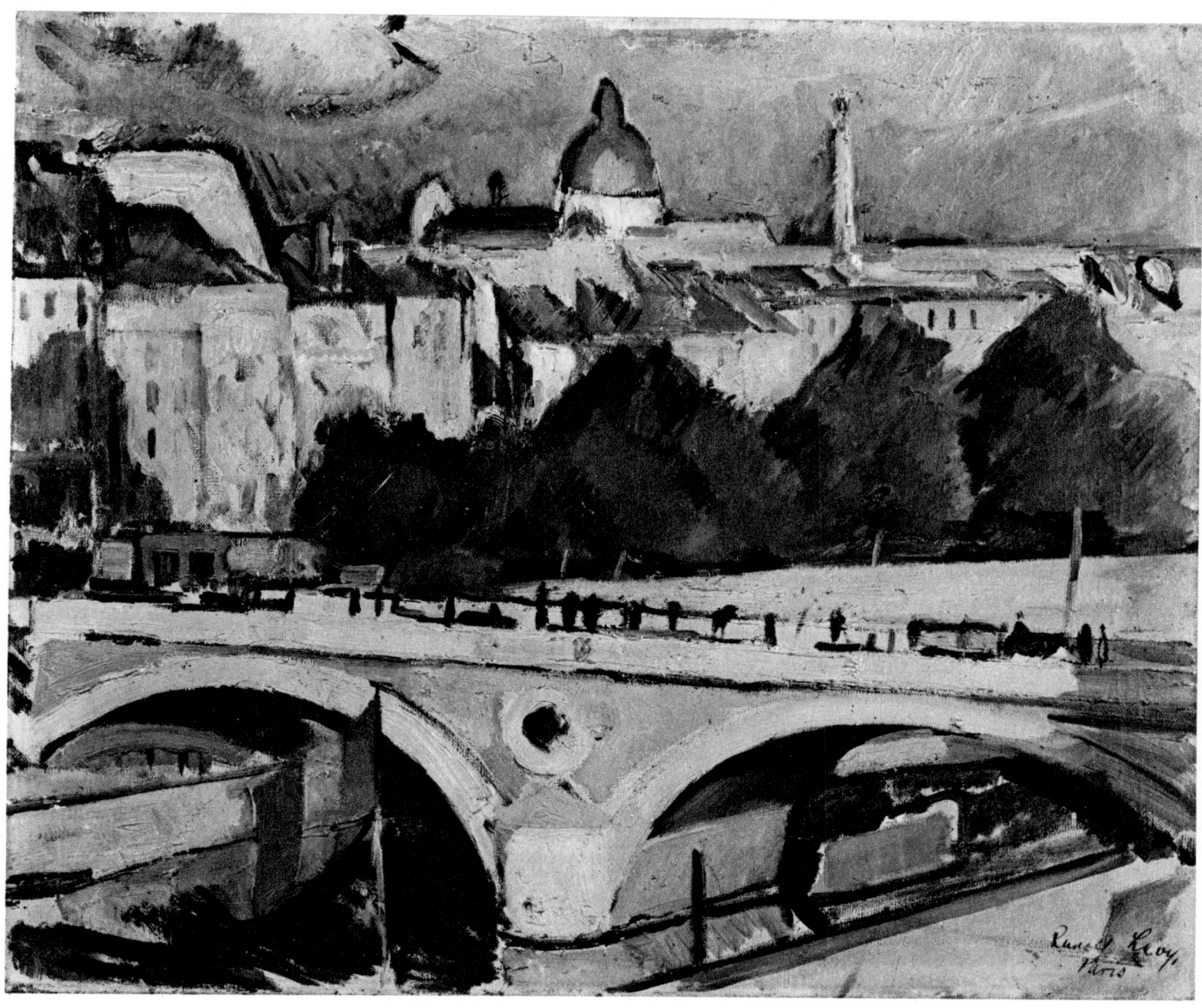

40. Rudolf Levy. AT THE SEINE IN PARIS. 1910. Oil on canvas, 18 1/8 × 21 5/8″. *Wilhelm-Lehmbruck-Museum der Stadt, Duisburg*

a new academic year in October, the rush of candidates forced him to organize a regular school with Purrmann as director.

The enthusiasm was entirely justified, for Matisse was then at the height of his fame. In the course of the year he exhibited watercolors and prints at the Stieglitz Gallery in New York, presented a total of thirty paintings, sculptures, and drawings at the Salon d'Automne—a rather unusual privilege—and finally organized a show of paintings at the Cassirer Gallery in Berlin. At the same time he lucidly stated his position in *Notes d'un peintre*, published in *La Grande Revue* of December 25, 1908, and soon translated into German in *Kunst und Künstler*, and into Russian in *Zolotoye Runo* (Golden Fleece), with a list of his works and an article by Mercereau pointing out his influence.

The expressiveness that he seeks, above all else, in the arrangement of the picture, through the composition and the drawing, by abandoning the literal representation of movement; the state of intensified sensation, the living harmony of color to which he aspires; the expressive quality of colors to which he is so sensitive; the desire to express, especially through the figure, the almost religious feeling that he has for life; the balanced, pure, and serene art of which he dreams, without preconceived notions of style—these, in his own terms, form the substance of the profession of faith which he drew up and which he tried to impart to his pupils during the weekly lessons. At the end of three years of sometimes unrewarded effort, tired and wishing to have more time to work and travel, he closes the Academy, of which Isaac Grünewald had become the *massier*.

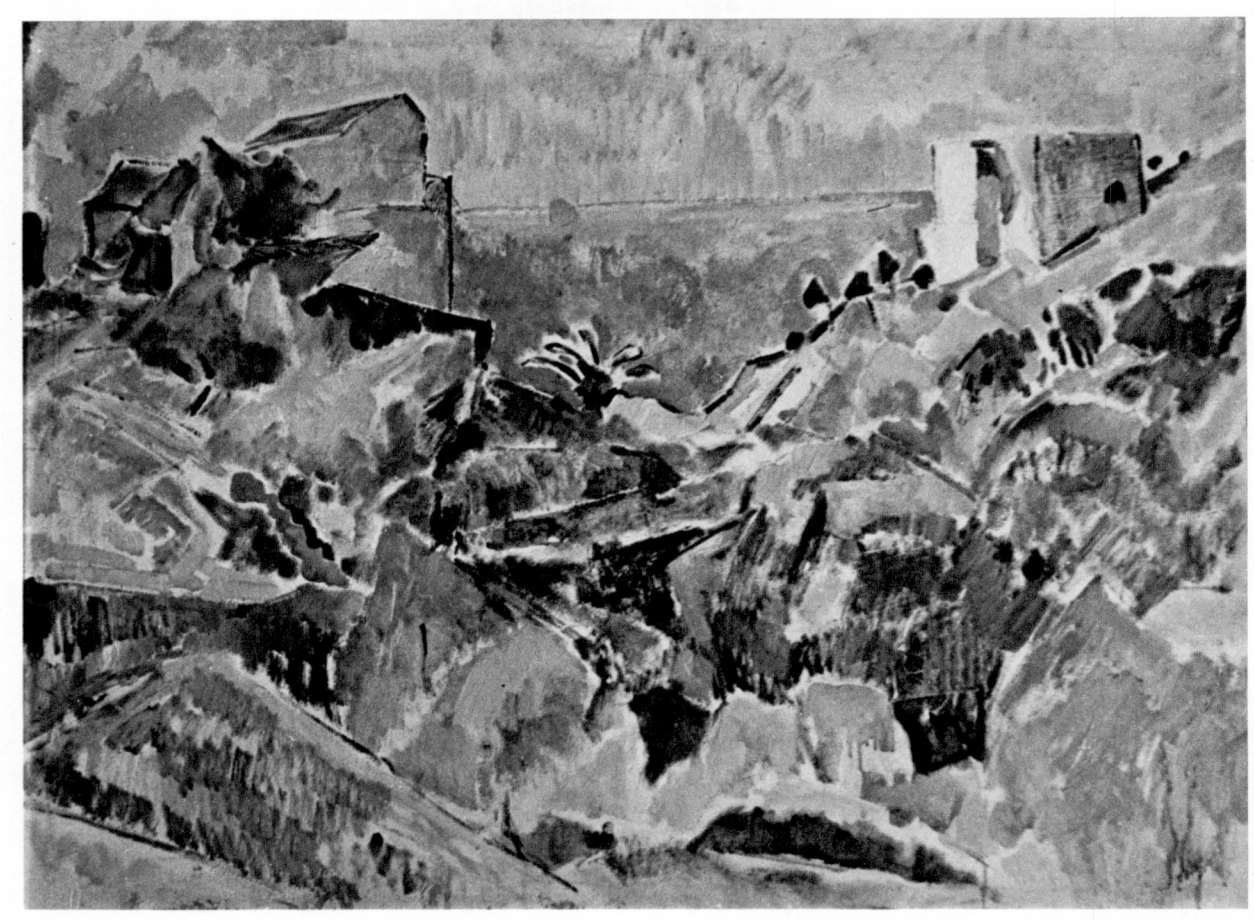

41. Oskar Moll. CÔTE D'AZUR. 1912–13. Oil on canvas, 29 1/2 × 39 3/4". *Städtisches Museum, Trier*

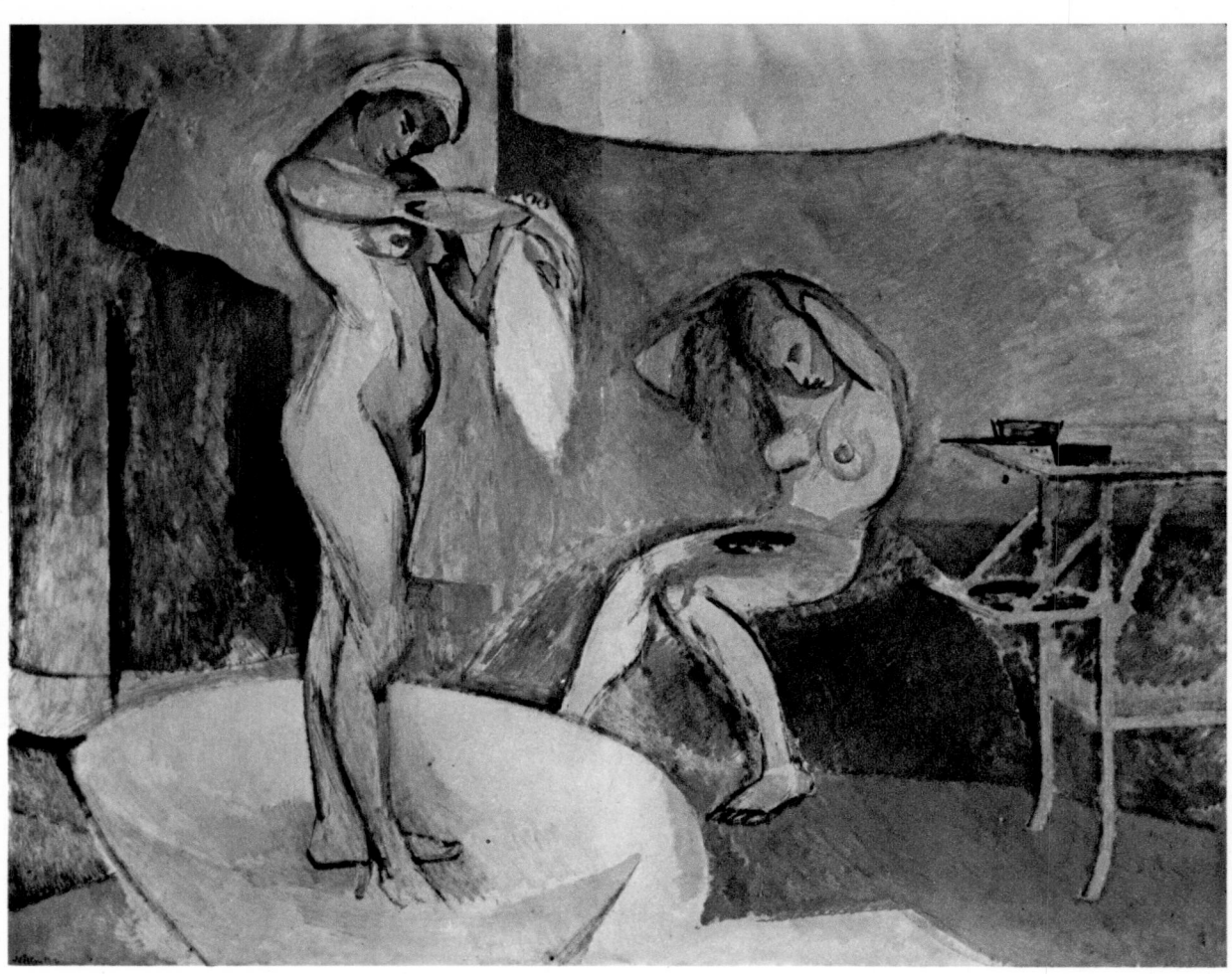

42. Franz Nölken. WOMEN BATHING. C. 1912. Oil on canvas, 23 1/4 × 32 1/4".
Collection Dr. Helene Gropp, Hamburg

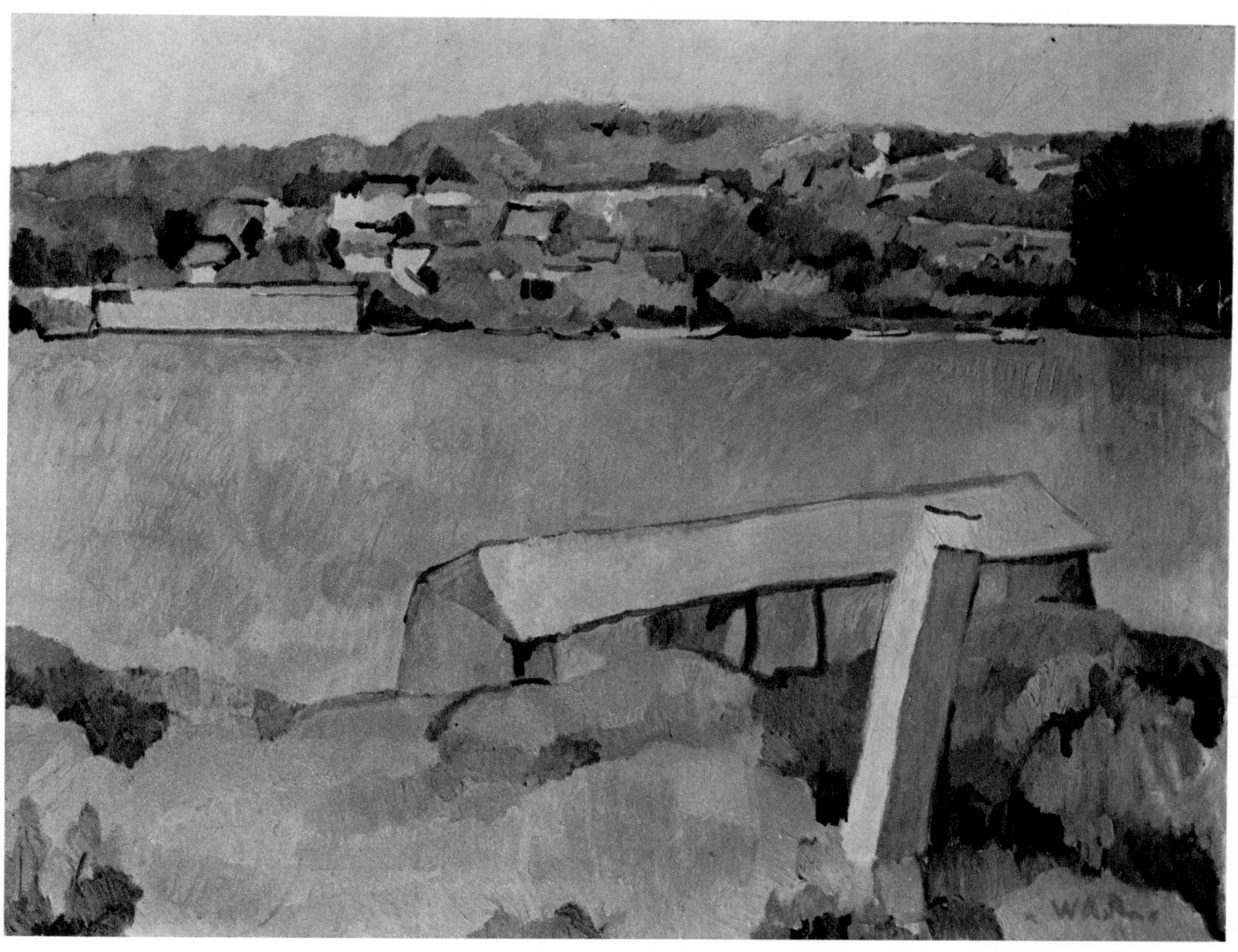

43. Walter Rosam. VIEW OF THE SEINE. 1912. Oil on canvas, 19 5/8 × 25 1/4".
Collection Lilo Streiff, Zurich

It is true that only some of the 120 students who frequented the studio on the Boulevard des Invalides until 1911 were converted to the song of life and color that Matisse tried to convey to them with his usual proselytizing ardor. But they swelled the ranks of those who were spreading and defending the spirit of Fauvism throughout the world. Among all these foreigners the Germans—who already formed a majority in the initial group with Purrmann, Oskar and Greta Moll, soon followed by Levy and most of the Dômiers—played a role whose importance has often been underestimated because some, including Franz Nölken and Walter A. Rosam, were killed during the war, while others were to be eliminated by the Nazis. Scandinavians also were well represented with Jean Heiberg and Carl Palme, who were present from the start and introduced their compatriots. Heiberg brought in the Norwegians Axel Revold and Henrik Sörensen, accompanied

by the more independent Per Krohg and Halvorsen and sometimes by Karsten, who remained faithful to his temperament and came as an old friend. Through Palme came a number of Swedes who, with the exception of Grünewald, were not to be greatly influenced: Einar Jolin, Nils de Dardel, and others. There were also Hungarians, the sculptor Brummer and the painters Robert Bereny and Vilmos Perlrott-Csaba, who soon attracted attention in the Salons. The Americans of the Dôme had been joined by Arthur A. B. Frost, the Icelander Jon Stefansson, the Englishman Matthew Smith at a later stage, and several Russians and Austrians. On returning to their own countries in 1910 or 1911, nearly all these artists were to contribute to the diffusion of the new trends. Paradoxically, the French play only a minor part in these developments. Their number includes Charles de Fontenay, later killed in the war, Albert Guindet, who had first met Matisse in

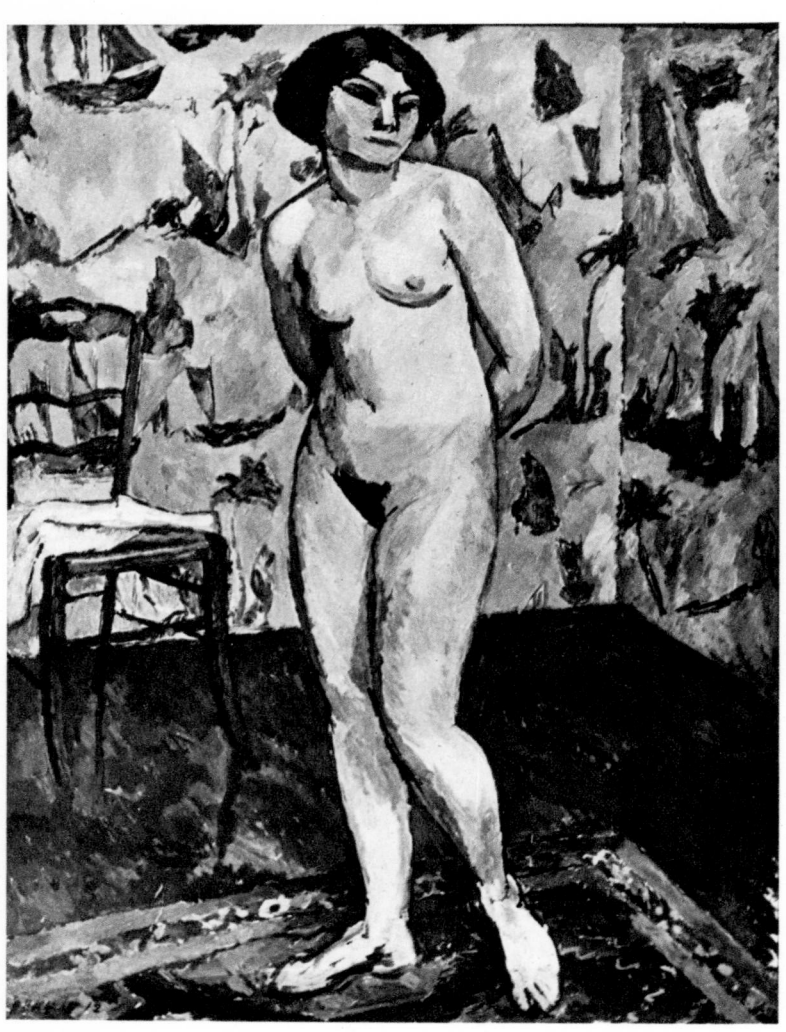

44. Jean Heiberg. NUDE. 1912.
Oil on canvas, 51 1/8 × 38 3/8".
Rasmus Meyers Samlinger, Bergen

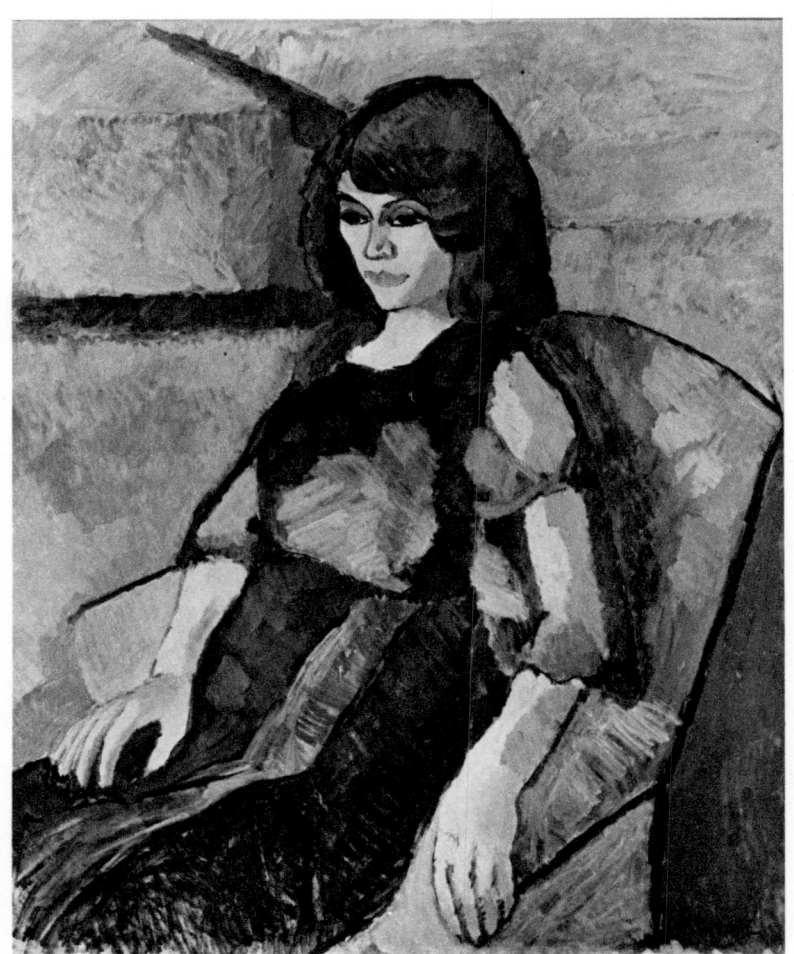

45. Axel Revold. ITALIAN WOMAN. 1914.
Oil on canvas, 36 1/4 × 29".
Nasjonalgalleriet, Oslo

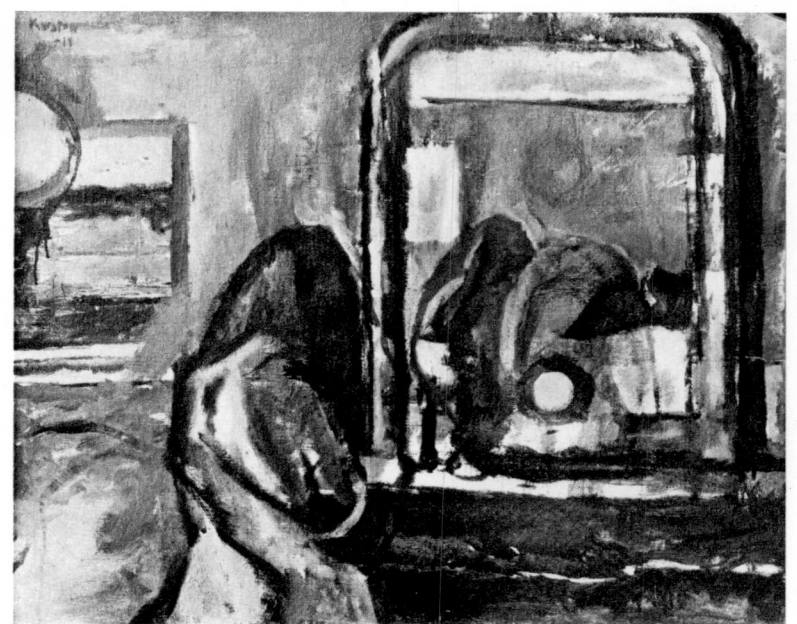

46. Ludvig Karsten. BEFORE THE MIRROR. 1914.
Oil on canvas, 25 5/8 × 31 7/8".
Nasjonalgalleriet, Oslo

Cormon's studio and who was likewise to become fascinated by North Africa, and finally Pierre Dubreuil, who became a close friend of Pascin and Gromaire.

This general survey would be incomplete without some mention of the importance of certain foreign contributions to the cultural life of Paris. The Salon d'Automne had made a custom of inviting a foreign group every year. In 1906 the Russian contribution organized by Diaghilev presented the Moscow school in particular, with Larionov, Pavel Kuznetsov, Korovin, and Milioti, of whom the last two were to reappear at the following Salon. In 1907 it was the Belgians' turn, with well-deserved honors going to Ensor and Evenepoel; in 1908 the Finns, in 1909 the Germans, with Max Beckmann, Wilhelm Gerstel, and others. At the same time, in May and June, 1909, the Russian Ballet opened its first season at the Châtelet. The spectators were amazed and Matisse enraptured by the riot of color it presented.

Thus an active series of exchanges steadily developed among all the different countries.

ABROAD

As it crossed frontiers and extended its influence into neighboring countries, Fauvism aroused curiosity and sympathy, and above all provided an artistic stimulus for painters who then tried to adapt it to their own needs.

Its reception in Germany is both eager and belated. The country, as we have seen, had close artistic ties with Paris despite the mutual hostility of the press. It could boast of being the first to acquire a Matisse (in 1912 by the Munich Museum), and it played an important role in the diffusion of the new aesthetic ideas. Yet, although Van Dongen was invited to Dresden in 1908, it is not until 1910 that the Fauves or Cubists are even meagerly represented at the Neue Künstler Vereinigung in Munich, and not until 1912 that they take part in any numbers in the Blaue Reiter exhibitions in the same city, in the Berlin Sezession, the impressive Sonderbund in Cologne, and the shows in Walden's Der Sturm gallery in Berlin. In 1913 they exhibit at the first German Salon d'Automne.

German Expressionism, it is true, attracts more attention. Fostered by Die Brücke, which originated in Dresden in 1906 and gained a hold in 1907, this movement, while retaining its individuality, had much in common with Fauvism. But the vehement nationalism that was long rampant on both sides of the Rhine led to persistent efforts to dissociate them and present them as rivals. In 1905 the young Expressionists are unaware of what is happening in Paris, and yet they react in the same way to the demands of the time and draw inspiration from the same sources: Van Gogh and Gauguin, whom they can admire at the

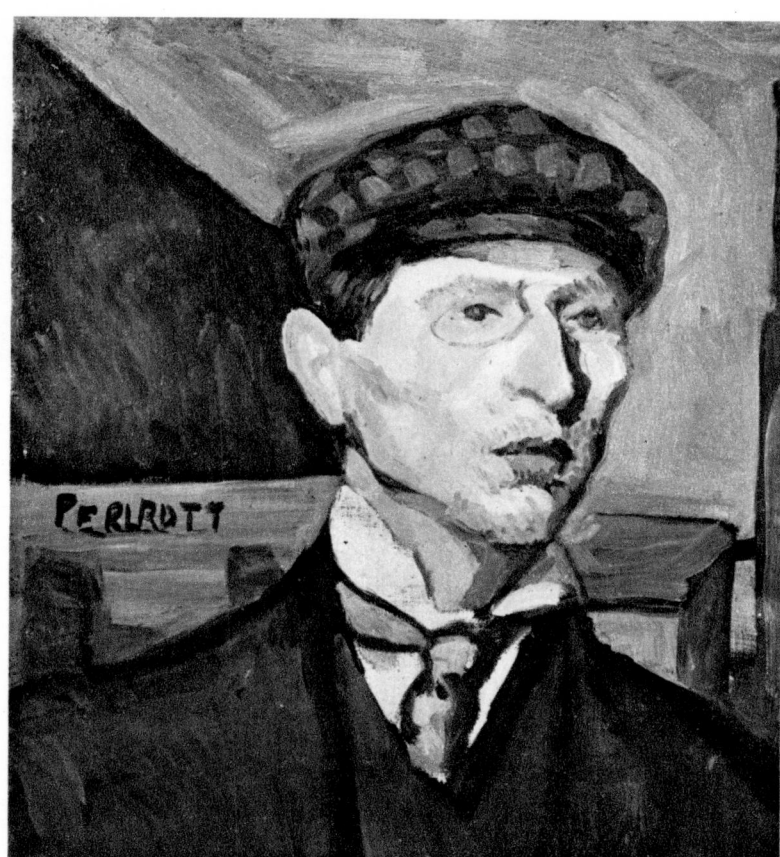

47. Vilmos Perlrott-Csaba. SELF-PORTRAIT. 1905.
Oil on canvas, 21 1/4 × 18 1/2".
Hungarian National Gallery, Budapest

Arnold Gallery, the primitive arts, and caricature, to which they add social concerns and the visionary anxiety of Munch. Self-taught, they are more radical, like Heckel or Schmidt-Rottluff, in their revolt against tradition, more virulent in the harshness of their prints, more carried away, like Nolde, by the magic of color, more united as a result of their communal life in improvised studios and the summers spent on the Moritzburg lakes. They share, however, a need—more arbitrary in their case—for transpositions, pure color, flat areas, and compelling outlines. After the example of Cuno Amiet, who was with them for a time, they sometimes reach a certain hedonism in their more peaceful moments. This is true even of Kirchner, the leader of the group, and still more of Pechstein, who was in France in 1907 and was influenced by Cézanne. It should be noted that outside this group other artists such as Erbslöh and Kanoldt occasionally adopt this attitude as well, to say nothing of Paula Modersohn-Becker, who was so strongly influenced just before her death by the Gauguin retrospective.

A traditional European crossroads and as such easily penetrated by outside trends, Munich is to be the meeting point for West and East from the moment that Kandinsky, Gabriele Münter, and Jawlensky take over the leadership of the Neue Künstler Vereinigung in 1909 and of the Blaue Reiter at the end of 1911. They were assisted by August

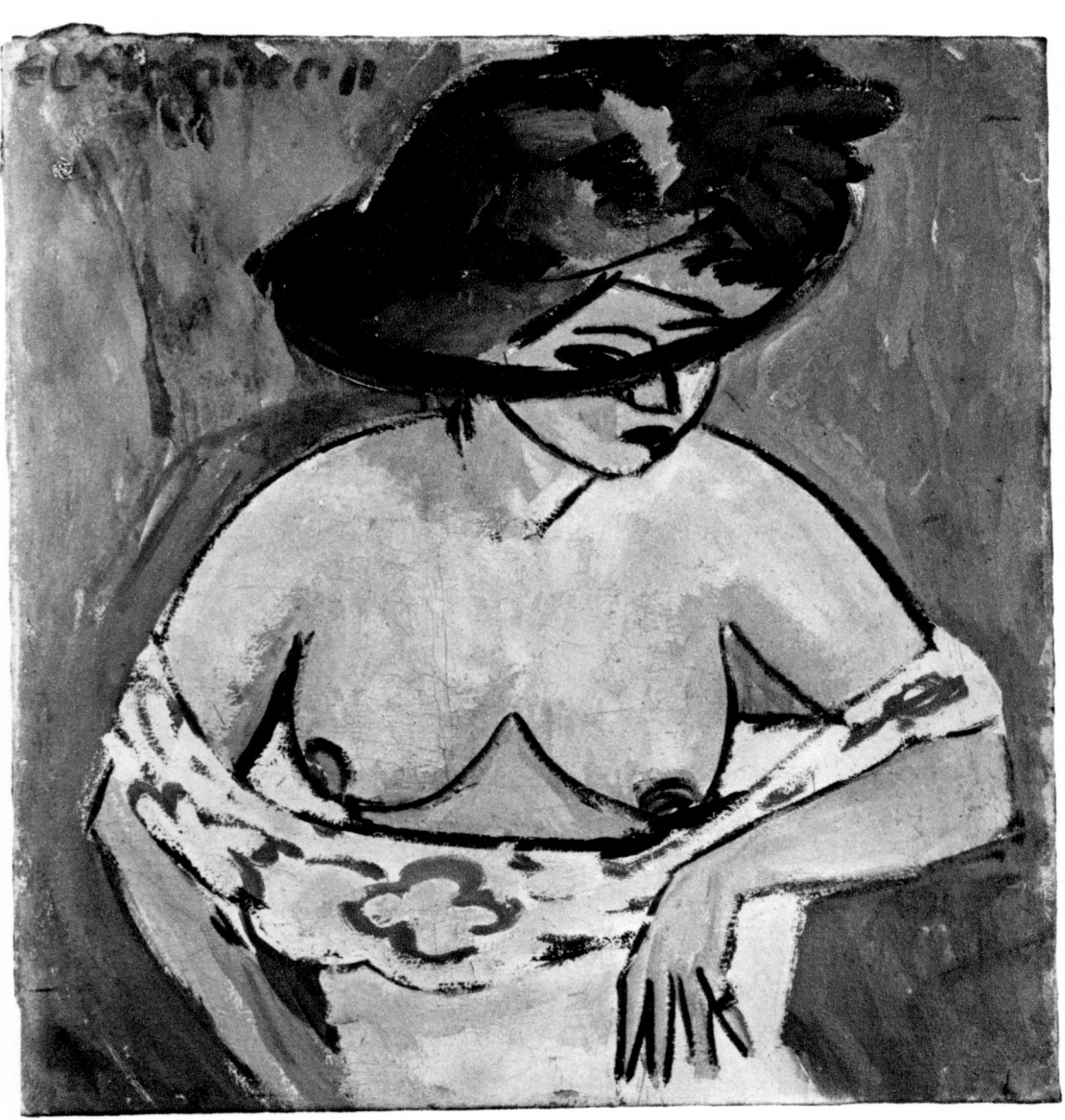

48. Ernst Ludwig Kirchner. WOMAN IN HAT WITH NUDE TORSO. 1911.
Oil on canvas, 29 3/8 × 27 5/8″. *Wallraf-Richartz-Museum, Cologne*

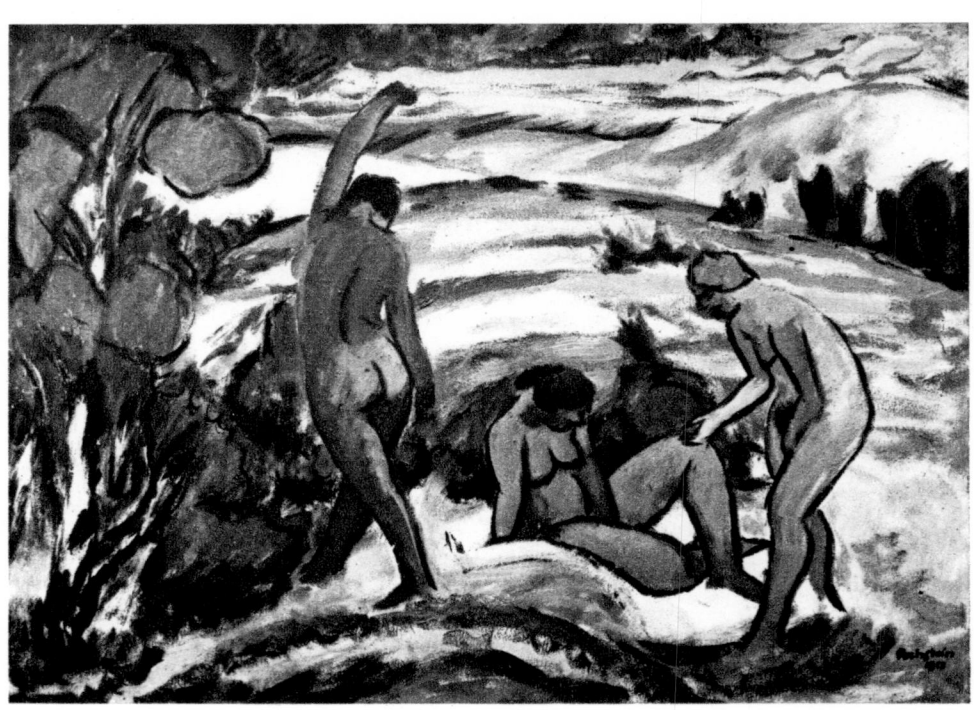

49. Max Pechstein.
LANDSCAPE WITH THREE NUDES. 1911.
Oil on canvas, 30 3/4 × 39 3/8″.
*Musée National d'Art Moderne,
Paris*

Macke and Franz Marc, who had made early and frequent trips to France and had established ties with Matisse and subsequently still more with Delaunay.

The Hungarians are the first to turn from the tradition of the Munich academies and send a growing number of artists to France. Already ardent supporters of Fauvism, they will later abandon it like so many others in favor of a return to Cézannian construction. It is Czóbel, living in Paris since 1903, who prepares the way for this unexpected influx. After his success at the previous Salon d'Automne, where he had been immediately accepted by the Fauves, he returns during the summer of 1906 to sow temptation and doubt among his old friends and companions of the Nagybanya School, who then rebel against the school's outmoded teachings. Before long Paris becomes the favorite place of residence or the object of frequent visits for many Hungarian artists, who often earn for themselves the best places in the Salons. Some, like Geza Bornemisza, and above all Perlrott-Csaba, hasten to Paris and become Matisse's most assiduous pupils. Others, both older and younger, end by joining Czóbel to form "The Eight" group in 1907, which was to exhibit a number of times in 1909 and then at the Budapest National Salon in 1911 and 1912. Most of these artists—Marffy, who made a very successful debut at the Salon d'Automne in 1906 and, like Czóbel, was for a long time a member of the School of Paris; Kernstok, with his powerful lyricism; Bereny, with his rigorous style; Czigany; Orban; and Tihanyi, who finally settled permanently in Paris—exert a great influence in their country, to which they remain deeply attached. Along with the poet Ady and the historian Fülep, they help to make their compatriots aware of the problems of the modern age.

The Poles seem hardly attracted by the new movement —Wojtkiewicz, appearing at the Salon d'Automne of 1907, only slightly, Grombecki, Weiss, and somewhat more Kisling, all latecomers to Paris, and Pankiewicz, despite his age, whose art blossomed fully in Spain during the war. The Rumanians had in Pallady an excellent permanent representative in Paris, who to the end was a faithful friend of Matisse while remaining independent in his ideas. Vienna, until then the closed bastion of the Sezession, opens up slightly to the Impressionists and Post-Impressionists in 1903, and beginning in 1908 is the scene of impetuous attempts at liberation under the determined leadership of Richard Gerstl and Egon Schiele, which soon lead to the triumph of Expressionism and Kokoschka. But it is only in Prague that every effort is made to achieve total emancipation. Full and fruitful exchanges are established with Paris, which, no doubt thanks to Mercereau, sends to the 1907 exhibition of the Mánes Art Society a complete panorama of late nineteenth-century art and in 1910 a selection of 122 paintings, most of them Fauvist. Czech painters were by then already involved in the movement, following the ex-

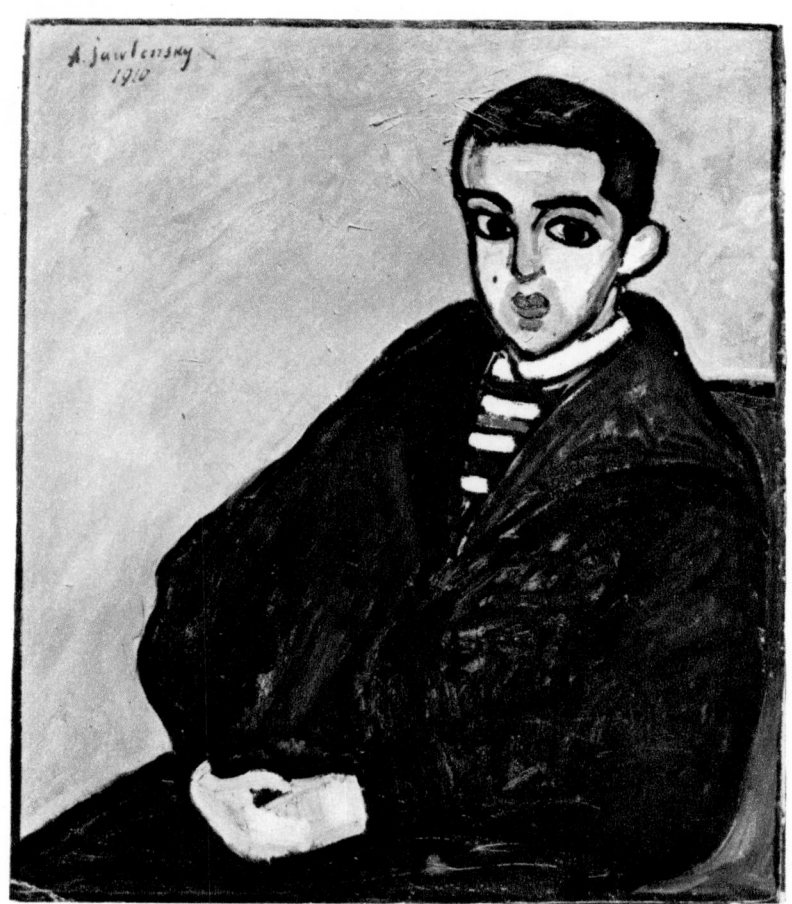

50. Alexej von Jawlensky. NIKITA. 1910.
Oil on cardboard, 33 7/8 × 29 1/8".
Städtisches Museum, Wiesbaden

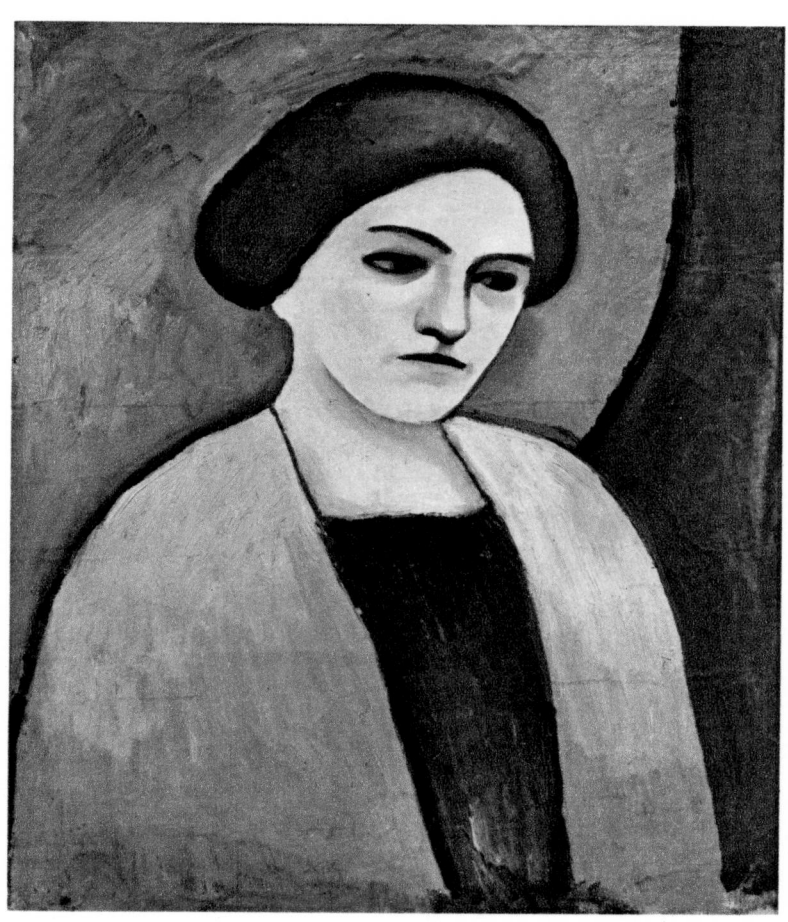

51. August Macke. PORTRAIT OF THE ARTIST'S WIFE. C. 1911.
Oil on canvas, 25 1/4 × 20 7/8".
Musée National d'Art Moderne, Paris

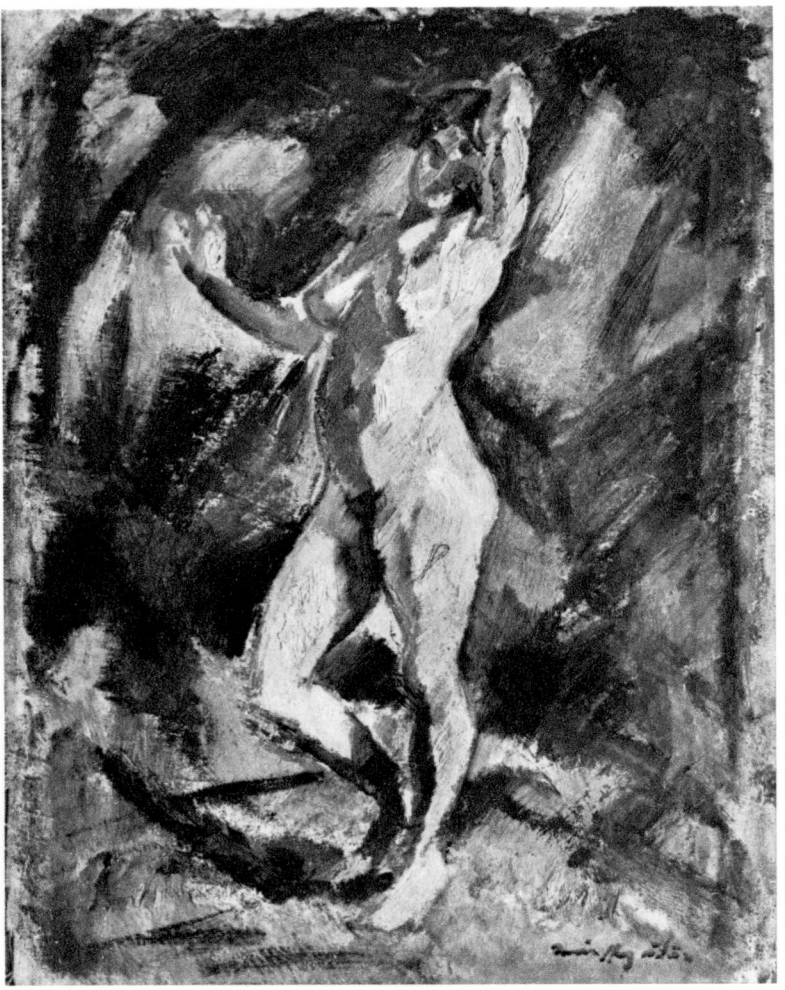

52. Odön Marffy. NUDE. 1910.
Oil on canvas, 23 1/4 × 17 3/4″.
Private collection, Hungary

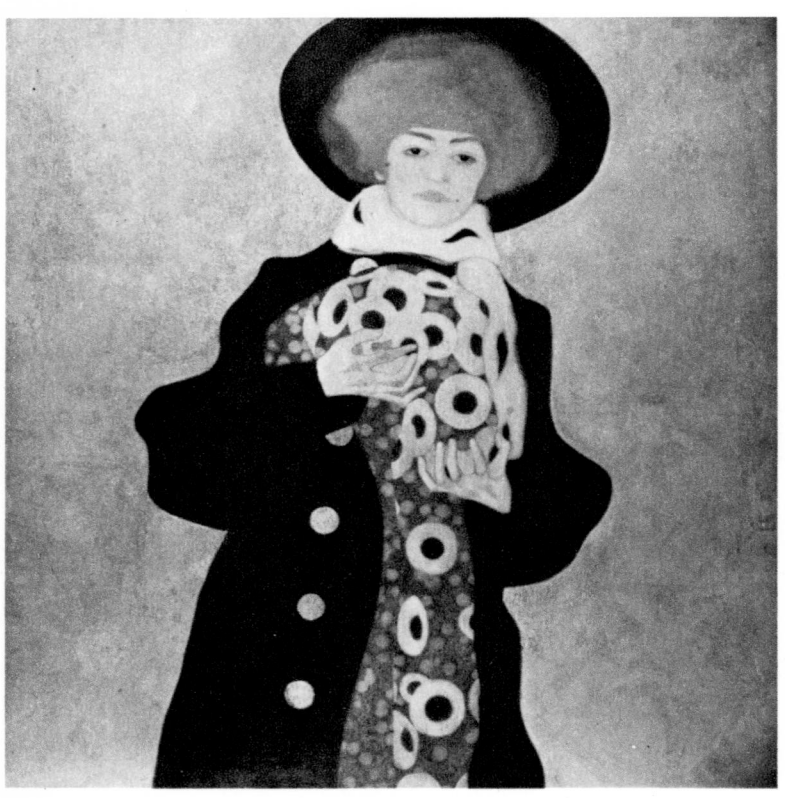

53. Egon Schiele.
PORTRAIT OF A WOMAN IN A BLACK HAT. 1909.
Oil on canvas, 39 3/8 × 39 1/4″.
*Georg Waechter Memorial Foundation,
Geneva*

ample of Kupka, a resident of Paris since 1895. Filla, another of their leaders and a member of "The Eight" group, is a frequent visitor to Paris at this time, and on his return communicates his zeal for experimentation to Procházka. Prucha, who works independently, and Spála, who joins the group in 1911 and goes to Paris, have early evolved in a similar direction toward a truly instinctive Fauvism which is soon to grow more disciplined.

The best evidence of this ancestral background linked with folklore is to be found in Yugoslavia with Jakopic, and the almost unique case of Nadezda Petrovic, who although trained in Munich expresses herself with a strong, impetuous touch long before going to Paris in 1910. There she acquires an even greater richness of color, thereby opening the way for the whole artistic future of her country.

In Russia, interest in the Fauves is aroused very early by the World of Art exhibitions, and develops rapidly through contacts with Paris and the purchases of collectors. The presence of about a hundred works by the Fauves and their immediate predecessors at the Salon of the Golden Fleece in 1908 and of a smaller number in 1909, combined with Mercereau's articles, encourages Russian artists, several of whom have already gone to Paris. Older painters such as Korovin, and the younger generation—Pavel Kuznetsov, strongly influenced by the Gauguin retrospective in 1906, Sarian, Milioti, and Sapunov—paint in a free and expansive style, using brilliant colors, and are intensely active in every artistic field. They are joined by Larionov, who exhibits his glowing *Bathers at Sunset* (fig. 58) at the Golden Fleece in 1908, and by Goncharova, Malevich, and Konchalovsky, who are soon to tend toward dynamism and the "Knave of Diamonds" group.

With the exception of Scandinavia, whose artists, already deeply committed, were later to move toward a monumental art, the countries closer at hand were much less affected by the movement. The large Post-Impressionist and Fauve exhibition held in London in 1910 seems to have had little impact, the only important link being established by Smith. In Switzerland, participation is limited but steady, Cuno Amiet sometimes prompting his faithful friend Giacometti to freer expression, while Von Tscharner occasionally attends the Matisse Academy, and during the summer of 1912 even goes to Hungary to seek inspiration at Nagybanya before returning to avail himself of the atmosphere of Paris. Although Italy was now given over to the international ascendance of Futurism, Boccioni had earlier made a brief incursion into Fauvism, brilliantly represented by Viani and Rossi. The first, during his various Parisian stays between 1907 and 1909, becomes closely associated with the Germans Nolde and Heckel, and the turbulent expressiveness of his work, particularly his prints, reveals their growing influence. Rossi, who goes to Paris in 1907 with the sculptor Arturo Martini, is gradually won over by the calm radiance of color, derived chiefly

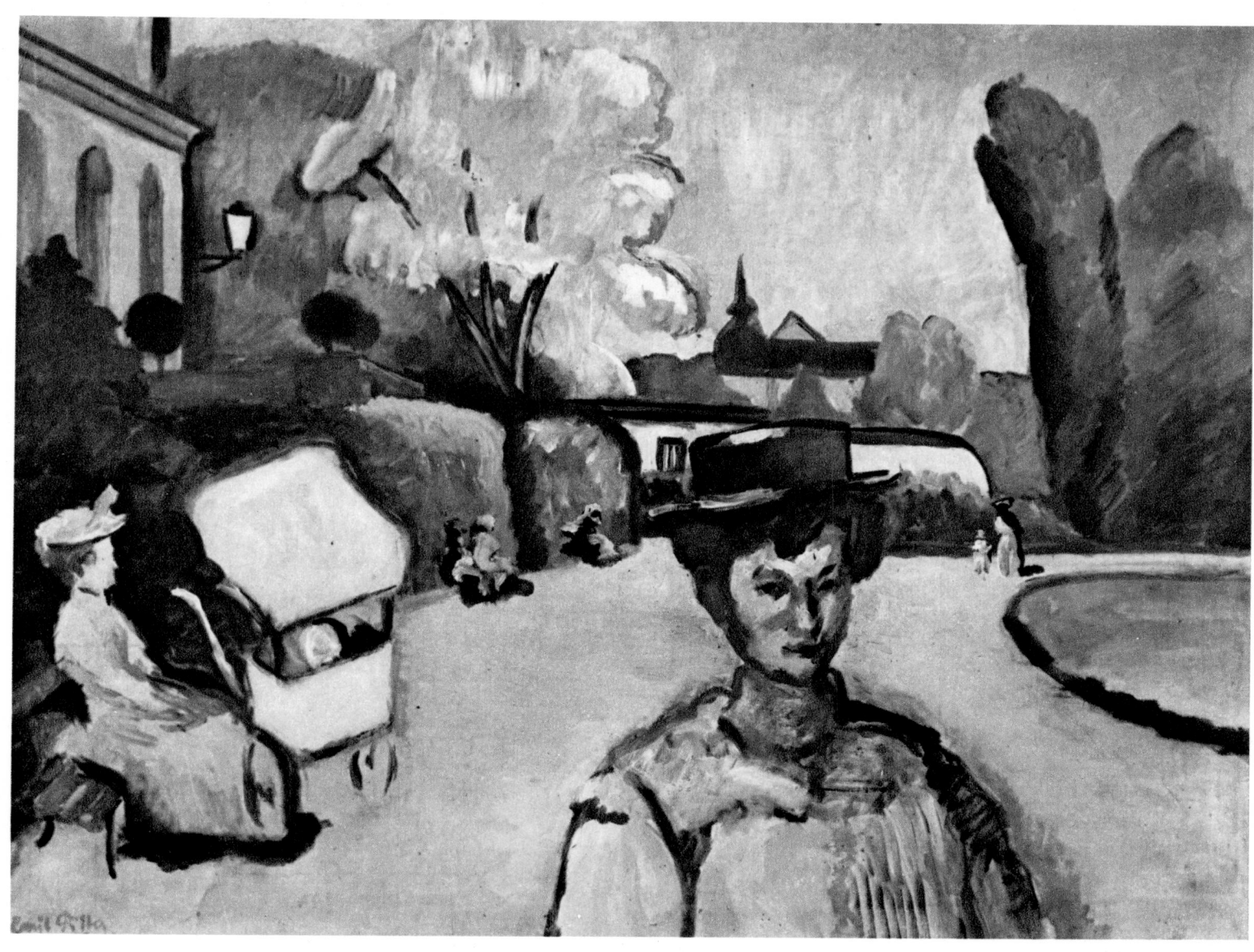

54. Emil Filla. THE CHILDREN IN THE GARDEN. 1910. Oil on canvas, 23 5/8 × 37". *National Gallery, Prague*

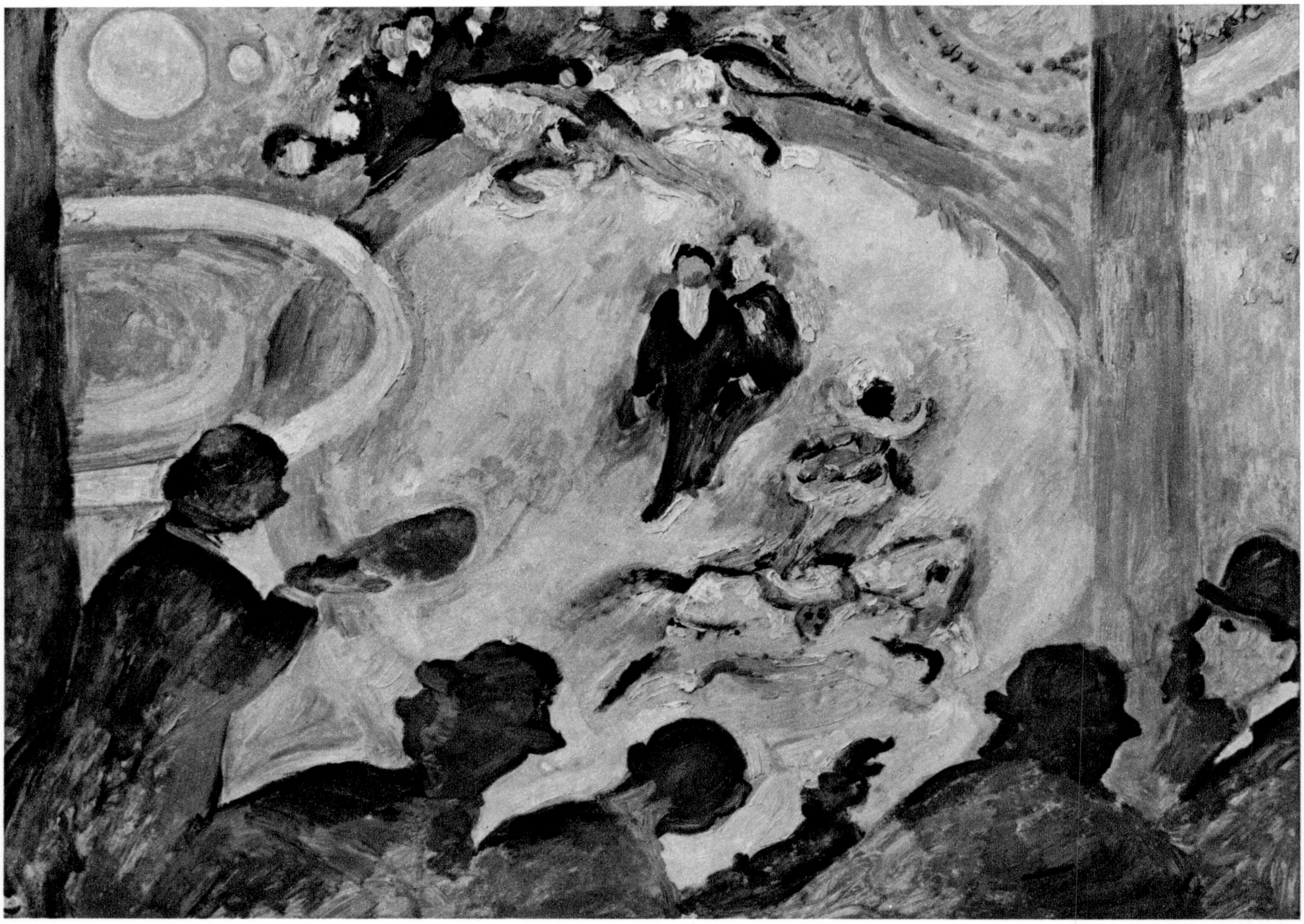

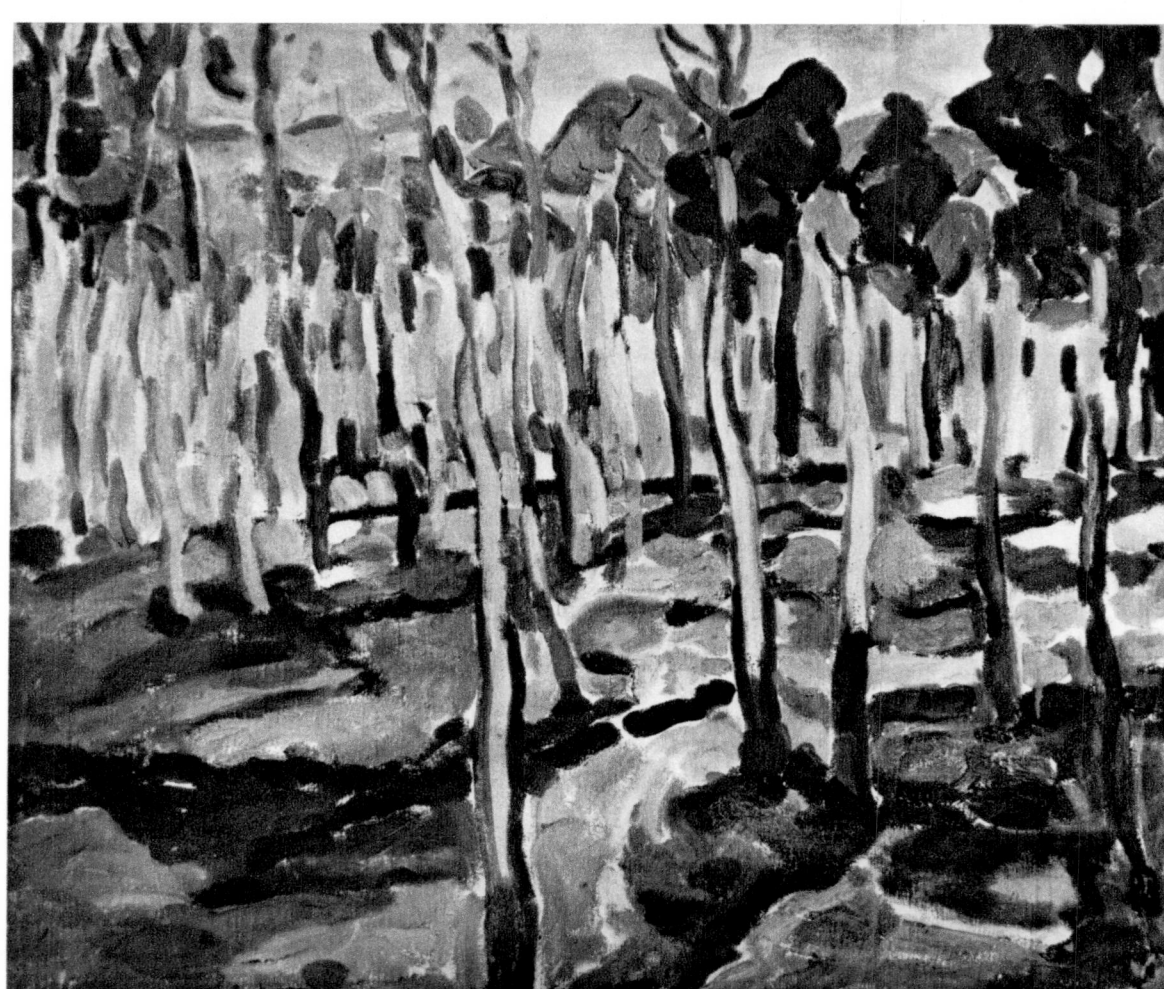

55. Antonin Procházka. THE CIRCUS. 1906–7. Oil on canvas, 18 3/4 × 25 5/8″. *National Gallery, Prague*

56. Friedrich Prucha.
BEECH FOREST. 1911.
Oil on canvas,
33 1/8 × 37 5/8″.
*National Gallery,
Prague*

from Gauguin, which he then preaches to the members of the "happy colony" on Burano.

Well before the Kunstkring exhibitions of international modernism in Amsterdam in 1911, two artists had brought back from their frequent trips to Paris and through their close friendship with Van Dongen the stimulus that was needed, even in these parts where Van Gogh was honored. In 1905 Toorop, always in search of a new idiom, and in the next year Sluyters, with a force of conviction that carried Mondrian with him, rallied temporarily to Fauvism, but both abandoned it two years later in favor of Luminism and experiments in construction.

In Belgium the spread of Fauvism was particularly favored by the work of Evenepoel, whose death was a sad blow, and by the Libre Esthétique exhibitions in Brussels, which presented a complete panorama of Fauvism in two successive series in 1906 and 1907. Yet Belgium was the last country to move toward Fauvism, and it did so with a reticence strongly emphasized by Wouters. In 1912 the Giroux Gallery began to reveal a movement led by the admirable Wouters, which in fact focused its attention as much on Ensor as on Paris. Schirren, the senior member of the group, was turning in 1906 to pure color in his paintings, especially his watercolors, but like Wouters he was more attracted by sculpture. He was to continue in this quiet, more restrained artistic tradition with Deroy, Paerels, and De Kat until after the war.

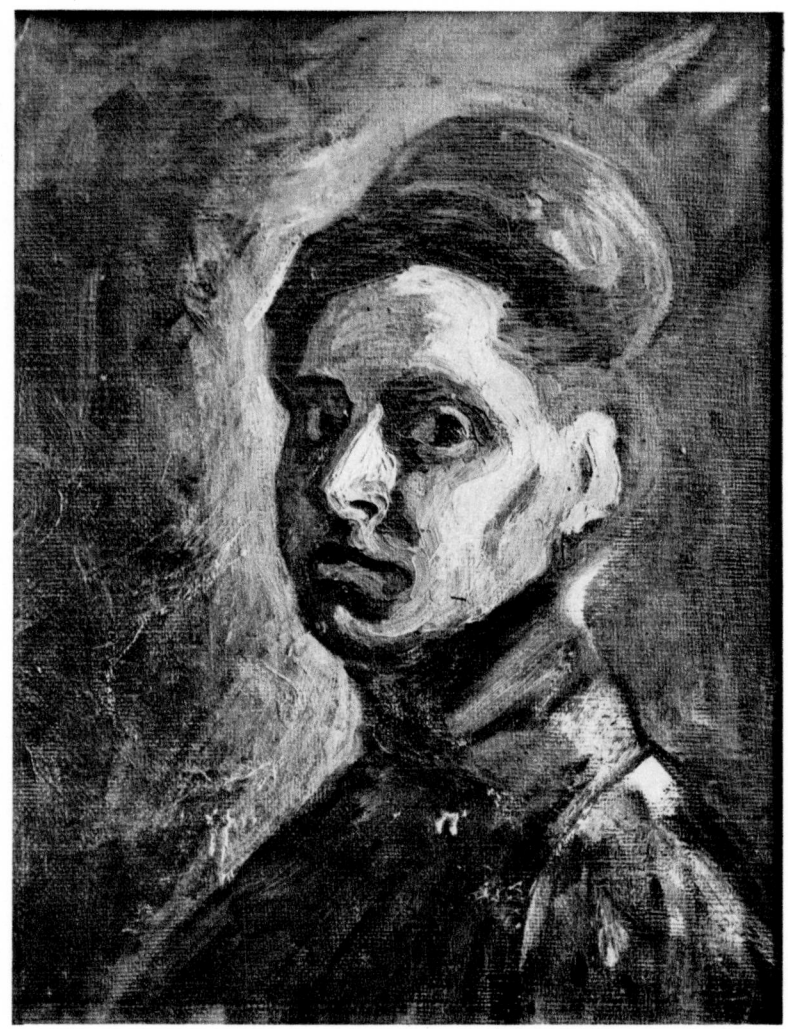

57. Nadezda Petrovic. SELF-PORTRAIT. 1907.
Oil on canvas, 25 5/8 × 19 1/4".
National Museum, Belgrade

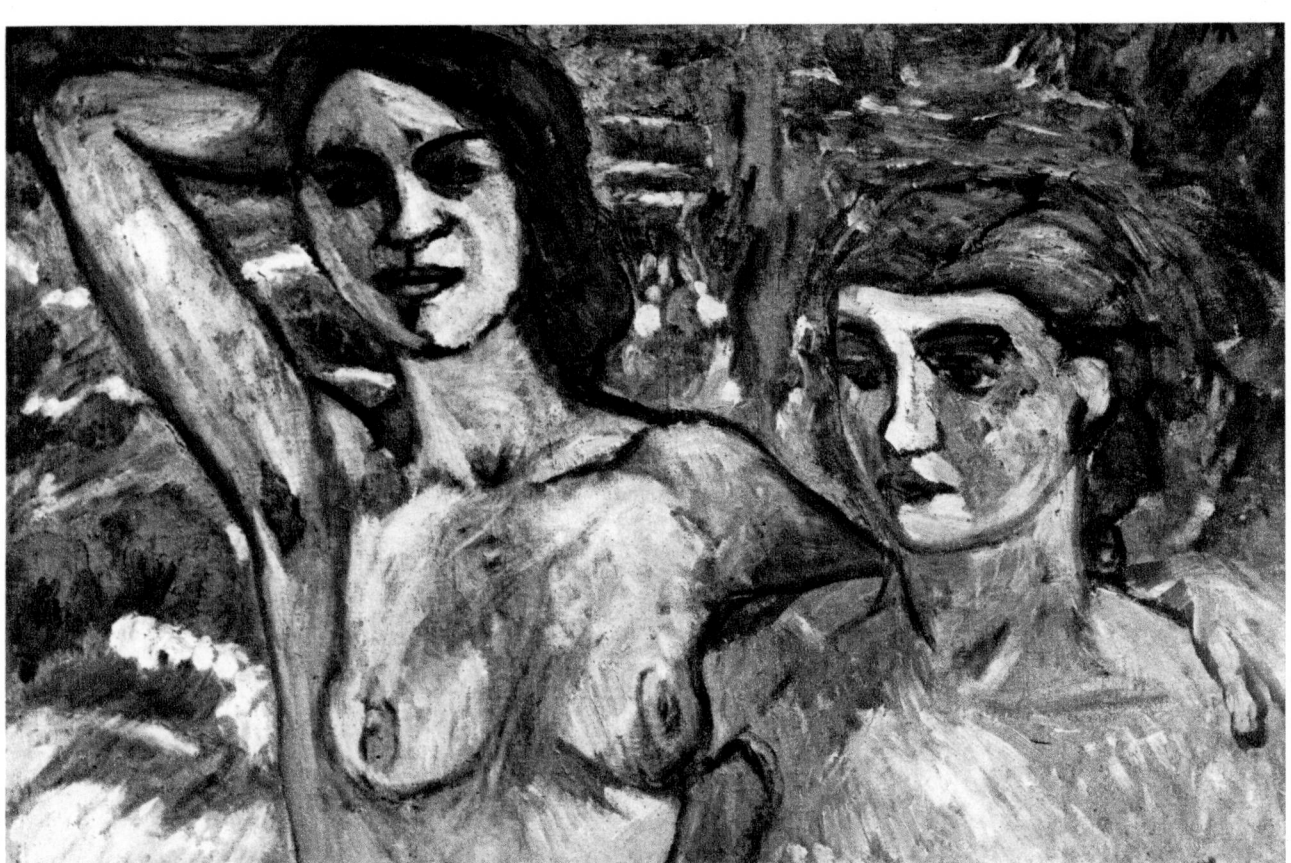

58. Michel Larionov.
BATHERS AT SUNSET.
1903–8.
Oil on canvas,
26 1/4 × 37 3/8".
*Private collection,
Paris*

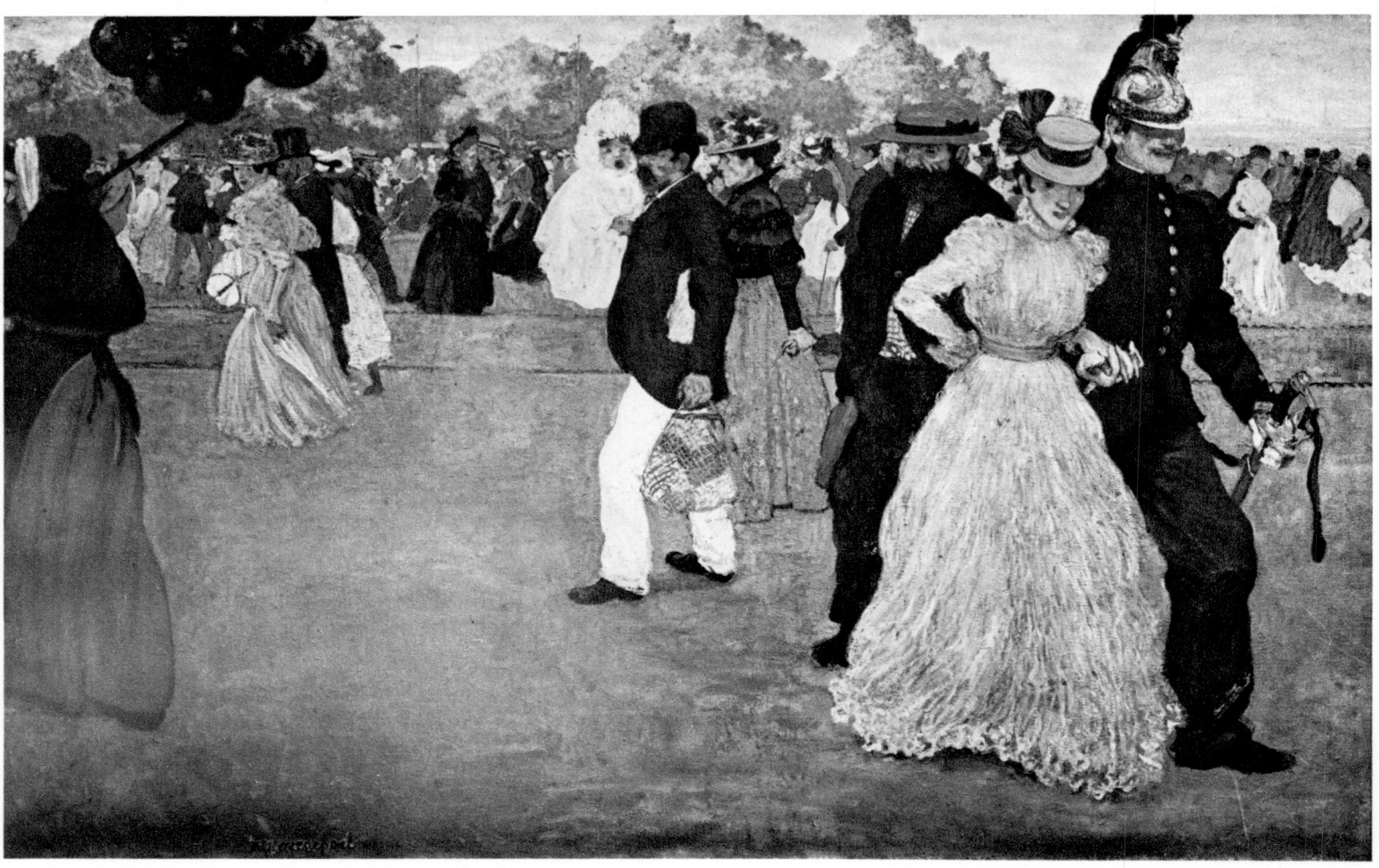

59. Henri Evenepoel. SUNDAY PROMENADE AT SAINT-CLOUD. 1899.
Oil on canvas, 74 3/4 × 118 1/8".
Musée des Beaux-Arts, Liège

At the end of this odyssey are we to conclude that Fauvism, whose historical role has ended, was nothing in France or the rest of the world but a brief flare-up soon extinguished or reabsorbed by the Cézanne tradition, Cubism, and the various recalls to order that took place before 1914? This would badly underestimate the potential forces which it held in reserve and would continue to release in many countries.

To return, for brevity's sake, to the movement's country of origin, it is true that the war, which annihilated and disrupted so many efforts, would seem to have dealt it a deathblow by trampling underfoot and desecrating everything that had formed the basis of its existence: a spontaneous joy of life, a serene rationalism, a warm belief in man. Even those who, like Matisse and Van Dongen, interpreted and explained Fauvism to the best of their abilities until the outbreak of the war seemed rather discouraged, changed, and ready to give in to the fallacious arguments of the critics who were exhorting them to return to healthy traditions.

Yet in them and the others, Manguin and Dufy particularly, the fire continues to smolder until it finally flares up again. From 1927 onward Fauvism is gradually reborn

from its ashes, resumes its place in the struggle and soon reaffirms, through the words and works of Matisse, the virtues of a necessary and constant revolt against convention. For Pignon, Estève, Manessier, Singier, Schneider, Vasarely, and many others, it becomes directly or indirectly the leaven that will quicken a whole generation before and after World War II. Grievously afflicted by events and his inexorable illness, even at death's door Matisse remains indomitable, and by his example his old friends and colleagues, from Camoin to Valtat, from Derain to Marquet, also regain at certain moments that vibrant sense of life and color that illuminated their youth.

During the dark war years I earnestly considered, in my first book on Fauvism, whether the movement should be regarded as the close of a cycle, an irrevocable conclusion to the efforts of the preceding century, or on the contrary as the beginning of a promising renewal. I confess that I found it hard then, despite many obvious signs given by both older and younger painters, to conceive of an art capable of soon offering these eagerly awaited rediscoveries.

48

In historical perspective the evolution of painting has itself provided the answer. The Fauves opened a new era and most certainly gave rise to a powerful and stimulating movement that has not ceased to disrupt outmoded habits and provide inspiration for the future.

Color has invaded our epoch, triumphing almost everywhere. We are inundated and obsessed by it. If we tolerate and even favor its universal presence, it is surely because it helps us to escape from our closed world with its steadily growing tensions and forebodings. Its Dionysiac virtues spread the illusion of youth and offer the solace of an overflowing vitality.

The magic of color leads us, through its inherent impetuosity and dynamism, to a better understanding of our times, by giving us access to the universal and popular language that alone can fulfill our present needs.

The quickening influence of Fauvism is still enriching and broadening artistic life.

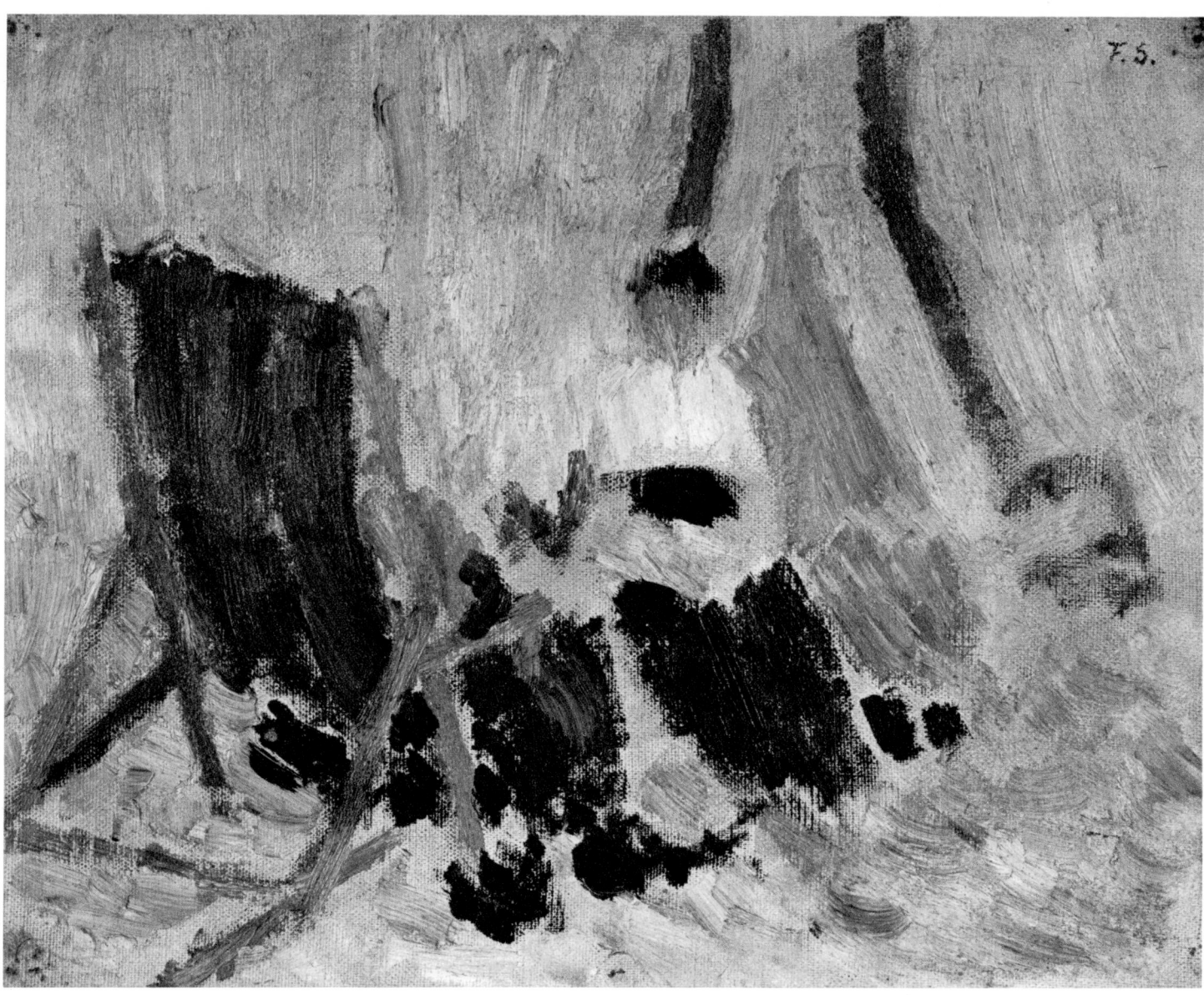

60. Ferdinand Schirren. ON THE SAND. C. 1906. Oil on canvas pasted on cardboard, 10 5/8 × 12 7/8″. *Private collection, Brussels*

DRAWINGS, WATERCOLORS, AND PRINTS

Unlike the German artists of Die Brücke or Der Blaue Reiter, who from the beginning strove to publish regularly their amazingly unified albums of plates, and to organize exhibitions of prints and drawings, the Fauves, with the possible exception of Matisse, were hardly concerned with the graphic arts in their own right, independently of painting, and attributed only minor importance to them.

Whereas the Dresden Expressionists worked in collaboration, individualism was the rule among the French. The only attempt at collective work was the one successfully undertaken by the ceramist Metthey for the Salon d'Automne of 1907, where each artist offered his individual collaboration and affirmed his personality in what was predominantly an exercise in painting.

Throughout the Fauves' work, however, there runs a certain family resemblance, discernible in the bold, synthetic appearance of line that characterizes the style of a period in which Japanese art, caricatures, and posters exercised a great fascination. This kinship would have become more obvious if the Fauves, like the Nabis, had used lithography, but no publisher—not even Vollard—approached them when the movement was at its height, and it was not until the period between the two wars and in some cases even later that they were able to show their potentialities and their undeniable talent in this technique as well as in etching. Woodcuts were in a better position, for they had been popular since Gauguin, Munch, and many others had revealed their rich possibilities, and Vallotton had followed their example. Several of the Fauves were attracted by this medium and made use of it—for example, Valtat as early as 1898—or took pleasure in experimenting with it. Here again, however, the commissions arrived belatedly, when Fauvism had disappeared and its former adherents had adopted a more rigorous style that moreover gave better results. The woodcuts that Kahnweiler commissioned from

Derain in 1909 to illustrate Apollinaire's *L'Enchanteur pourrissant* and in 1911 for Max Jacob's *Les Oeuvres de Frère Matorel* anticipate other, later successes, particularly the *Pantagruel* of 1945 that was to be the fitting conclusion to his work; Dufy's illustrations of 1911 for Apollinaire's *Le Bestiaire* are an excellent preamble to his later work for Poiret; then there are Braque's *Le Piège de Méduse* of 1921 and Vlaminck's various woodcuts, also from the postwar period. But this unfortunately brings us far from the Fauve period, to which it is time to return.

Marquet was unquestionably the most gifted of all, a true virtuoso whom his friends dubbed "our Hokusai." A dedicated draftsman, he started very early to note down in pencil, or with a brush like the Japanese, silhouettes, scenes, crowds caught on the spot. He is a past master at rendering the flow of movement and his intelligence and sharpness of observation are extraordinary. His highly condensed, elliptical way of depicting a whole scene is both supremely elegant and profoundly human. More than with any of the others, one can only feel sorry that his gifts as an illustrator were not exploited earlier.

Although in the beginning Matisse often worked with his friend Marquet and used the same thick line with equal skill, his manner and aims are very different. He introduces more violence and sensuality into his simplifications. His passion for drawing is more an exercise through which he conducts parallel experiments involving light, expression, and space in concert with his ceaseless research on form, color, and volume and with his work in sculpture and engraving. Yet line is for him an end, an absolute, a creation in itself, and he was almost the only artist to reserve an important place for his graphic work in the Salons and in his exhibitions. In 1908 he held a show at the Stieglitz Gallery in New York consisting exclusively of engravings, lithographs, watercolors, and drawings. He gradually developed the sustained, melodic line which is his special characteristic, and which he used to trace his wonderful, slender arabesques on copper, stone, or linoleum when, after 1932, he received an increasing number of commissions for illustrations.

Derain's skill is early apparent in the drawings that he produced in 1902 and 1903, while still in the army, for his friend Vlaminck's books. A notebook dating from the Fauve years shows a marvelous verve and assurance, but, overtaken by qualms, he already combines his bold improvisations with traditional elements that he will soon introduce into his first etchings.

The graphic style of most of the other Fauves early reflects the personal ideas to which they will remain faithful. Valtat gives expression to his youthful and ebullient vitality with a happy spontaneity. Friesz feels the need for self-expression combined with a desire for accurate observation and a certain restraint, and this will lead him in the postwar period to show a frequent preference for the waxy, flexible lithographic crayon in his illustrations. Dufy acquires an early mastery of the light, cursive, and playful touch that is a prelude to his later dynamic shorthand and by which he will achieve many striking effects, particularly in his etchings, lithographs, and ceramics. Manguin's remarkable drawings and watercolors, by which he always set great store, betray the demanding will, the tenacious effort that he manages to conceal under the guise of a happy, steadily evolving serenity. Firmly entrenched in his convictions and certitudes, the prolific Vlaminck expends himself in a craftsmanship that he will later abundantly develop.

Finally, Van Dongen is the only one who, even in his many illustrations, long maintains a difference, or, so to speak, a distance between painting and drawing. Having begun as a draftsman, he feels more at home, more free to express himself in this medium, to which he gives a satirical or biting turn as he sees fit. He gives color free rein in his watercolors before he ventures to do so in his canvases. Taking up the larger medium, he uses his painting to pour scorn on a large part of humanity, thus revealing his true predilection.

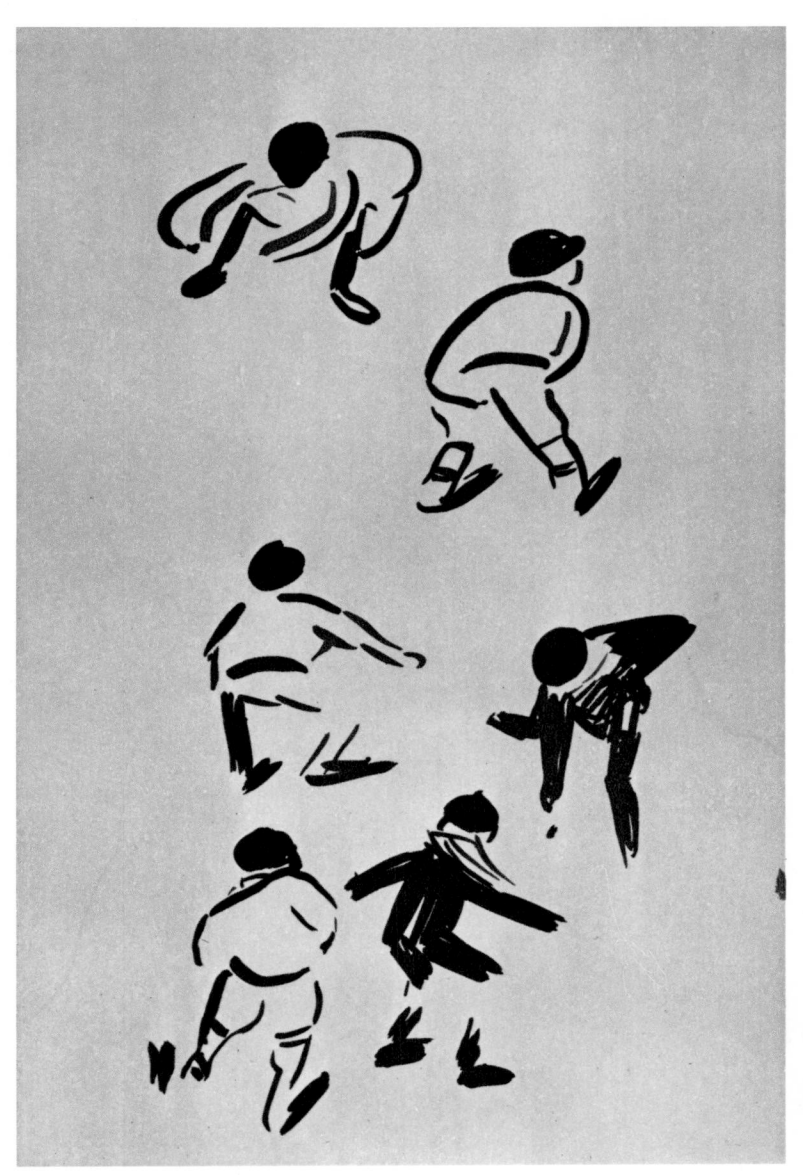

61. André Derain. CHILDREN'S GAMES. C. 1903.
Brush with India ink, 11 3/4 × 7 7/8″.
Musée National d'Art Moderne, Paris

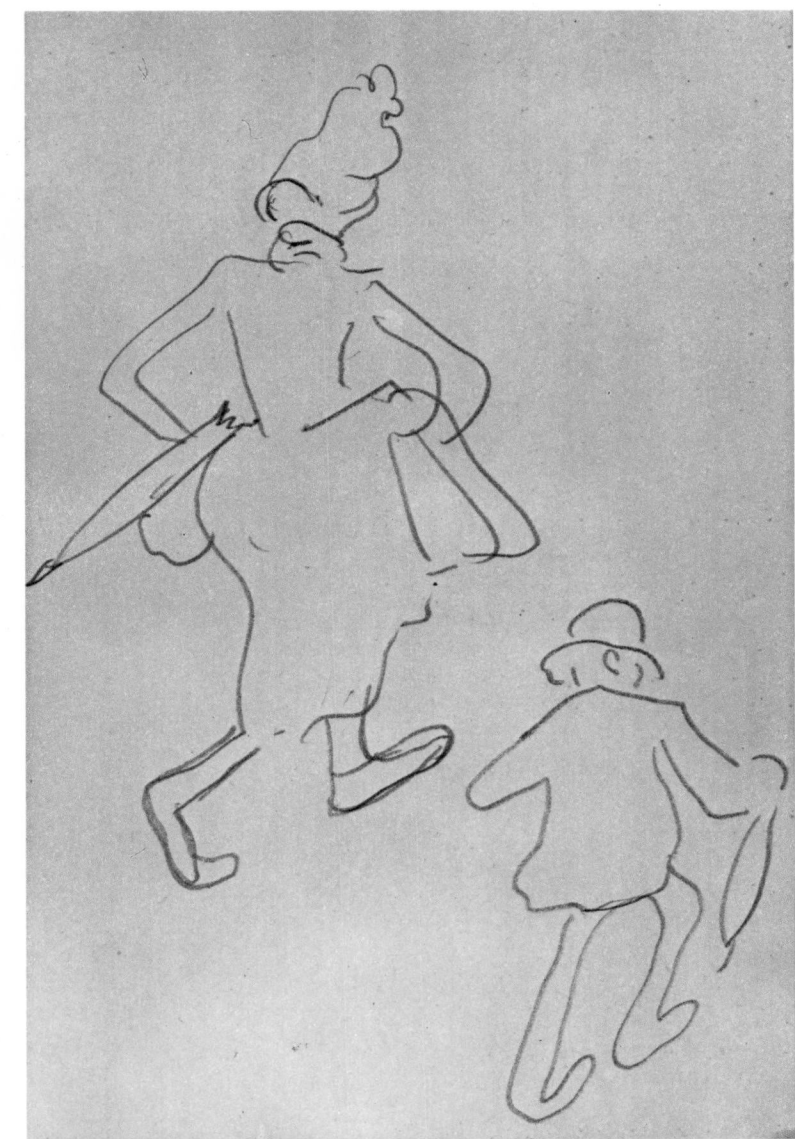

62. André Derain. STREET SCENE. 1905.
Pencil, 11 3/4 × 7 7/8″.
Musée National d'Art Moderne, Paris

53

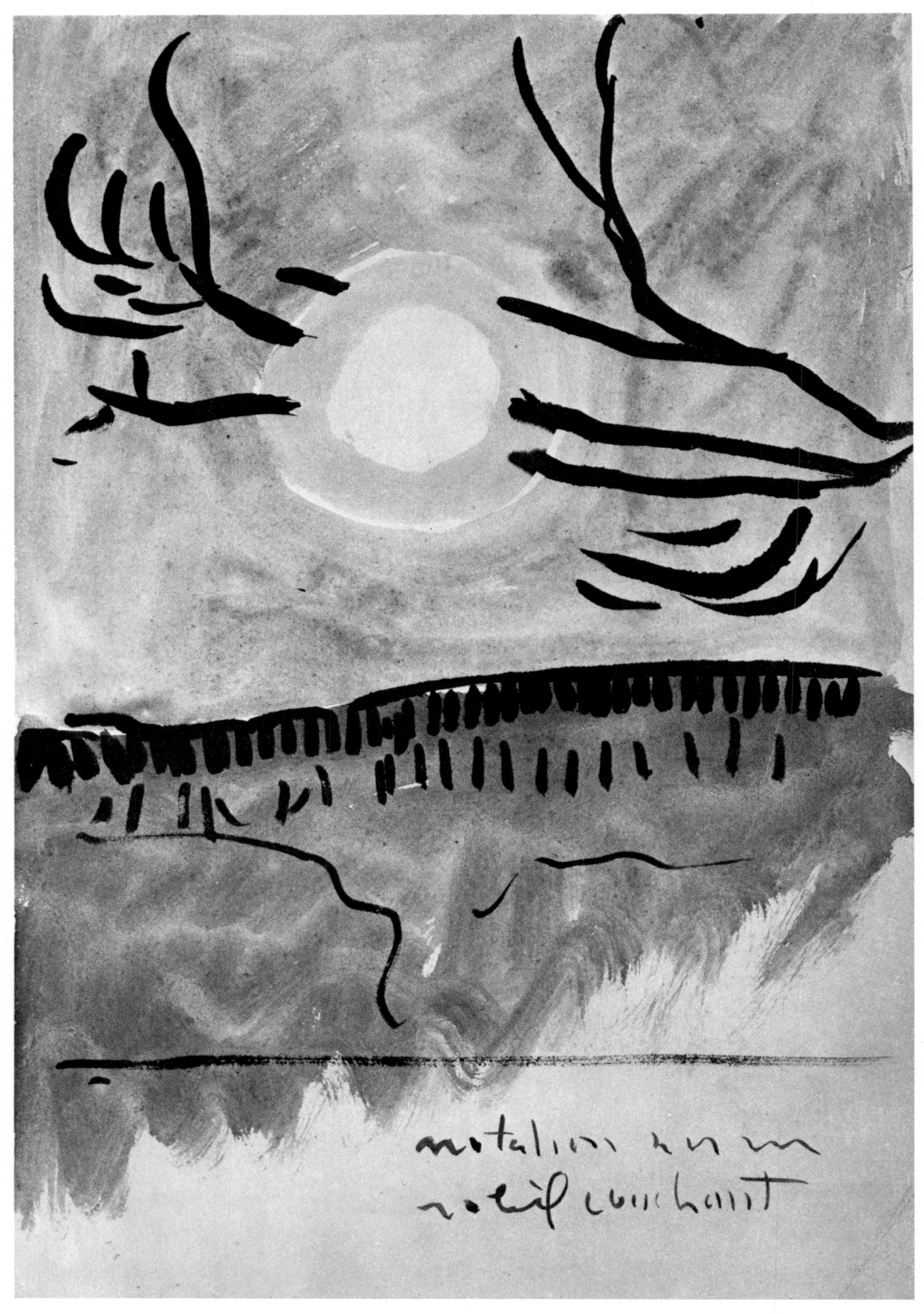

63. André Derain. NOTES ON A SETTING SUN. 1905. Watercolor, 11 3/4 × 7 7/8″. Musée National d'Art Moderne, Paris

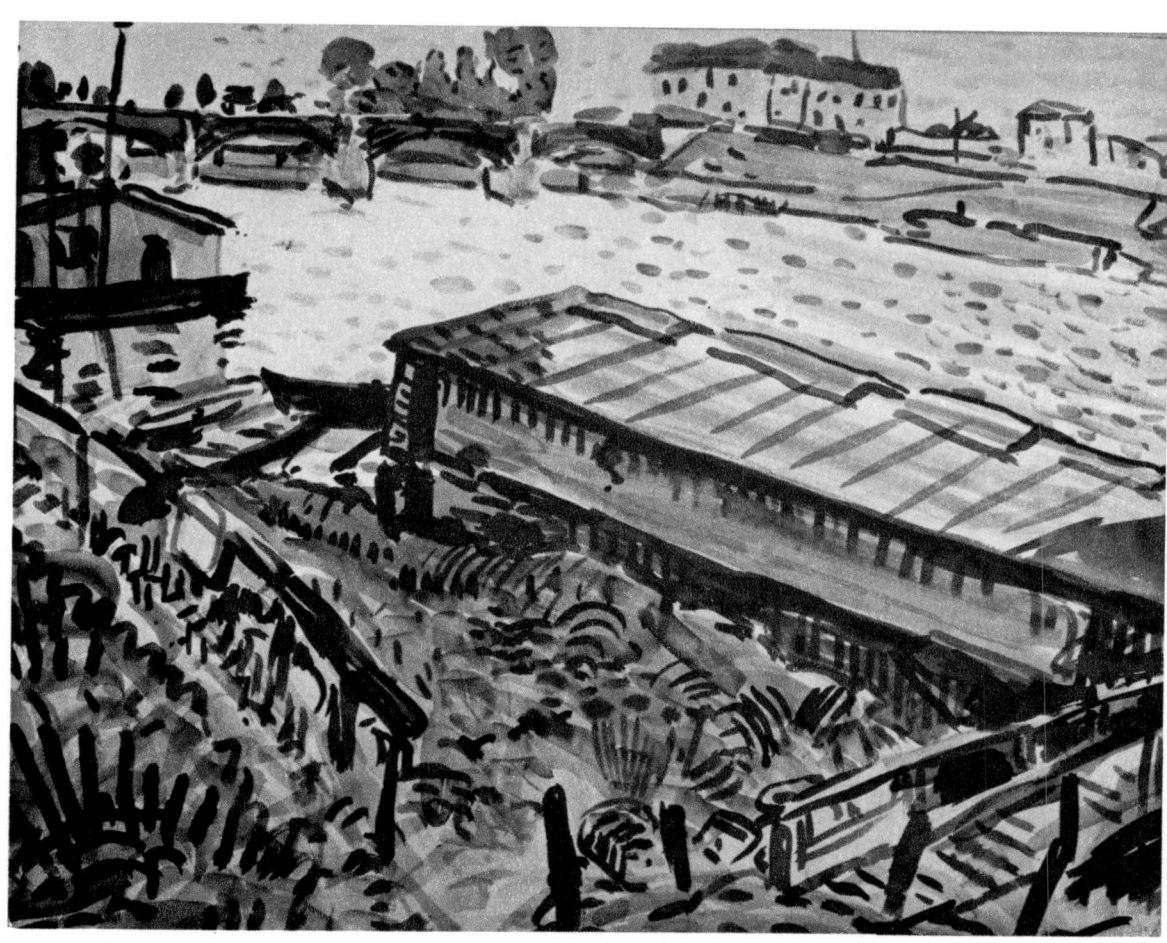

64. André Derain.
THE BRIDGE AT CHATOU. 1905.
Watercolor, 18 1/2 × 22 1/2".
Private collection, Paris

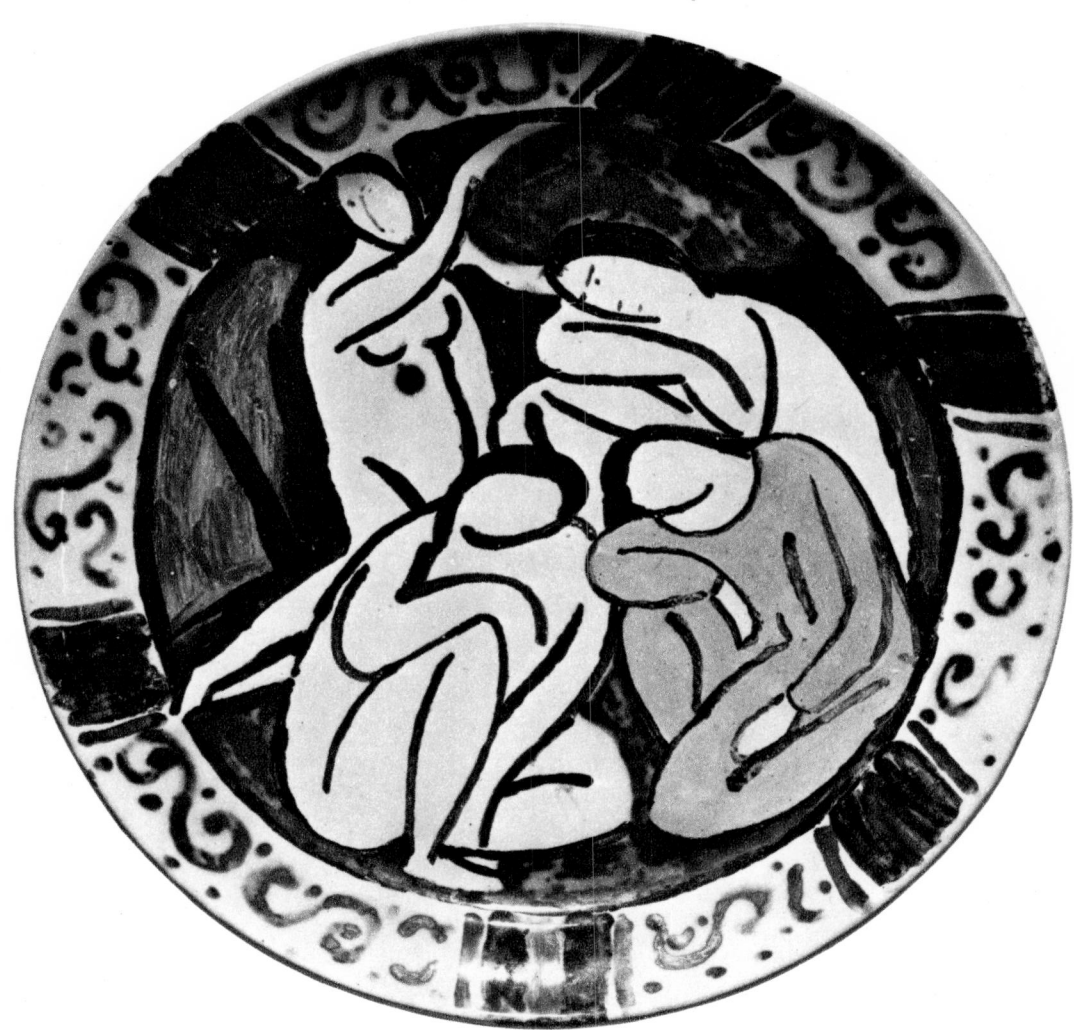

65. André Derain.
BATHERS. 1907.
Decorated porcelain plate,
diameter 9".
Collection Samuel Josefowitz, Lausanne

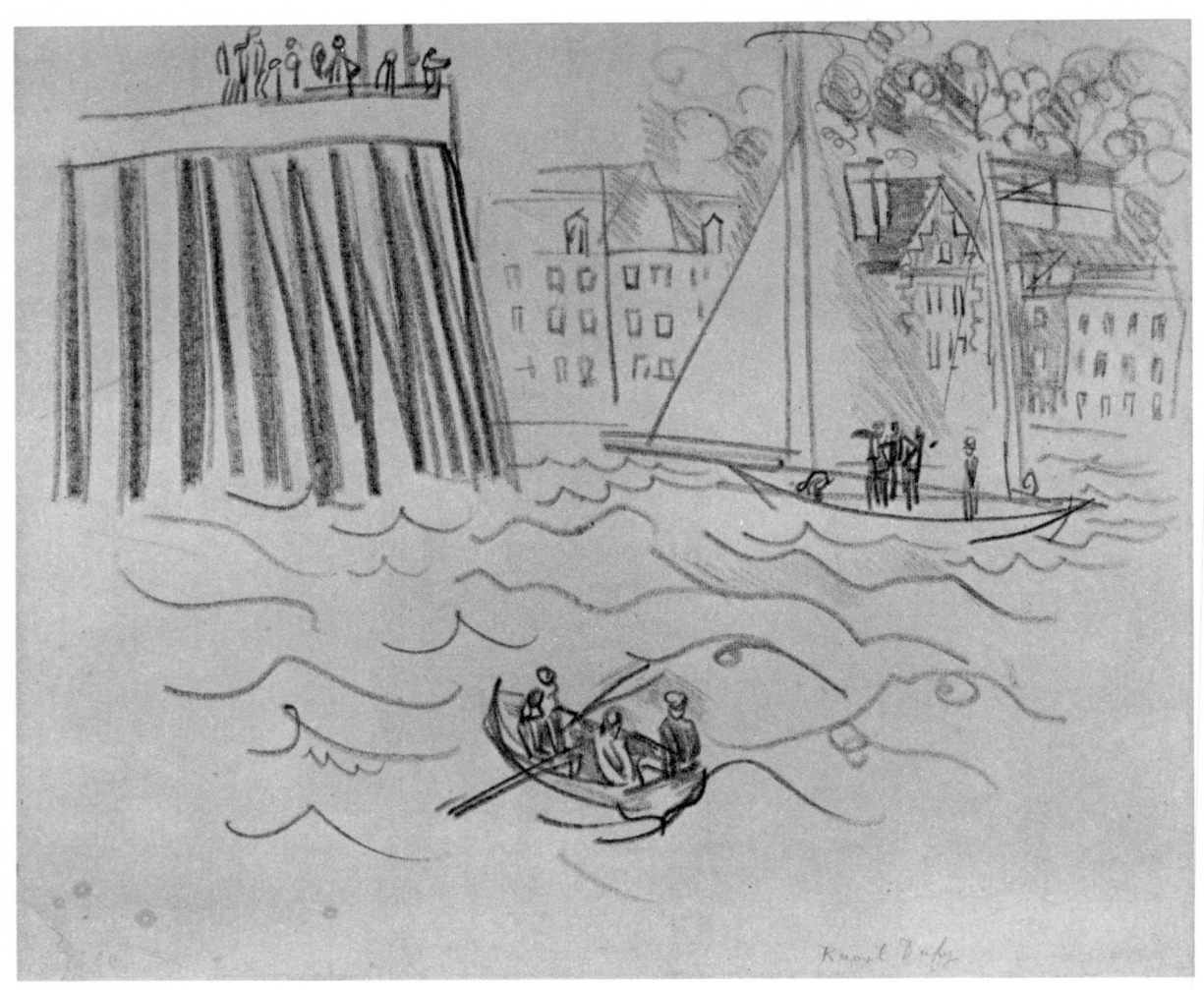

66. Raoul Dufy. BREAKWATER. C. 1910–12.
Charcoal, 18 1/2 × 22 1/2".
Nouveau Musée des Beaux-Arts, Le Havre

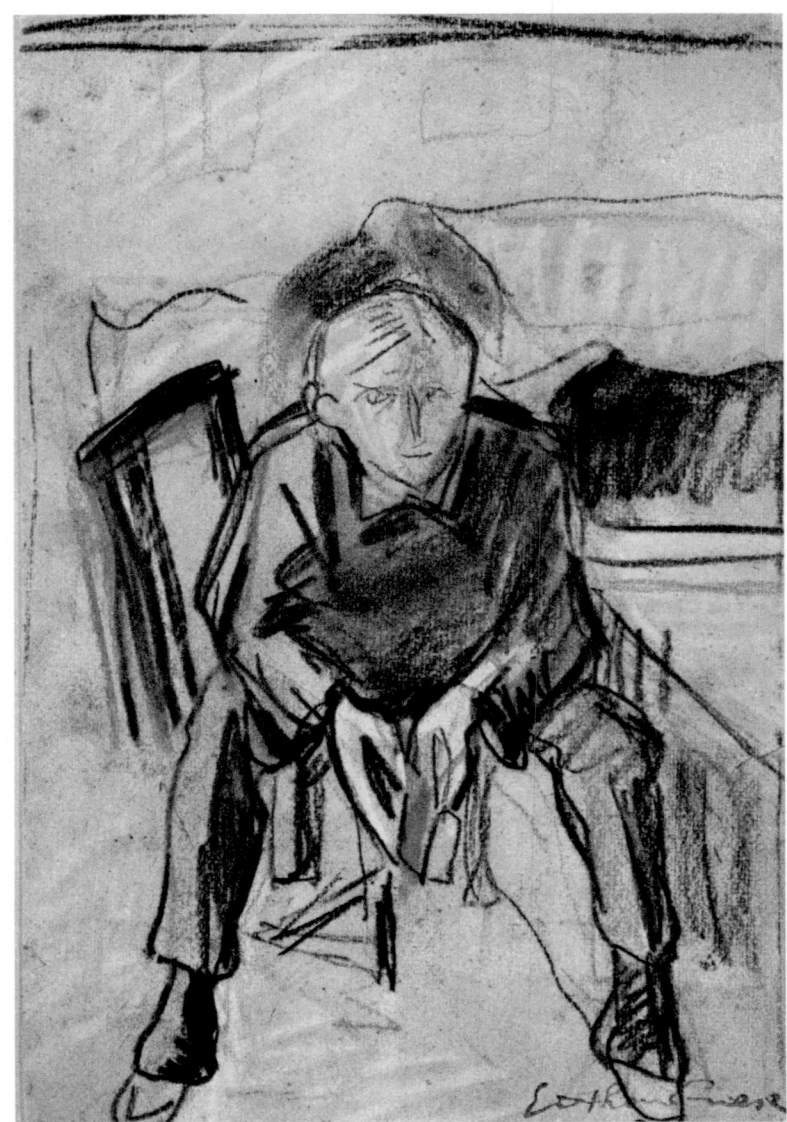

67. Othon Friesz.
STUDY FOR PORTRAIT OF FERNAND FLEURET. 1907.
Colored pencil on beige paper, 14 1/8 × 9".
Musée National d'Art Moderne, Paris

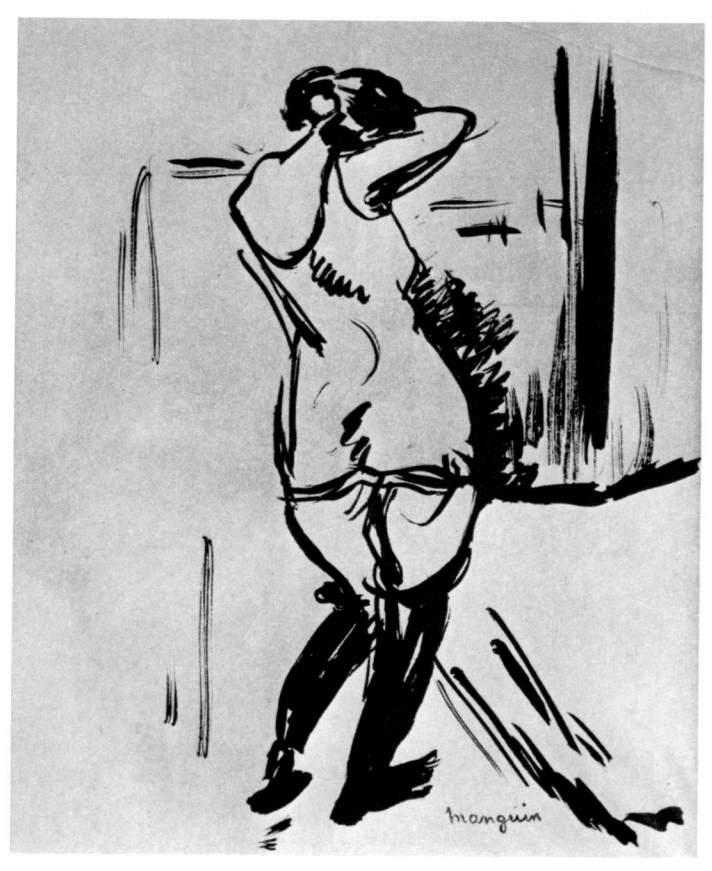

68. Henri Manguin. NUDE WITH BLACK STOCKINGS. 1903.
Brush with India ink, 11 × 8 5/8".
Galerie de Paris, Paris

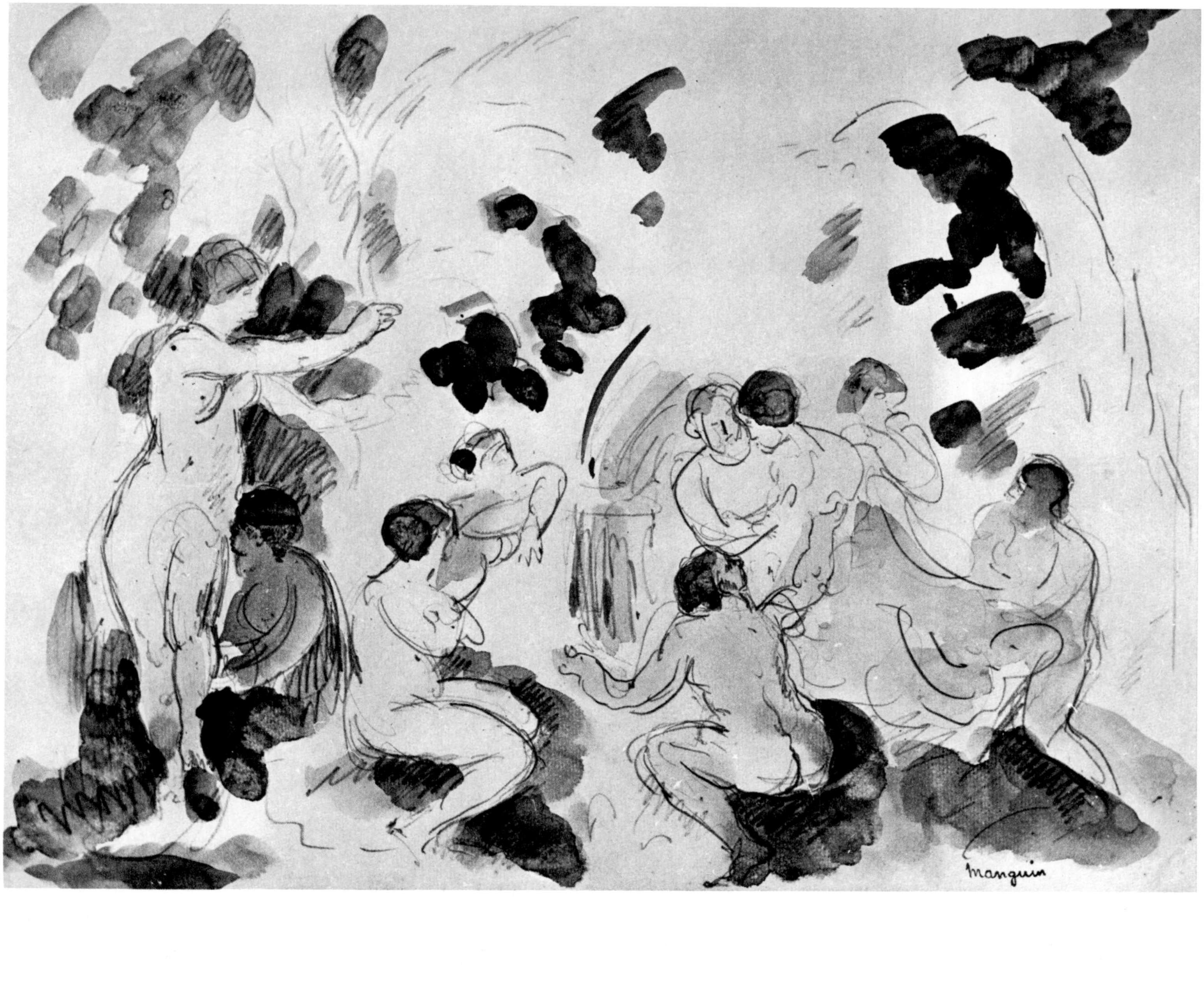

69. Henri Manguin. BATHERS. 1905.
Watercolor, 13 3/4 × 17 3/4".
Galerie de Paris, Paris

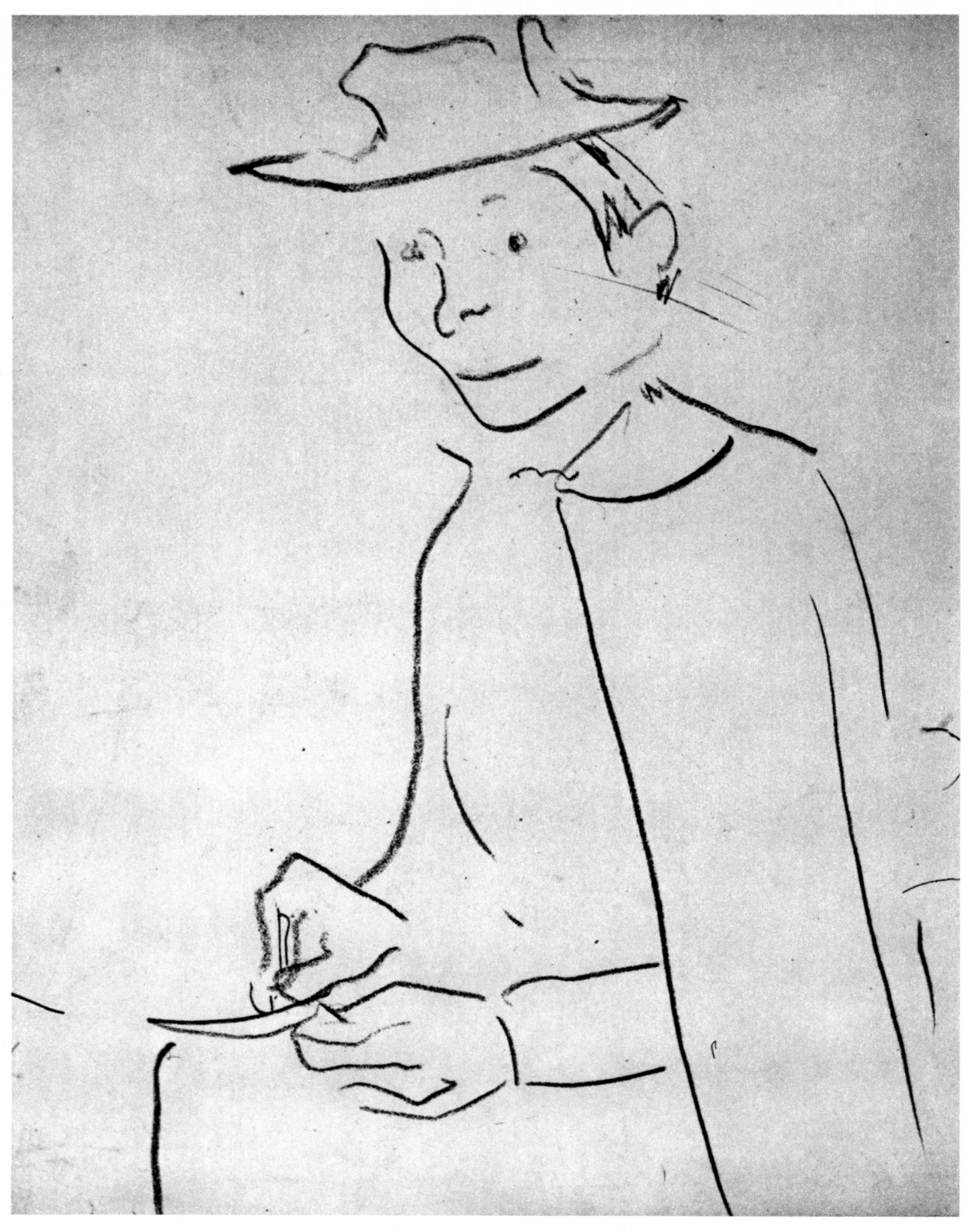

70. Albert Marquet. SILHOUETTE OF JACQUELINE MARVAL. c. 1901. Pencil, 11 3/8 × 8 5/8″.
Musée de Peinture et de Sculpture, Grenoble

71. Albert Marquet. WOMAN WITH BASKET. 1904.
Brush with India ink, 8 3/8 × 6 1/4".
Musée des Beaux-Arts, Bordeaux

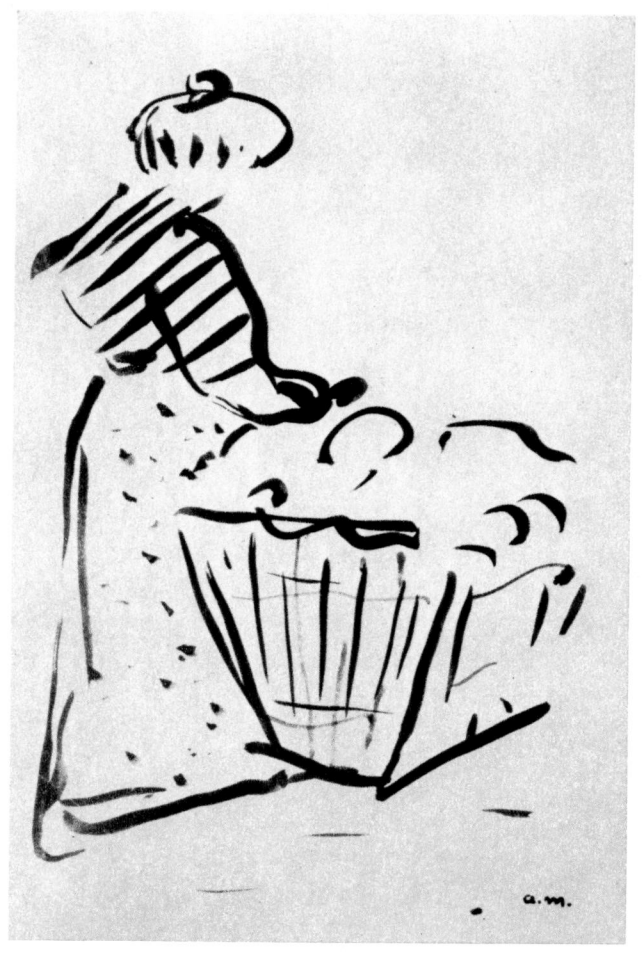

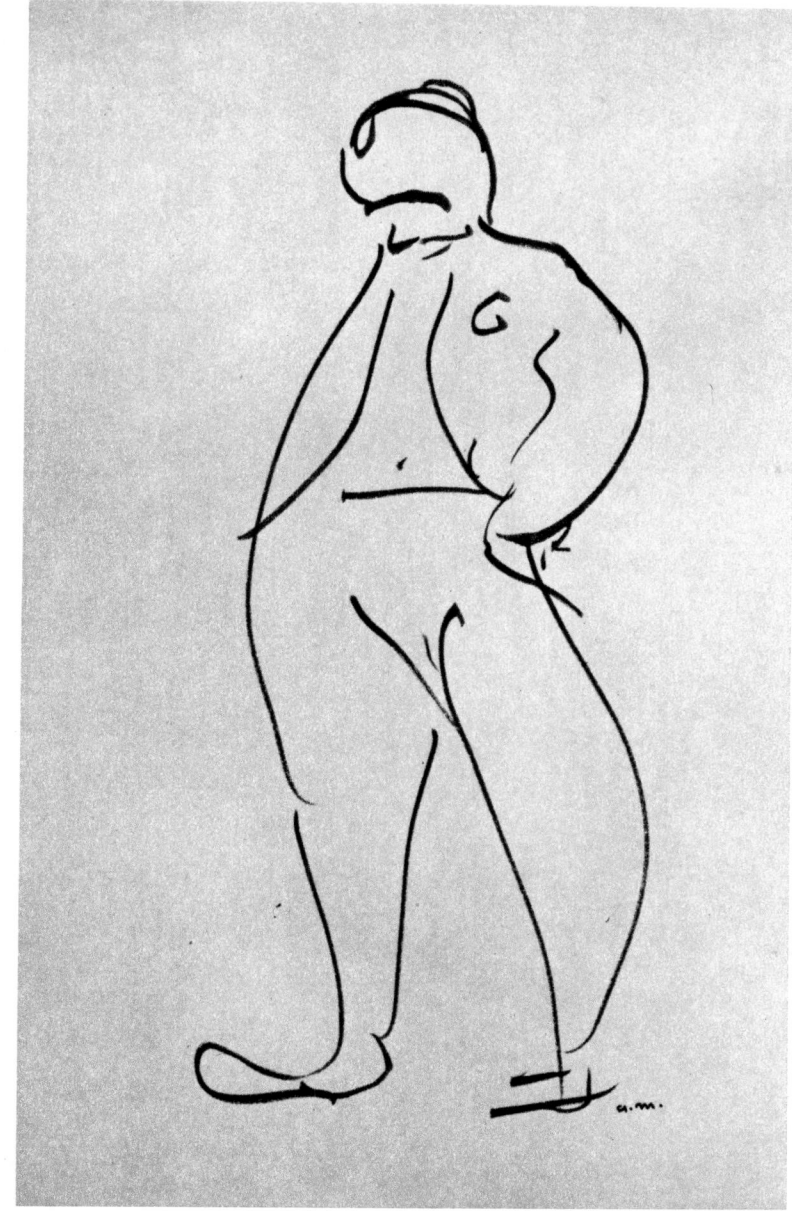

72. Albert Marquet. MAN STANDING.
c. 1905.
India ink on cream-colored paper,
13 × 8".
*Musée National d'Art Moderne,
Paris*

73. Albert Marquet.
CARNIVAL AT COLLIOURE. 1908.
Brush with India ink,
5 1/8 × 7 1/8".
*Musée des Beaux-Arts,
Bordeaux*

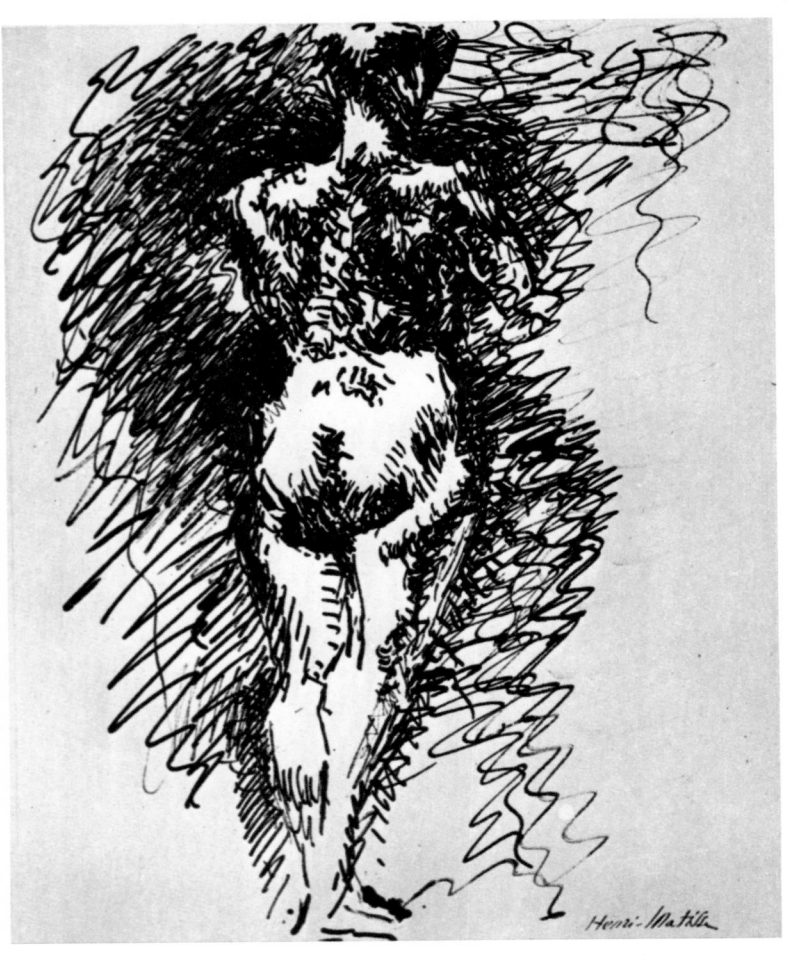

74. Henri Matisse. NUDE SEEN FROM THE BACK. 1903.
Pen and ink, 10 5/8 × 7 7/8".
Musée de Peinture et de Sculpture, Grenoble

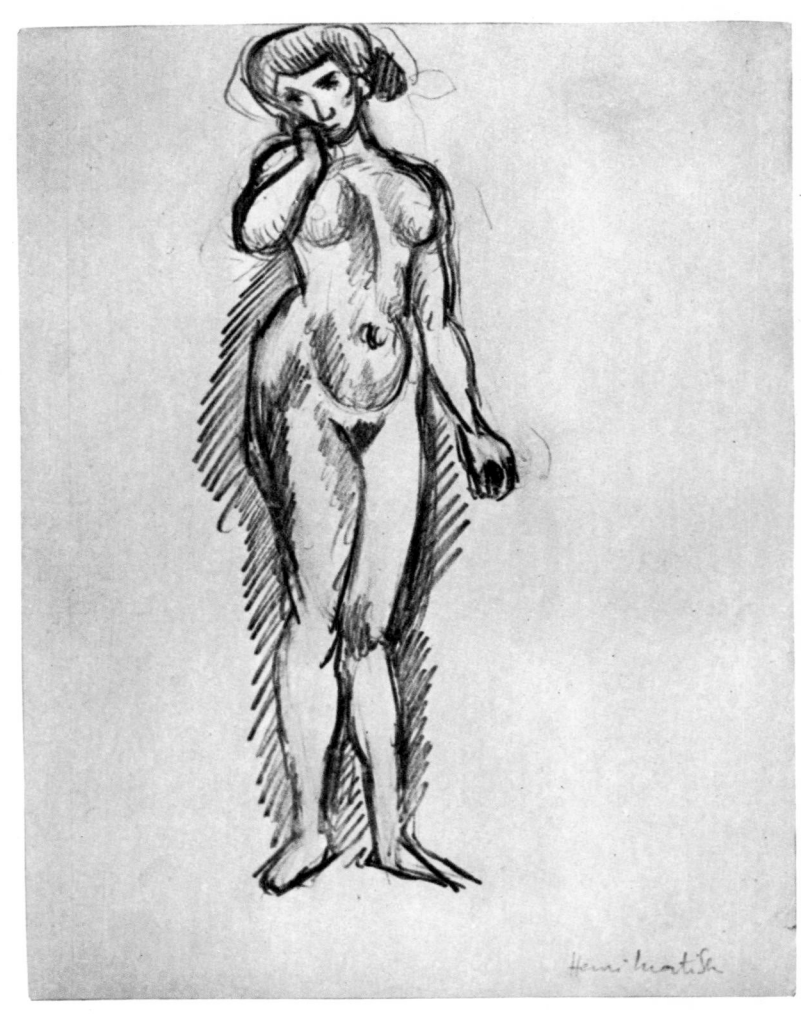

75. Henri Matisse. NUDE. C. 1908.
Black lead, 12 1/4 × 9".
Musée de Peinture et de Sculpture,
Grenoble

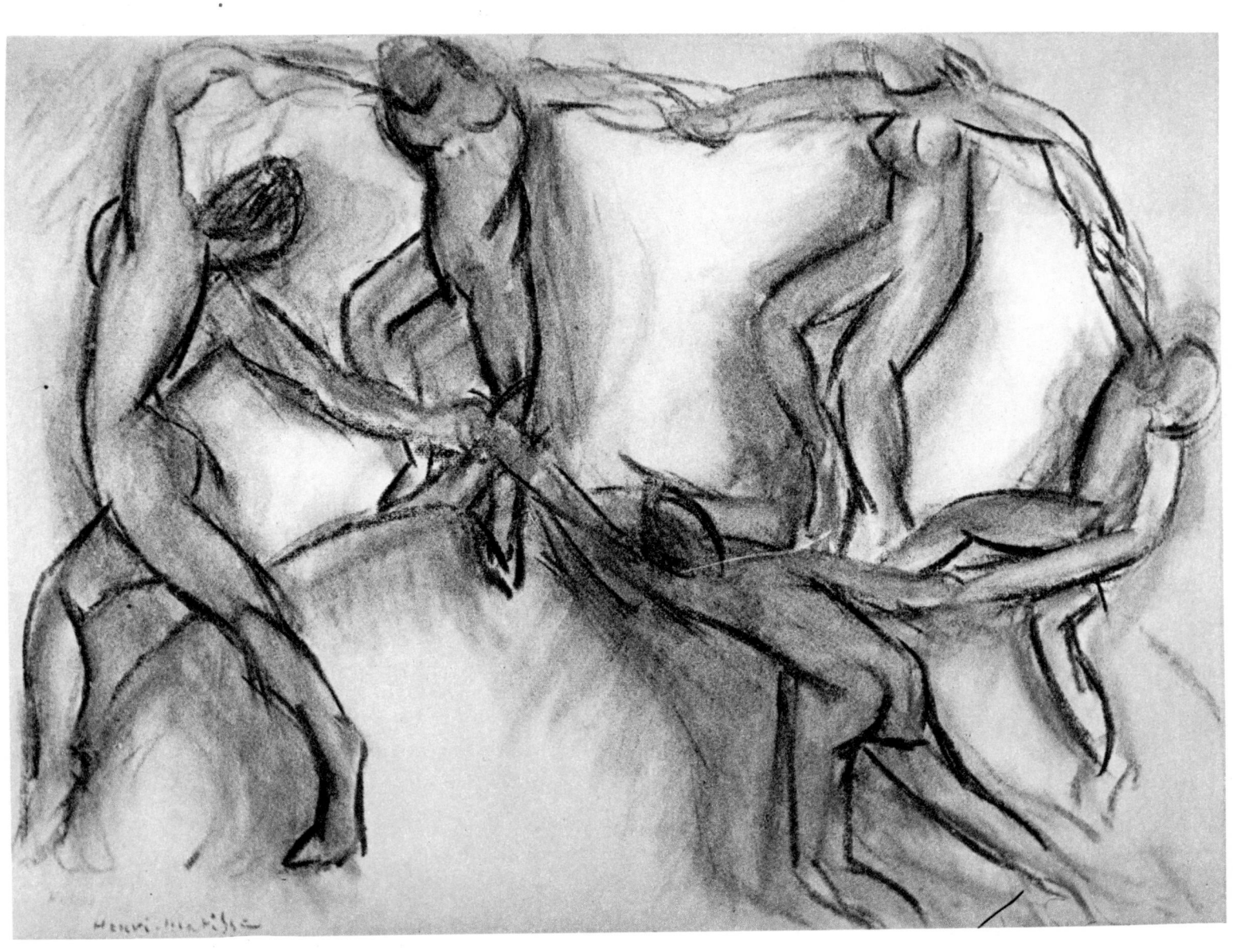

76. Henri Matisse. DANCE. 1909. Charcoal, 18 7/8 × 25 5/8″. *Musée de Peinture et de Sculpture, Grenoble. Gift of Agutte-Sembat*

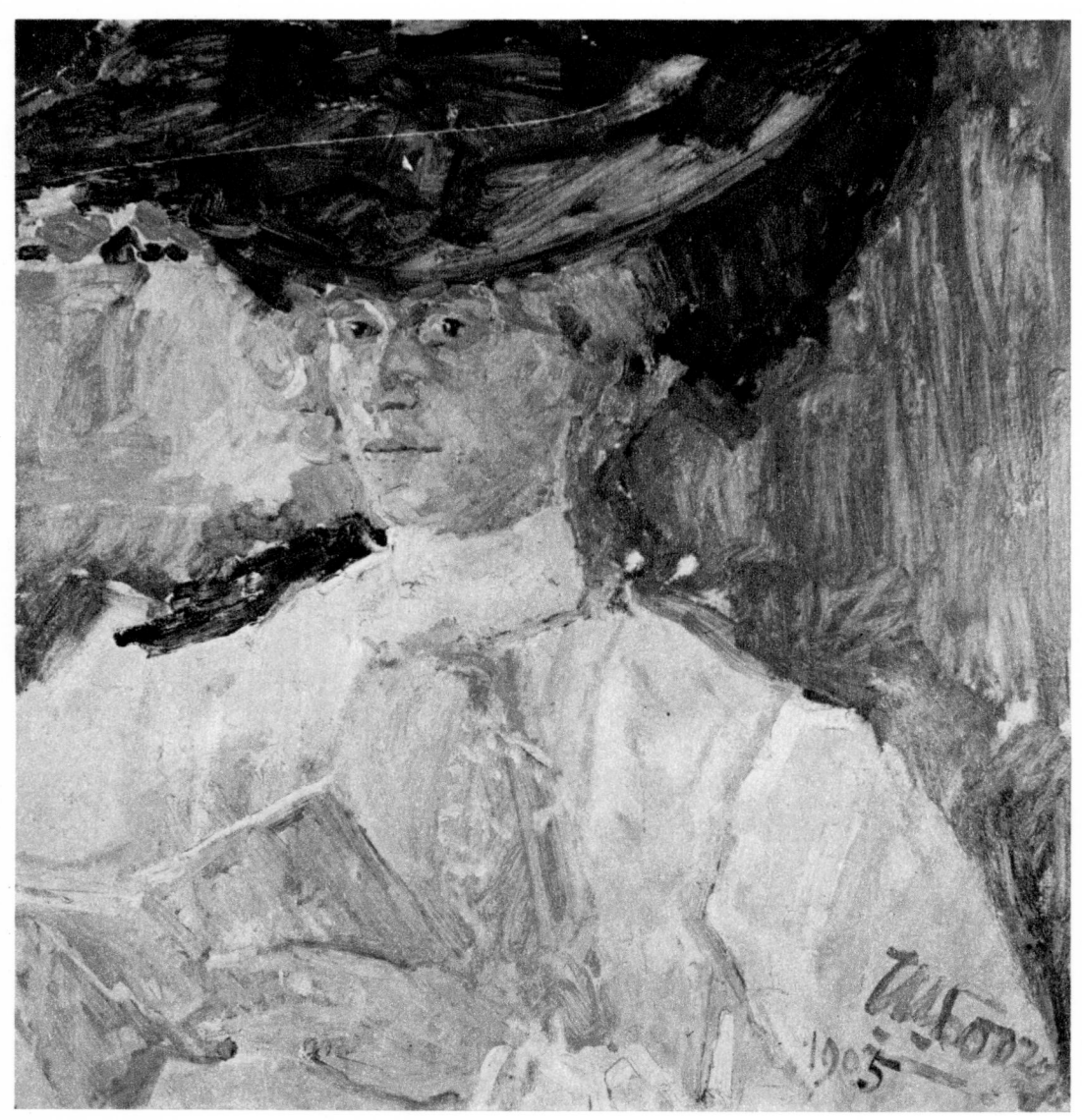

77. Jan Toorop. PORTRAIT OF MME LUCIE VAN DAM VAN ISSELT. 1905.
Oil on canvas, 27 3/8 × 25 1/4″. *Gemeentemuseum, The Hague*

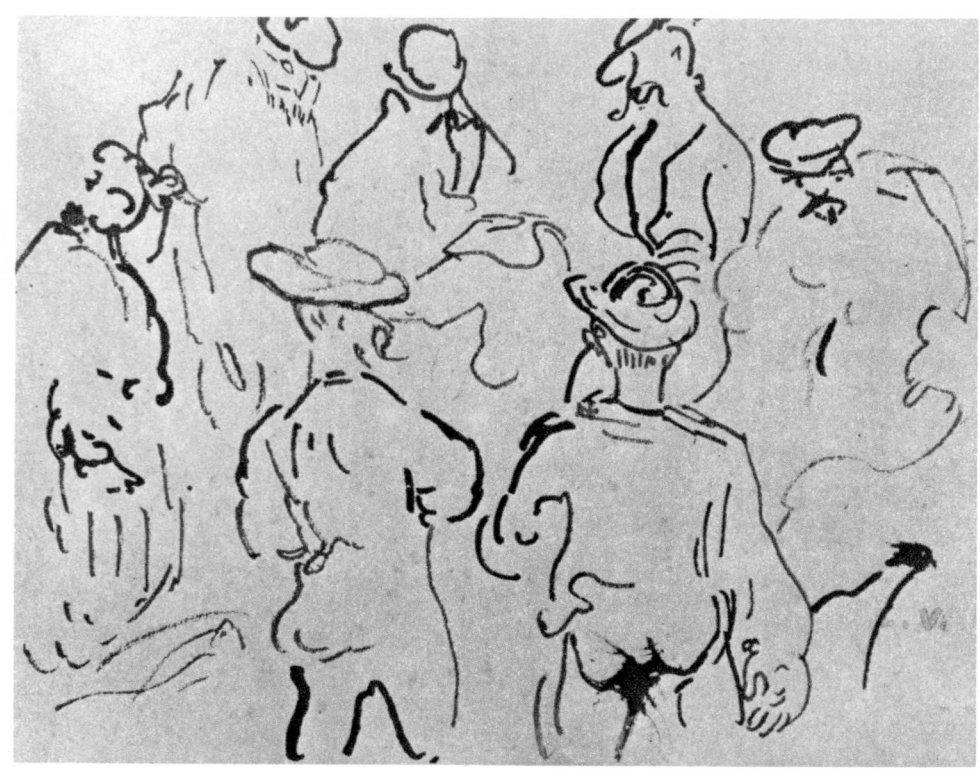

78. Louis Valtat.
SPANISH SILHOUETTES. 1894.
India ink, 6 1/4 × 9 7/8″.
Private collection, Switzerland

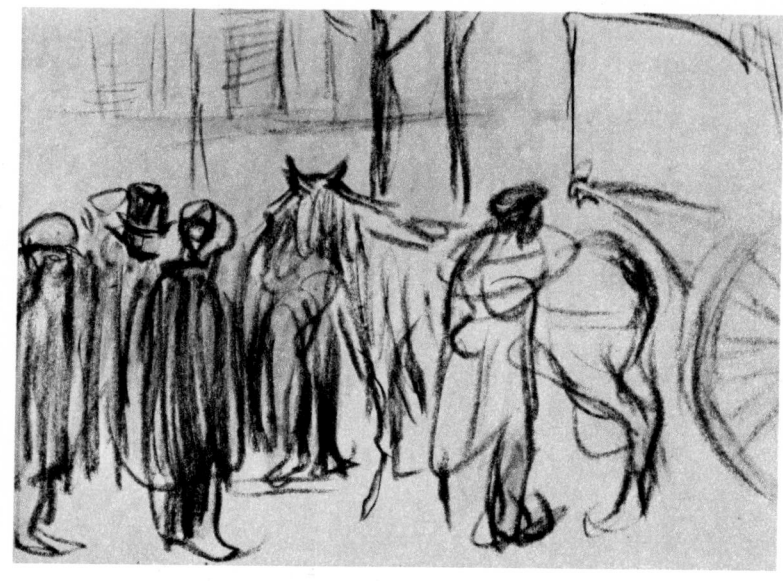

79. Kees van Dongen. THE PRODUCE VENDOR. C. 1902.
Charcoal, 11 3/4 × 17 3/4″.
Private collection, Paris

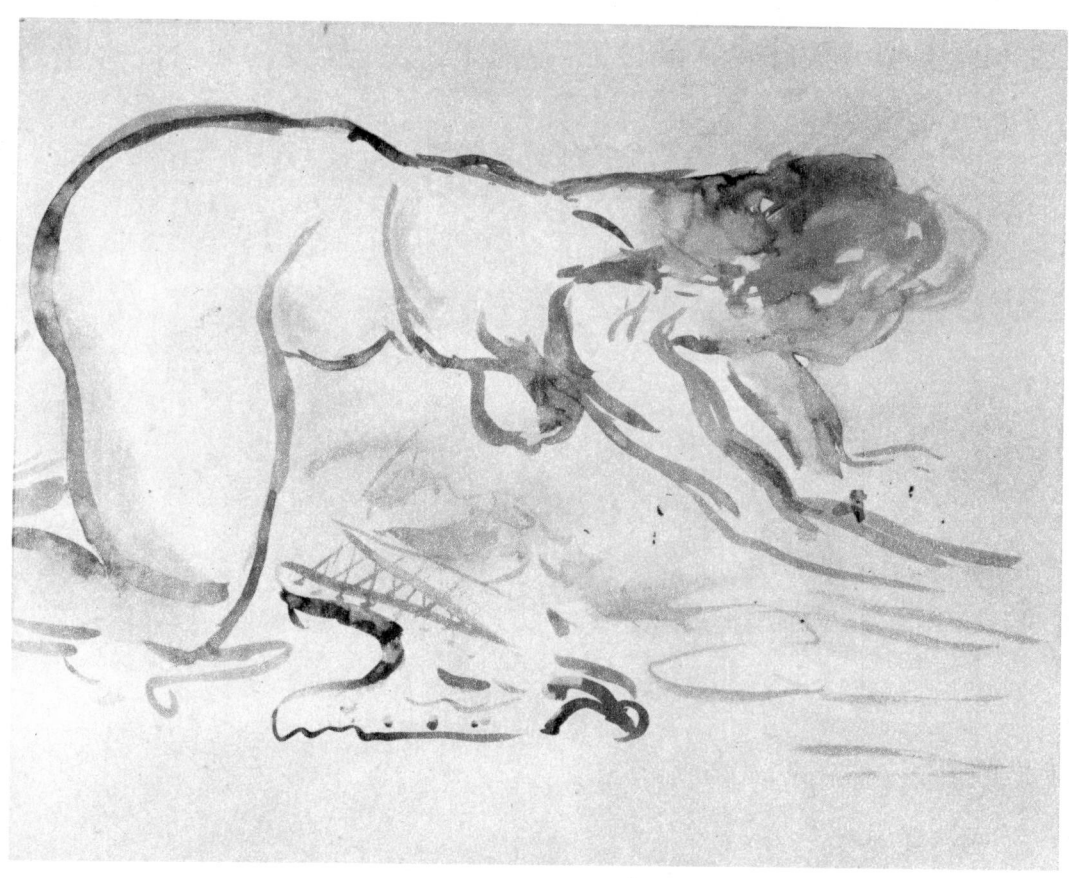

80. Kees van Dongen.
NUDE WITH CORSET. C. 1904.
Watercolor, 17 3/4 × 21 5/8″.
Private collection, Paris

81. Kees van Dongen. NUDE. 1907.
Decorated porcelain plate,
diameter 9″.
*Collection Samuel Josefowitz,
Lausanne*

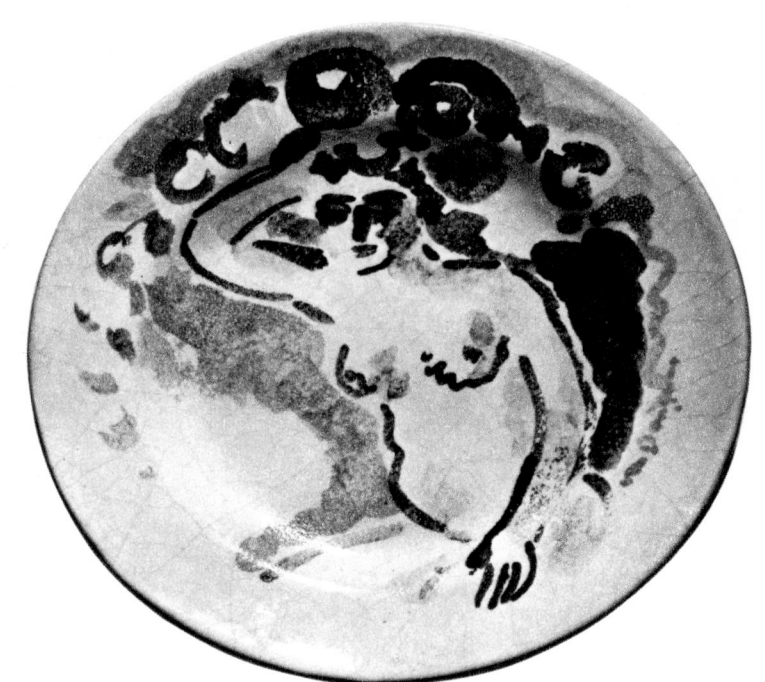

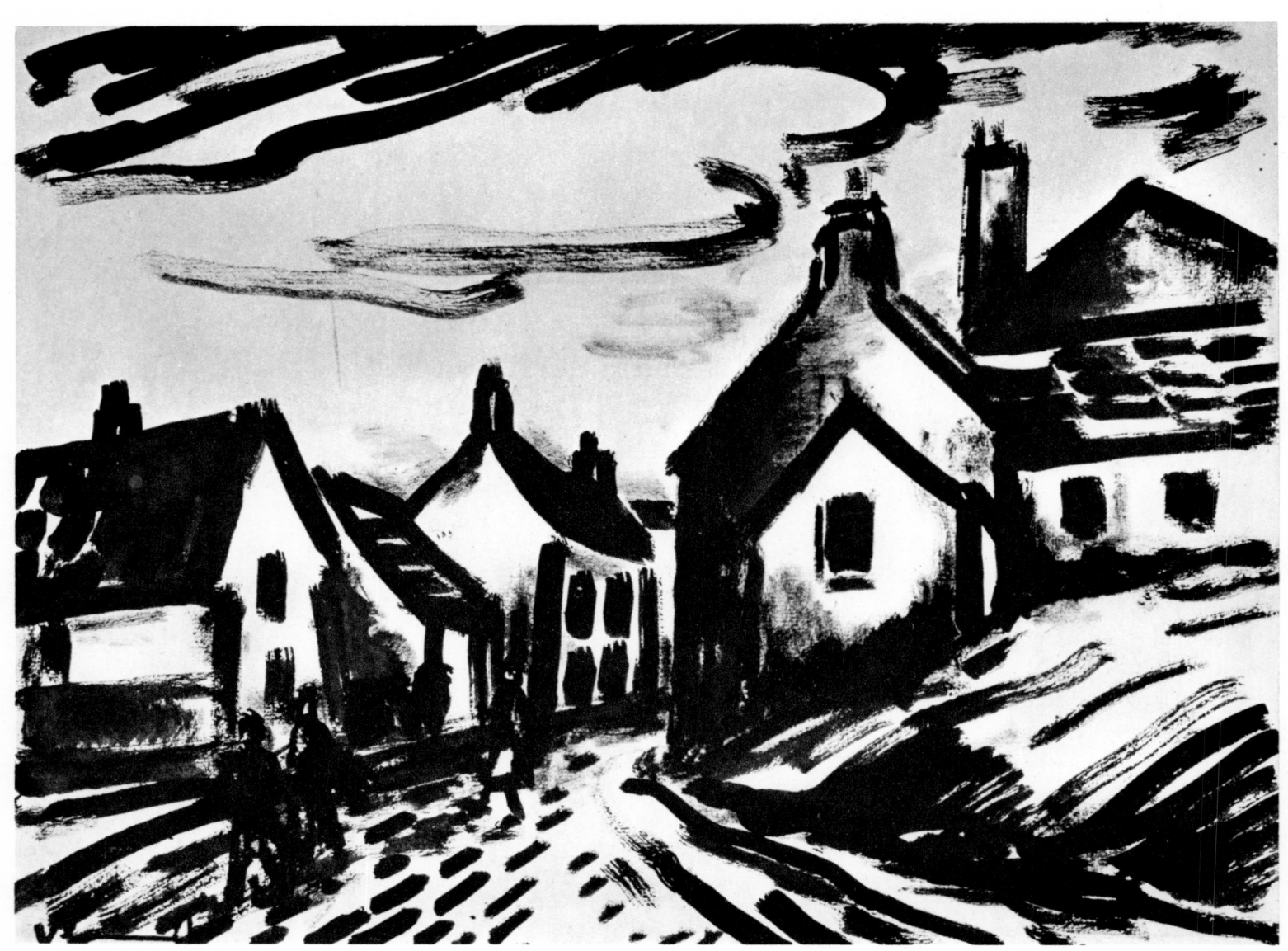

82. Maurice de Vlaminck. A VILLAGE STREET. C. 1907. Brush with India ink, 9 3/4 × 12 5/8″. *Private collection, Paris*

CHRONOLOGY

1895–98   A friendly nucleus forms in Gustave Moreau's studio, Matisse and Marquet, already good friends, being joined by Evenepoel, Manguin, and Camoin.

Beginning of 1898, Matisse goes to Corsica. Death of Moreau in April. Matisse and Marquet embark on Pre-Fauvism. Friesz enters Bonnat's studio.

1898–1901   In Carrière's studio, Matisse has a strong influence on Biette, Derain, Chabaud, Karsten, and Puy.

Late 1900, Derain and Vlaminck meet and work together at Chatou. Dufy at the Ecole des Beaux-Arts. Arrival of Braque in Paris.

1901, Matisse and Marquet exhibit at the Indépendants, where Valtat had preceded them. In the following years they are joined by Manguin, Camoin, Van Dongen, and others, Van Dongen having settled permanently in Paris at the end of 1899.

1901, at the Van Gogh retrospective, Derain introduces Vlaminck to Matisse.

1902   First group exhibitions at Berthe Weill's. In Munich, Kandinsky presides over "Die Phalanx."

1903   Matisse and Marquet exhibit at the new Salon d'Automne, where they are subsequently joined by Valtat, Camoin, Manguin, and others. Death of Gauguin.

Works of Cézanne, Gauguin, and Van Gogh at the Berlin Sezession.

The Post-Impressionists at the Vienna Sezession.

1904   In April, group show of the works of Camoin, Manguin, Marquet, Matisse, and Puy at Berthe Weill's. Matisse has an exhibition at Vollard's in June and spends the summer with Signac at Saint-Tropez, where he experiments with Neo-Impressionism. Vollard, who had signed a contract with Valtat in 1900, organizes a show of his work; exhibits Van Dongen in November.

Having finished his military service, Derain again works with Vlaminck.

1905   Seurat and Van Gogh retrospectives at the Indépendants. The new painting begins to take hold, and Matisse's Pointillist canvas causes a sensation, prompting many of his friends to go in their turn to Saint-Tropez during the summer.

In Dresden, formation of the Brücke association by the architecture students Heckel, Kirchner, Bleyl, and Schmidt-Rottluff; Van Gogh exhibition.

Jawlensky in Brittany and Provence.

Matisse and Derain are filled with enthusiasm at Collioure, where they are able to admire Gauguin's works at Daniel de Monfreid's.

The works painted at Saint-Tropez and Collioure, glowing with color, are assembled with those of Vlaminck, Van Dongen, Czóbel, at the Salon d'Automne in one room, which Vauxcelles christens the Fauves' den. In late October Berthe Weill opens a show for the whole group in her gallery, and Prath & Magnier follow suit, after first holding a Friesz exhibition. Van Dongen shows in November at the Druet Gallery. Jawlensky and Kandinsky take part in the Salon d'Automne.

1906   Matisse moves to the Rue de Sèvres, to the ex-convent of Les Oiseaux. Here he paints *Joy of Life*, which causes a stir at the Indépendants and establishes his authority over the whole group. Success of his large exhibition at Druet's in March. Trip to Biskra. Braque shows for the first time at the Indépendants and goes to Antwerp with Friesz. Derain in London.

Brilliant success of the Fauves' room, with the addition of Friesz, Dufy, Marinot, and others, at the Salon d'Automne, which also pays ample tribute to Gauguin and offers a display of Russian art. Kandinsky and Gabriele Münter settle for a year in Sèvres and exhibit at the Salon d'Automne. Arrival of many foreign artists in Paris.

The Berlin Sezession invites Valtat.

In Dresden, Pechstein, Nolde, and shortly thereafter Cuno Amiet and Axel Gallen-Kallela, join Die Brücke; the group publishes its first album of prints, and organizes an exhibition of paintings in the autumn and another of graphic works in the winter.

Works of the Neo-Impressionists and Gauguin exhibited at the Arnold Gallery.

1907   At the Indépendants the Fauves—among whom the critics class the newcomers Bereny, Delaunay, and Metzinger—are the center of attention; they are even more so at the Salon d'Automne, where Braque has joined them, and already their works are distributed in several rooms.

In March and November, exhibition of the whole group at Berthe Weill's; another exhibition at the Blot Gallery.

The Fauves take part, as in the previous year, in the Salon de la Libre Esthétique in Brussels. Marquet and Friesz have one-man shows at Druet's, and Camoin and Van Dongen at Kahnweiler's. In Dresden, Die Brücke exhibits at the Richter Gallery.

Matisse, who has started to teach a few pupils, is obliged by their growing numbers to move to the Boulevard des Invalides in the fall and to organize a real academy.

1908   Several of the Fauves do not take part in the Indépendants and the critics congratulate those who show a change of approach. Their group is fully represented, however, at Le Havre, Toulouse, and abroad—particularly at the Golden Fleece Salon in Moscow.

Total dispersal at the Salon d'Automne, where Matisse presents a collection of his works. He has a show of graphics in New York, and of paintings in Berlin; in December he publishes *Notes d'un peintre*.

Van Dongen, who has a show at Bernheim's, is invited to exhibit with Die Brücke; Pechstein visits France. Czóbel exhibits at Berthe Weill's, Braque at Kahnweiler's.

1909   Another, smaller exhibition of the Fauves at the Golden Fleece Salon in Moscow.

Kandinsky and his friends found the Munich Neue Künstler Vereinigung, which exhibits the works of several French artists the following year: Braque, Derain, Van Dongen, and others.

The Russian Ballet performs in Paris.

A group of German painters is invited to the Salon d'Automne.

1910   Large Matisse retrospective at the Bernheim-Jeune Gallery and a second exhibition of graphics in New York.

The Fauves are represented at the Mánes Society in Prague.

Fourth album and new exhibition of Die Brücke in Dresden.

Matisse and Marquet in Munich.

1911   French artists take part in the Berlin Sezession.

In Munich, a group of artists answers the protest by the painter Winnen against the invasion of French art.

A number of French artists are represented at the Blaue Reiter exhibition in December, and in the album subsequently published.

1912   The former Fauves are well represented at the Berlin Sezession, and still more so at the Sonderbund in Cologne, the Grafton Gallery in London, at St. Petersburg, and Zurich.

1913   Exhibition in Berlin of the works of Matisse and Friesz.

Important French contribution at the Armory Show in New York.

COLORPLATES

PAUL GAUGUIN (1848–1903)
Painted in 1894
The Day of the God (Mahana no Atua)
Oil on canvas, 27 3/8 × 35 3/8"
The Art Institute of Chicago

Many artists set a fundamental example for the Fauves in their rejection of outmoded traditions and their enthusiastic discovery of the impact of color: Delacroix, Monticelli, on occasion Ingres and Manet, the Impressionists and the Japanese, these latter two coming into their own at the end of the nineteenth century. In the previous generation, there were such obvious predecessors as Ensor and Munch, without there being, however, any actual contact. For some of them, Gustave Moreau was to be the most effective inspiration and guide for their youthful efforts.

Greatest of all was the attraction of Van Gogh and Cézanne, but even this cannot eclipse the overwhelming influence of Gauguin on the whole group, and particularly on Matisse to the end of his career. This influence operated on two different levels—one technical, the other spiritual and aesthetic—which cannot be dissociated. This is apparent in *The Day of the God*, finished during Gauguin's stay in Paris, which sums up all his leading aspirations.

By means of subtle gradations, Gauguin's highly saturated color here achieves its greatest richness. He applies it in skillfully interwoven planes where there is a play of complementary colors. The extraordinary luminosity of the foreground brings out the predominantly ultramarine background, heightened by contrasting vermilions, yellows, and slightly tinted whites. The alternating bands of color, enclosed by their sinuous outlines, admirably define a suggested space without detracting from the effectiveness of the flat areas boldly introduced from the bottom upward to unify and harmonize the whole composition.

The deliberate symbolism and the disturbing presence of the tutelary god vanish before the enchantment of a primitive life in which the golden hue of naked bodies, music, and dance are mingled in a peaceful spectacle of everyday existence that vividly evokes the original concept of paradise.

Such were the rejuvenating examples that inspired the Fauves. Matisse especially, who in 1905 saw Gauguin's last paintings at Daniel de Monfreid's at Collioure, was spellbound, and henceforth exploited this eloquence of color while often indulging in the same exotic dreams. He never ceased to reflect this image of an eternal paradise in his interiors, with their luxuriant plants, and in his dreams of flower maidens. In 1930 he made the journey to Tahiti, and not long before his death he vividly re-created in tapestry his dazzled memories of the South Sea lagoons.

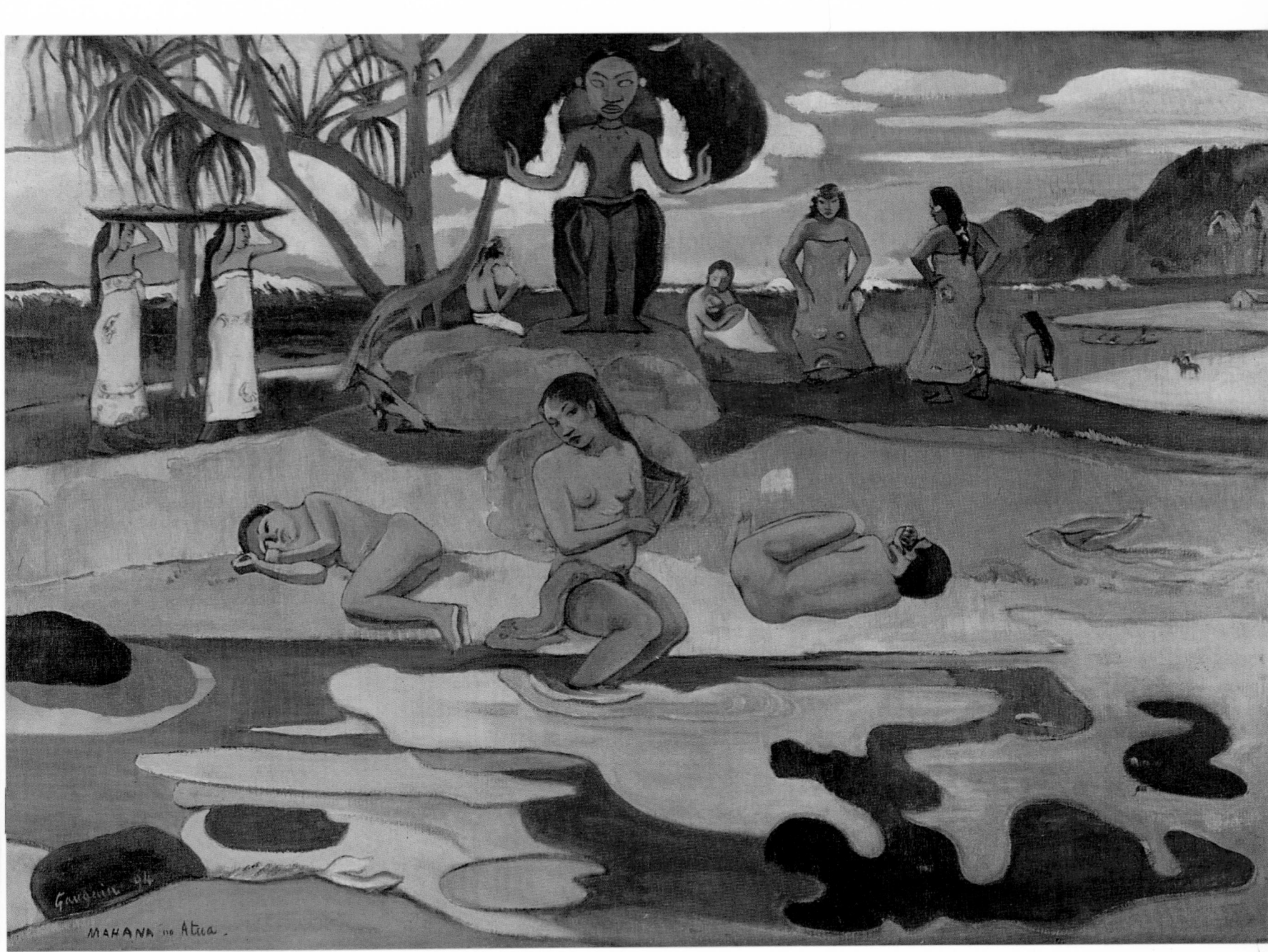

ARMAND SÉGUIN (1869–1904)

Painted in 1894
The Two Cottages
Oil on canvas, 23 5/8 × 35 7/8"
Collection Samuel Josefowitz, Lausanne

The younger generations had little opportunity to see Gauguin's work during his lifetime except for his exhibition in November, 1893, at Durand-Ruel, and that of 1903 at Vollard's. It is therefore not surprising that the large retrospective at the Salon d'Automne in 1906 should have been such a dazzling revelation to so many artists, particularly those from abroad. Yet Gauguin's influence becomes apparent at an early date, and during the last decade of the nineteenth century many painters undertake to transmit his precepts with varying degrees of understanding.

The first to be exposed to his influence and to publicize his merits are the future Nabis. As early as November, 1888, even before they have formed a group, Sérusier brings back from his stay at Pont-Aven his famous *Talisman*, painted under the master's direction at the Bois d'Amour, and communicates his enthusiasm to his young companions at the Académie Julian. Sérusier was later to return to Brittany with Jan Verkade and Mogens Ballin, to work with Gauguin before and after his voyage to Tahiti. In 1895 his paintings still reflect this influence, which he will soon throw off. The only member of the group who long remains faithful to Gauguin is Maillol, the quality of whose paintings has too often been neglected, as is apparent from *The Wave* of 1898 (Musée du Petit Palais, Paris), with its stylized flat areas and rich blues.

Very few of the Pont-Aven group—as the artists who had gathered round Gauguin were called—were to have a consistent influence on the younger painters, for some of them, like Emile Bernard, changed their orientation, while others, such as Charles Laval or Meyer de Haan, disappeared from the scene. Schuffenecker and Filiger continued to exhibit at the Salons, but the first always with restraint and the second enclosed in a narrow symbolism. Three artists were finally to play a more important role: the Swiss Cuno Amiet, who later will enjoy great popularity in his own country, the Irishman O'Connor, who accompanies Gauguin in 1894 and later appears regularly at the Salon d'Automne as one of his rather distant followers, and Armand Séguin. Having moved into the Pension Gloanec in 1890, Séguin introduced his two friends to this milieu. In 1895 he had a one-man show at Le Barc de Boutteville that included this painting. As he explained in his introduction, the picture is to some extent influenced by Gauguin but is also significantly related to the developments of the moment. The warmth of the colors, the accentuation of the outlines, the sweeping arabesques seem by their very freedom to suggest the quest on which the Fauves were to embark a few years later. Séguin's early Pointillist technique also serves as a reminder that this movement always aroused lively interest among the younger artists and provided an indispensable springboard for their final development.

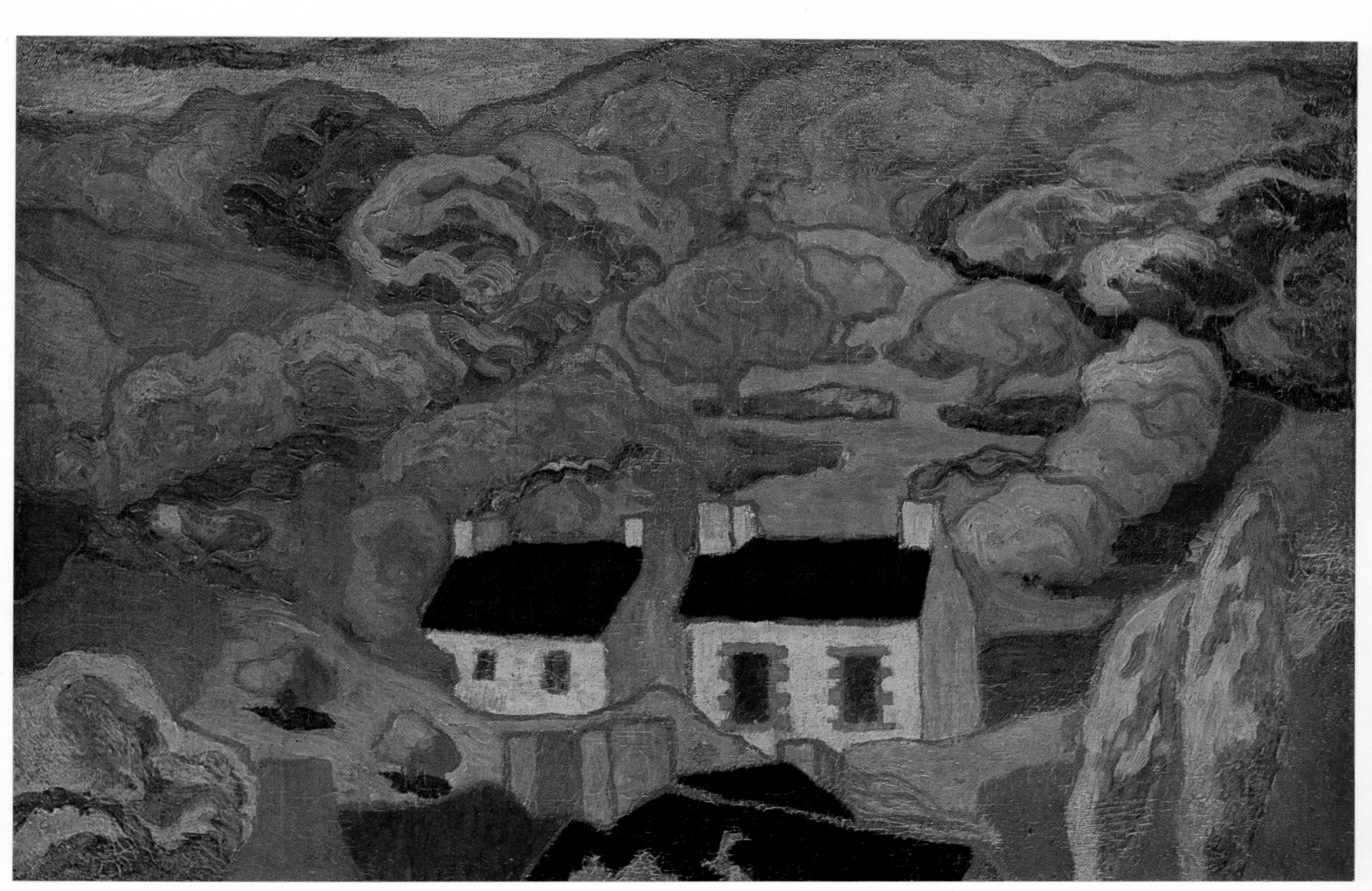

LOUIS VALTAT (1869–1952)

Painted in 1894
Nude in a Garden
Oil on canvas, 17 3/8 × 21 5/8"
Collection Dr. Jean Valtat, Paris

Valtat was born on August 8, 1869, of a family of shipowners, and when his parents settled in Versailles in 1880 he started his classical studies at the Lycée Hoche. His parents strongly encouraged his early artistic tendencies, and in 1888 he went to study under Dupré at the Académie Julian, where he met the future Nabis. He then attended the Ecole des Beaux-Arts for a time and was awarded a medal there.

In 1889 he begins to exhibit at the Indépendants, and the following year takes a studio of his own in the Rue de la Glacière, where he does vigorous renderings of street scenes and figures, and goes boldly beyond Impressionism and Neo-Impressionism, although their combined influence is at times still apparent.

In October, 1894, he travels to England, and then spends the whole winter at Banyuls and Collioure, where he makes friends with Maillol, and later goes to Llansa in Spain with Daniel de Monfreid. These two artists, particularly the second, already in constant touch with Gauguin, have a deep influence on the young man, as do, in the same place ten years later, Matisse and Derain.

Nude in a Garden, probably executed at this time, with its splashes of pink and orange, its graduated luminous greens, its powerful outlines, the raised horizon, and even the curiously coiled figure, clearly suggests a sudden and ardent admiration for Gauguin, about whom Valtat had already heard a great deal from Sérusier. Its joyful brilliance of color anticipates by a number of years the course that the Fauves were to follow.

Too isolated in his research—he was always to remain rather aloof, suspended between two generations and two groups—he feels the need to seek companions among the Nabis. He works with Albert André and Lugné-Poë on the sets for *Le Chariot de terre-cuite*, and furnishes drawings and woodcuts for the review *L'Omnibus de Corinthe*.

His elegant series *Les Jeunes Femmes au bois*, almost Baroque in style, brings him success but distracts him from his earlier objectives. After building a house in 1899 at Anthéor, where he is henceforth to spend a part of each year, he pays frequent visits to Renoir, works with him at Manganose, and is to some extent drawn by him into a kind of Mediterranean euphoria.

He recovers himself, however, using a swift, dense, but very light touch during a trip to Venice in 1902. After staying with Signac in 1903 and again during the winter of 1904, he works with heightened vigor and color. Several of his paintings once more anticipate the birth of Fauvism. Thus at the Salon d'Automne, although his five paintings are still far from the Fauves' room, having been hung in Room XV with the works of Biette, Marinot, Jawlensky, and Kandinsky, one of his seascapes is nonetheless pilloried in *L'Illustration* along with the canvases of Matisse, Derain, and Manguin. A hostile press forcibly, but quite justifiably, included him among the Fauves.

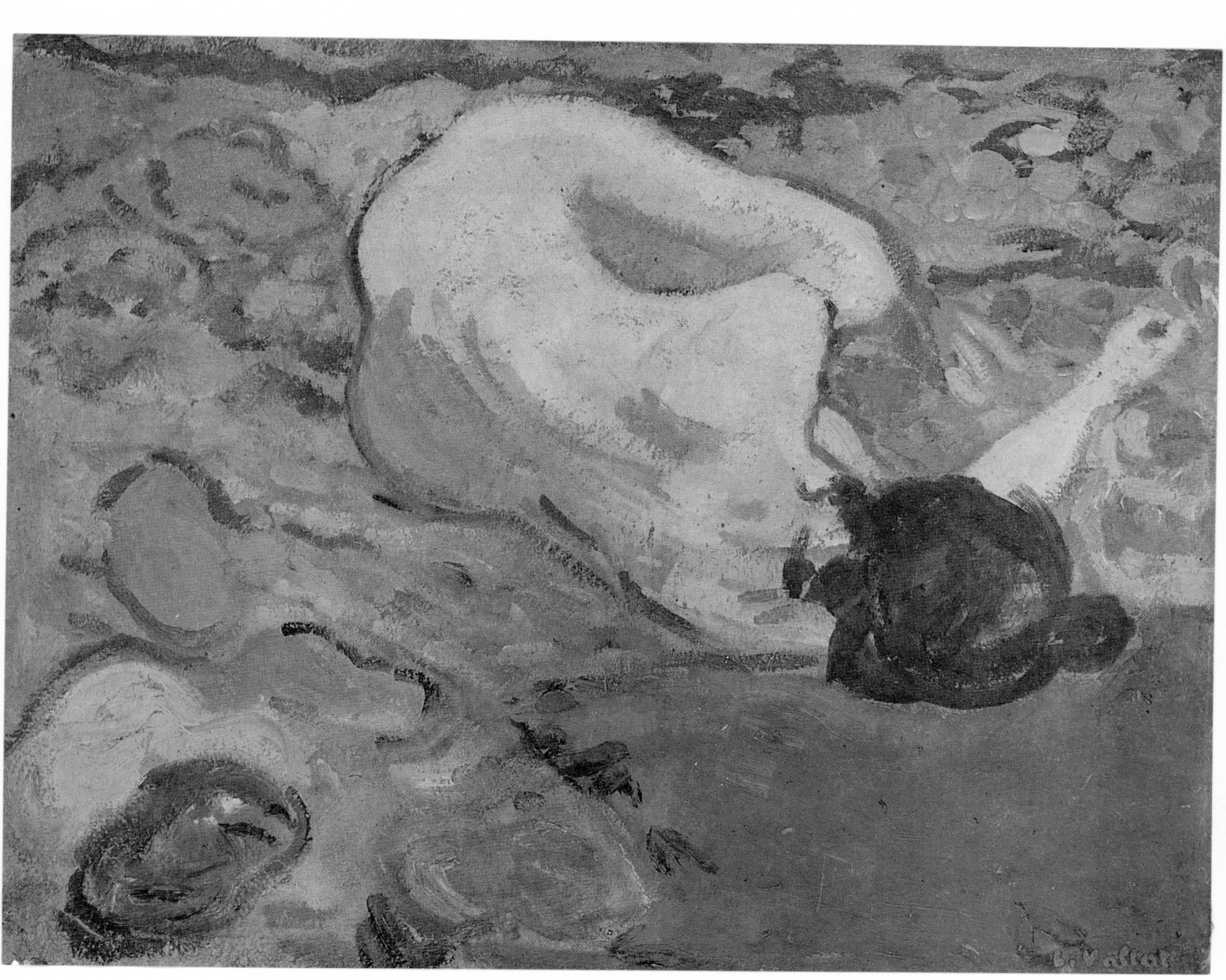

LOUIS VALTAT (1869–1952)

Painted in 1906
Algiers
Oil on canvas, 9 × 7 1/2"
Collection Dr. Jean Valtat, Paris

Valtat probably did not appreciate having been classed by the critics among the outcast Fauves at the 1905 Salon d'Automne, for he had been a successful artist for a number of years and had already acquired a certain fame. In any case, he made no effort to associate himself with them, and took no part in the shows at Berthe Weill's or the Prath & Magnier Gallery.

In 1903 he sets up a studio in Montmartre in the Rue Girardon and subsequently takes up sculpture under Renoir's guidance. In order to be closer to Renoir, then living in the Rue Caulaincourt, he moves to the Place Constantin Pecqueur in 1907.

He sends some important works to the 1906 Salons. He has eight canvases at the Indépendants in Room IV with Signac and Van Rysselberghe, which Vauxcelles praises in his review: "The style is broad but without exaggeration; his figures offer the singular attraction of concentrated strength combined with a soft and smiling grace." His ten canvases at the Salon d'Automne, placed in Room XVI with that of Dufrénoy, earn him similar eulogies: "His work is acquiring greater brilliance. . . . The flowers, the young woman with the boa, the truculent *Faun* . . . constitute luminous and dynamic painting." At this time he is even invited to exhibit with the Berlin Sezession.

As shown by this sketch, brought back that year from his second journey to Algiers (his first having been in 1903), he still keeps his lead over the other artists. In full command of his technique, he has now acquired a remarkable maturity. Note the spontaneous verve, the skillful composition, the controlled brushwork bringing out the slightest contrasts, and the use of brilliant color.

It matters little to him that Fauvism finally catches up with him and sometimes even outstrips him in his most ambitious aims. He continues on a parallel but slightly removed path where he remains independent, free to capture the enjoyment of the moment, the pleasure of sunlit hours that have been enhanced by the birth of his son. Vauxcelles comments on his contribution to the Salon d'Automne of 1908: "Some fine Valtats, brilliantly colored and boldly conceived."

In the course of a career that is very active until illness bars him from further work, he does not hesitate to change his attitude as he sees fit; but, far from the South of France, which he abandons once and for all, in Normandy, Brittany, and more often in Paris, he keeps the same broad, generous approach inspired by his love of painting, his impulsive eloquence, and his insatiable need for color, which today make it possible to place him as a precursor of the great events of the century.

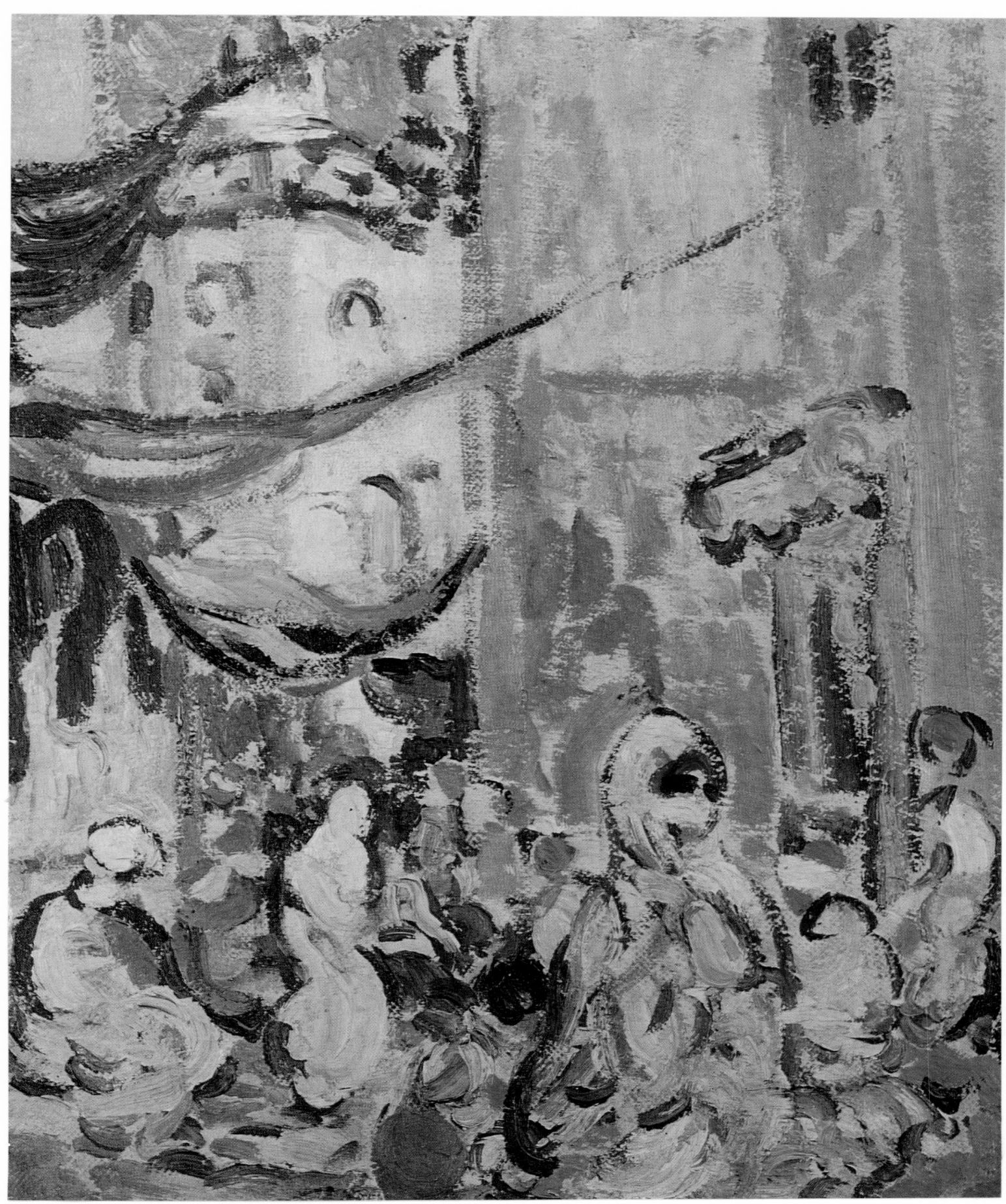

HENRI MATISSE (1869–1954)

Painted about 1900

Notre Dame

Oil on canvas, 15 3/4 × 13″

Collection Mr. and Mrs. Alexander M. Lewyt, New York City

Henri Matisse was born on December 31, 1869, at Le Cateau. He seemed in no way destined for an artistic career, and prepared for his law examinations in Paris, passing them in August of 1888. After an acute attack of appendicitis, he began to paint chromos.

In 1890 he paints his first still lifes, but it is not until 1892 that his father finally gives in to his growing determination to take up painting and allows him to go to Paris, where, on October 10, he enrolls for evening classes at the Ecole des Arts Décoratifs. Here he soon meets Marquet, and the two become lifelong friends. After a course at the Académie Julian that proves thoroughly useless to him, he attends Yvon's classes at the Ecole des Beaux-Arts, which enable him finally to enter Gustave Moreau's studio, where he is officially admitted in March, 1895. He is thus twenty-six before he begins to study seriously.

He rapidly acquires a solid technique by doing numerous copies in the Louvre, from Chardin to Poussin, from De Heem to Raphael and Carracci, several of which will be bought or commissioned by the State. He becomes passionately interested in the rendering of space by the play of values and at times reinforces his color planes, as in *La Desserte* (Collection Stavros S. Niarchos, Paris) of 1897 or some of his seascapes, under the double influence of Moreau and particularly John Russell, a friend of the Impressionists and admirer of Van Gogh, whom he had met at Belle-Ile.

On the occasion of his marriage in January, 1898, he goes to London on Pissarro's advice to examine the works of Turner, another artist obsessed by light, and spends several months in Corsica and then in the neighborhood of Toulouse. Solitude helps him to free himself from an outworn scholasticism and to give vent to the violence of his emotions, which he tries to express spontaneously in the warm and magical setting of the Mediterranean. A radiant color invades the landscapes painted in Corsica in 1898 and in the Toulouse region, where he returns in 1899 for his wife's confinement.

Using the freedom of touch and the impastos that he had adopted earlier, he seeks, partly in Pointillism and above all in Cézanne, a more disciplined construction through contrasting color planes. He undertakes a series of lavish still lifes and powerful nudes which by their expressiveness and the use of pure tones mark the culminating point of that Pre-Fauvism in which he is engaged, often in Marquet's company.

From the studio at 19 Quai Saint-Michel, which he has occupied since 1895, he also takes advantage of the splendid view toward the Pont Saint-Michel and Notre Dame. Already concerned with the problem of plunging perspective, he uses color to highlight the receding lines of the embankments in contrast with the cathedral, treating the whole in great vibrant masses.

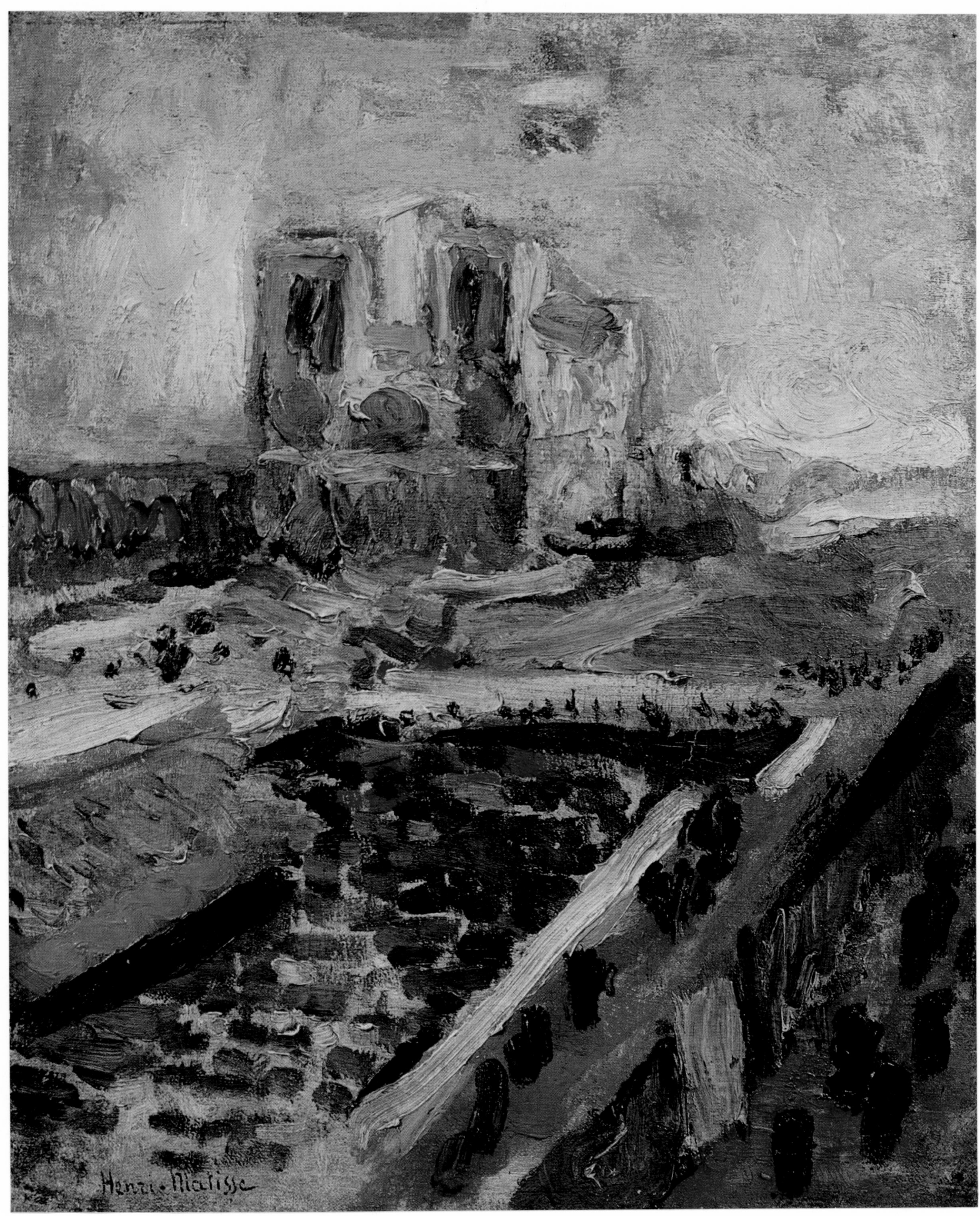

HENRI MATISSE (1869–1954)

Painted in 1904–5
Luxe, calme et volupté
Oil on canvas, 37 3/8 × 45 5/8"
Private collection, Paris

Full of enthusiasm, and now even taking up sculpture, Matisse has nonetheless had to contend with serious difficulties for some time past. Cut off from official circles, he has little hope of selling his work and is forced to make money by working with Marquet in the studio of the decorator Jambon for the Universal Exposition while his wife manages a milliner's shop in the Rue de Chateaudun.

Far from being discouraged, he redoubles his efforts, communicating his enthusiasm to his friends and exhibiting in turn at the Indépendants under Signac's chairmanship, at Berthe Weill's, and at the Salon d'Automne. His need to assert himself is so strong that in 1904 he sends six paintings to the Indépendants, exhibits a collection of forty-six pictures at the Vollard Gallery in June with a catalogue preface by Roger Marx, and shows fourteen canvases and two sculptures at the Salon d'Automne.

As he told me later, he tried to paint "by establishing zones of influence that created reactions and then proceeding by progressive gradations. Unfortunately, once I had placed my dominant color I invariably introduced the reactive color just as strongly. I would be doing a small landscape with spots of color, but being unable to achieve my light harmony according to the prescribed rules, I was always having to start over again. As I was starting with white light, the painting would grow dark and I invariably killed all my colors. . . . Above all I was no longer able to control my line and was tempted to overdo it. Cross, who witnessed my fruitless attempts and saw that in my canvases the contrasting colors ended up as strong as the dominant ones, told me that it was useless for me to go on with Neo-Impressionism."

He might perhaps have given up these inconclusive efforts on his return to Paris had he not had the occasion to see a large Signac exhibition at the Druet Gallery, where Luce and Cross had previously shown. The exhibition revived his enthusiasm, according to Jean Puy. He decides to push forward in the experiment more systematically and goes back to several works, using a faithful Pointillist technique and brighter colors. During the winter he devotes himself especially to this more spacious version of the sketch from life entitled *Luxe, calme et volupté* (Collection John Hay Whitney, New York City).

Exhibited at the Indépendants in 1905, the importance of the work is clear to all. It leads to Matisse's appointment as chairman of the organizing committee, is bought by Signac, who keeps it for many years in his villa "La Hune." Among both critics and artists, it arouses considerable excitement. Most of Matisse's friends immediately adopt the Pointillist formula, several going in their turn to spend the summer of 1905 at Saint-Tropez.

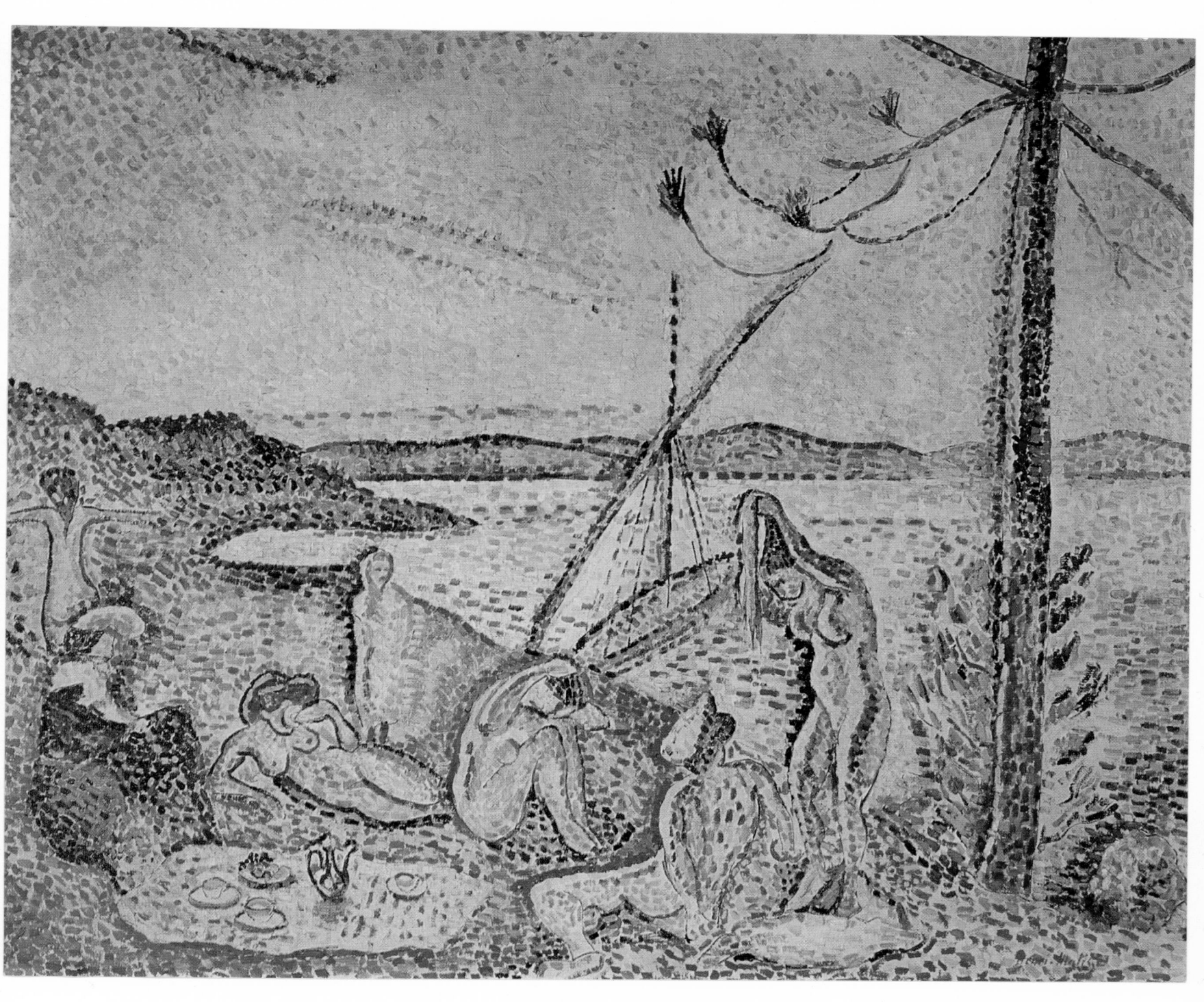

HENRI MATISSE (1869–1954)

Painted in 1905
Open Window, Collioure
Oil on canvas, 21 5/8 × 18 1/8"
Collection John Hay Whitney, New York City

Far from being satisfied by this public recognition, partially due to his apparent conversion to Neo-Impressionism, Matisse is already prepared, as usual, to reexamine his whole approach. This he does in the light of the revelations afforded by this same Salon des Indépendants of 1905 through the twin retrospectives of Seurat and Van Gogh, which he has had ample opportunity to study while directing the arrangement of the exhibits. Seurat's desire for simplification and transformation of space and Van Gogh's powerful lyricism now lead Matisse to abandon a formula that merely enabled him to give vibrancy to his contrasts and to exploit the white background of the canvas.

To have time to reflect and also for reasons of economy, he leaves Paris in the spring and spends several months at Collioure. At first, in a final bout of Pointillism that marks the end of his attachment to this technique, he produces a number of canvases where the square blotches are carefully aligned in the prescribed manner. Soon, however, he frees himself from this formula and begins to handle his brush with a certain feverishness, as is especially evident in *Madame Matisse or The Japanese Woman at the Seashore* (fig. 24).

He is filled with a sense of intoxication largely due to the atmosphere in which he is living, to the particular spectacle of the Catalan countryside, the rustic charms of which are revealed to him by Maillol in the course of long walks, and to the companionship of Derain, whose youthful enthusiasm is aroused, so he writes to Vlaminck, by these magical surroundings, where the slightest color contrasts are accentuated under the blazing sun.

As Matisse later confessed to me: "We were like children in the face of nature and expressed ourselves freely, even if we did not always paint directly from nature. I deliberately made a mess of everything and worked as I felt, exclusively with color."

Color certainly invades the works that follow, unfolding itself in joyful, triumphant tones to produce an extraordinarily buoyant impression through the blending of comma-shaped strokes, long streaks, and expanses of pure color with the whites retained in the canvas, as in the magnificent *Open Window, Collioure*.

Despite its small size, the painting, exhibited at the 1905 Salon d'Automne, where Fauvism first received its name, perfectly incarnates the hedonistic trend that gave birth to the whole movement. A feeling of elation emanates from these fresh harmonies, heightened by the skillful alternating of complementary colors. It seems incredible now that this work should have seemed so scandalous at the time that *L'Illustration* immediately held it up to ridicule.

HENRI MATISSE (1869–1954)

Painted in 1905

Woman with a Hat

Oil on canvas, 31 7/8 × 25 1/2"

Collection Mr. and Mrs. Walter A. Haas, San Francisco

Working with a will, Matisse accumulates canvases and sketches, and all of them, even the vigorous *André Derain* (The Tate Gallery, London), convey the happy abandon that takes possession of him at Collioure: *The Pastoral* (Musée d'Art Moderne de la Ville de Paris), where Maillol's influence is already apparent, *The Siesta* (Private collection, Ascona), the sketch for *Joy of Life* (Collection Mr. and Mrs. Walter A. Haas, San Francisco). The last two works clearly reveal another predominant influence from which he has been able to benefit on the spot, that of Gauguin, and this accounts for the bold flat areas and discreet outlines that he begins to use, his new manner of rendering space merely by color relationships, and even the choice of the Arcadian theme, where beside the conventional idyllic figures, embracing couples, and pipe players, a nude woman with a long garland of flowers unexpectedly takes her place.

In the course of his excursions in the region with Maillol, he had many opportunities to visit the property of Saint-Clément, where Daniel de Monfreid kept a large collection of Gauguin's last works. No doubt they went as far as Béziers to see other canvases belonging to Gustave Fayet, who was soon to take an interest in Matisse's work. For Matisse, who has long been a keen admirer of Gauguin, this influence is a providential one and helps him to overcome all his doubts and finally to dismiss the importunate memories of Pointillism. As he was to admit soon after to Purrmann: "At that time only Gauguin could extricate me from it."

As soon as he returns to Paris he sets to work feverishly, wishing to present an imposing array of works at the Salon d'Automne and to test the real value of his analyses by trying to convince his friends of their merits. It is not so much a simple application as a difficult demonstration that he undertakes in having his wife pose for him wearing a huge hat laden with flowers and various other ornaments, according to the fashion of the day. As we see, this enables him to juggle very freely with quite a wide color range. A little later he renews the attempt, simplifying it and carrying it almost to its ultimate limits in the *Portrait with a Green Line* (Royal Museum of Fine Arts, Copenhagen), where the distinct areas of color and the juxtaposition of warm and cold tones enliven and heighten the contrasts to the highest degree.

Less extreme in the subtle gradation of its background, which sets off the iridescent richness of the dominant tones, *Woman with a Hat* was no doubt the work that best represented the new Fauvist movement by its explosive lavishness. It served as a target for all the quips of the press and was given the place of honor in *L'Illustration*. Leo Stein immediately bought it, however, and subsequently exchanged it with Sarah Stein, who remained very attached to it. Thus Matisse established relations with the American community in Paris and could look forward to the future with somewhat more confidence.

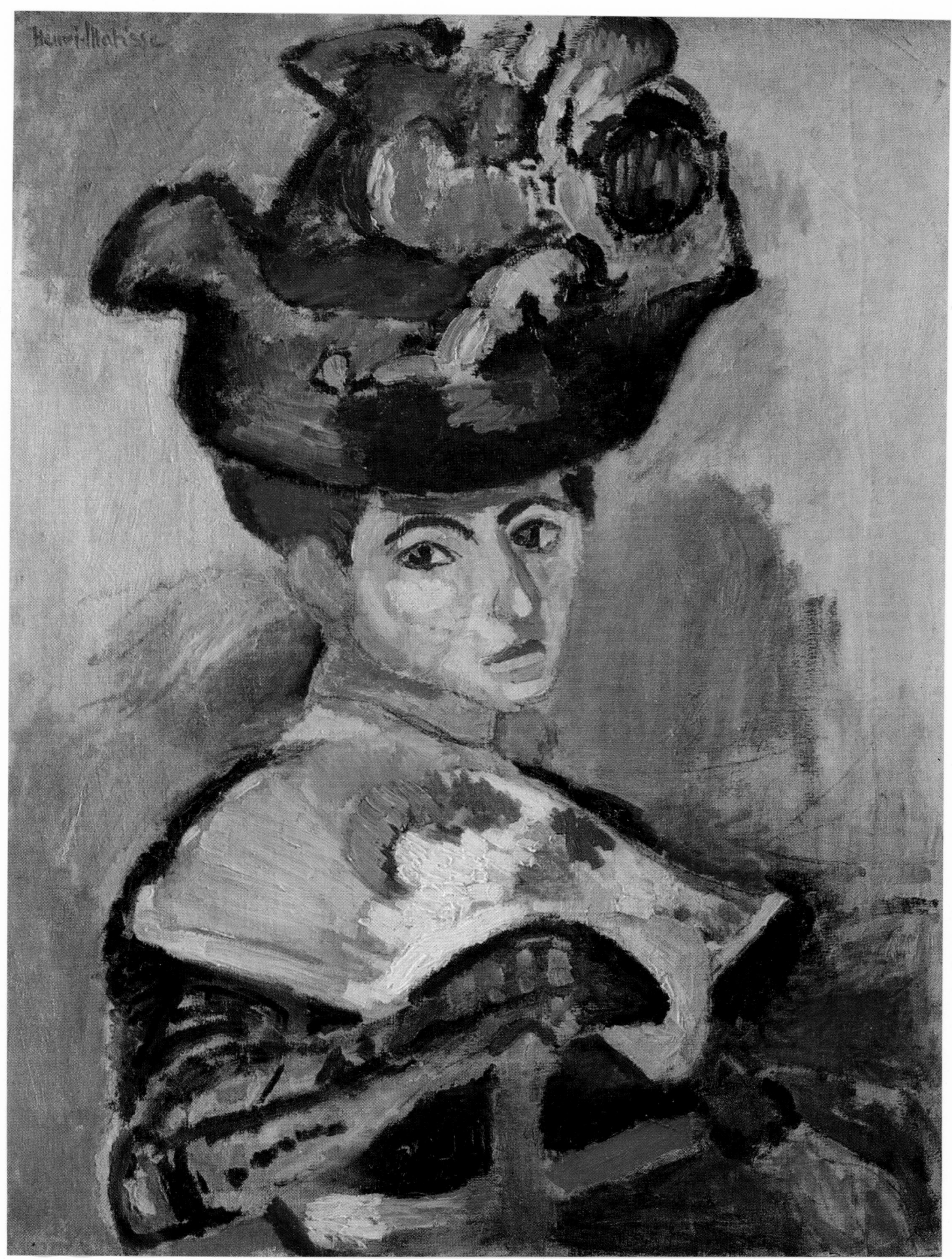

HENRI MATISSE (1869–1954)
Painted in 1908
The Red Sideboard
Oil on canvas, 70 7/8 × 86 5/8"
The Hermitage, Leningrad

Far from being overly theoretical, as his enemies claim, Matisse strove to recapture his original emotion in all its freshness by progressively refining his means of expression. "Fauvism," he confided to me, "was for me a testing of means: to place side-by-side, combining in an expressive way a blue, a red, and a green. It was the result of a growing inner need and not of a deliberate attitude, a deduction, or a line of reasoning, which are quite irrelevant to painting."

In 1906 he has a show at the Druet Gallery, a panorama of his efforts in different fields— painting, sculpture, and engraving—but the success of the exhibition is eclipsed by the stir caused by the vast canvas *Joy of Life* (fig. 25), presented at the Indépendants. He has prepared this ambitious synthesis so meticulously that he is later able to detach and use its main elements in a large number of canvases (such as *Le Luxe*, fig. 35; *The Blue Nude; Dance; Music*). His *Self-Portrait* (fig. 6), dating from the same period, clearly reveals his steadfastness.

He now concentrates on solving two complementary problems, one material and the other spiritual. By the simple play of color harmonies and line, he aims both at re-creating perceptible, plastic space and at transcending his means of expression in order to achieve a more direct impact on the spectator, from whom he expects a certain cooperation. "What I dream of," he wrote later in the *Grande Revue*, "is an art based on balance and purity . . . by which the businessman . . . will be mentally soothed."

In 1908, after much research on color and line, he proposes a bold solution in the form of this vast composition, which he exhibits at the Salon d'Automne under the title *Decorative Panel for a Dining Room*. Starting with a familiar theme that he has already treated in 1896 (*The Breton Serving Girl*) and more elaborately in 1897 (*La Desserte*, Collection Stavros S. Niarchos, Paris), he proceeds to simplify it rigorously, keeping only the essential. First he paints the whole composition with blues and then reworks it using subtle gradations of brilliant reds and oranges, blues and greens. The floral arabesques are deliberately used to create a complex space where the eye wanders at will before discovering the rigid contrast of the window frame and the presence of a second ambiguous space in which the values are admirably established.

As he explains in a general way in his *Notes d'un peintre:* "The various elements that I use must be balanced . . . the relationship between the tones has to be established in such a way that they sustain each other. . . . I am forced to transpose, and this is why my picture is thought to have changed completely when, after a series of modifications, red has replaced green as the dominant color."

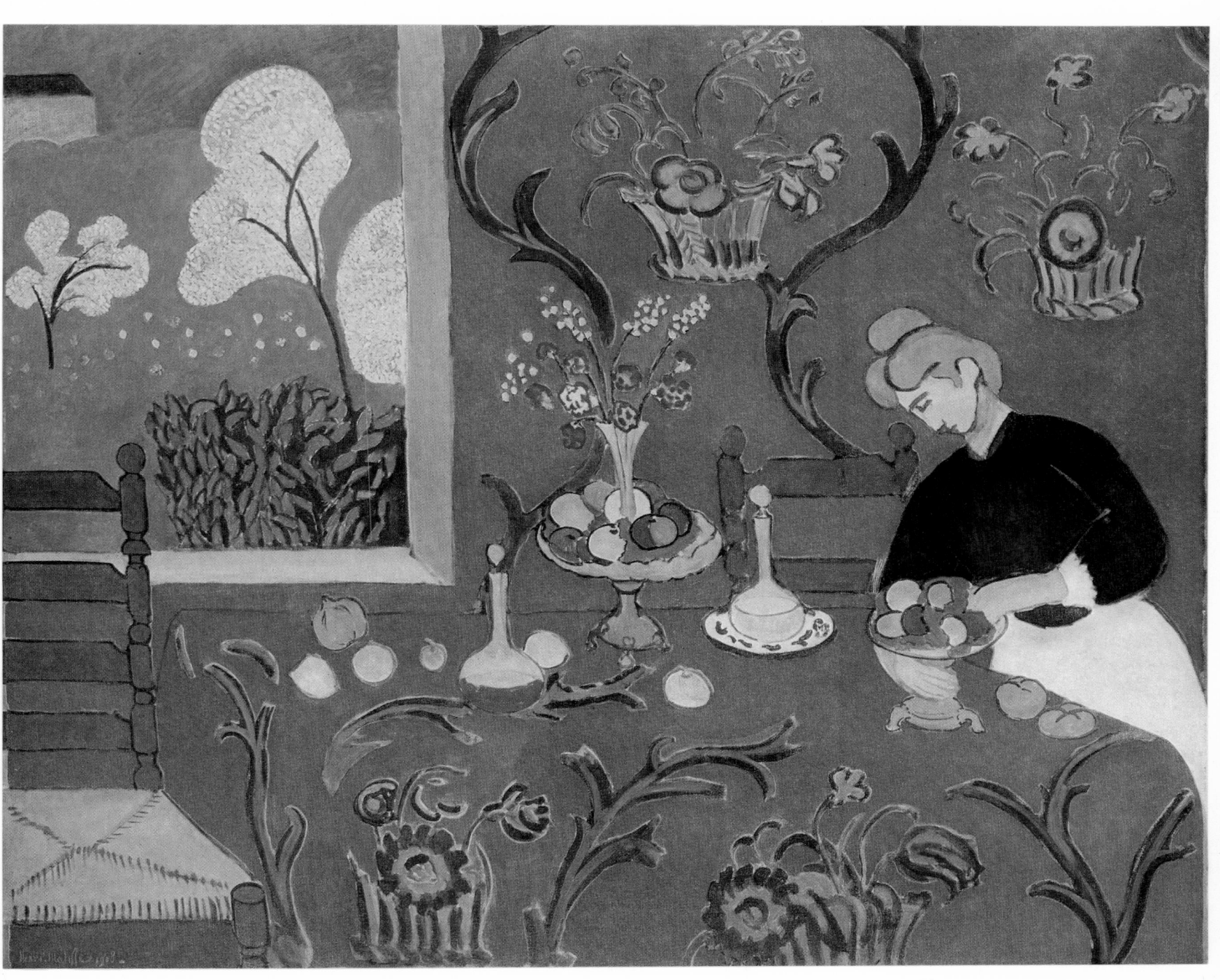

HENRI MATISSE (1869–1954)
Painted in 1910
Music
Oil on canvas, 8′ 6 3/8″ × 12′ 9 1/8″
The Hermitage, Leningrad

At the 1907 Salon d'Automne Matisse presented the first version of *Music* (The Museum of Modern Art, New York City), which was catalogued as a sketch. An offshoot of the pastorals of this period, it depicts two dancers and an attentive listener grouped around a violin player. In 1909 he executes another idea, again realistic, for *Dance* (The Museum of Modern Art, New York City), and submits it to the Russian collector Shchukin. The latter is enthusiastic, and in a letter of March 31 confirms his decision to brave public opinion by commissioning Matisse to paint the two panels.

Matisse comments on these projects to the journalist Estienne, who reproduces his remarks in *Les Nouvelles* of April 12, 1909, as follows: "I have to decorate a studio. There are three floors. I imagine the visitor who comes in from outside. The first floor confronts him. An effort should be made to give a feeling of relief. My first panel represents the dance, that flying round relay over the hill. On the second floor you are really inside the house; in its spirit and silence I see a music scene with attentive listeners; finally, on the third floor, there is complete tranquility and here I'll paint a scene of repose, people stretched out on the grass, talking or dreaming. I shall do this using very few means and very simple ones, those which best allow the painter to express his whole inner vision." Matisse even specifies his exact approach beforehand: "I want to achieve serenity through the simplification of ideas and plasticity. The general effect is my whole ideal. . . . It's a question of learning and perhaps relearning a style that is one of line. . . . The modeling will convey the emotion as directly as possible and by the simplest means . . . three colors for a vast panel: the blue of the sky, the pink of the bodies, the green of the hill."

He does in fact use only these three colors, carried to an extraordinary degree of saturation, in the two brilliantly luminous, monumental panels which he exhibits at the Salon d'Automne in 1910. These spectacular results—especially in the case of *Dance*—were achieved not without difficulty after the usual process of transposition, elimination of superfluous details from the original sketches, and more rigorous schematization of the figures.

As Matisse explained to me in a letter of December, 1953, Shchukin was far from satisfied with the panels and even proposed commissioning a smaller version of them. He gave his approval only during his return journey to Moscow, and Matisse was therefore able to leave for Spain with his mind more at rest. The controversy between them did not end there, however, and it was not until 1912 that Shchukin finally accepted the paintings.

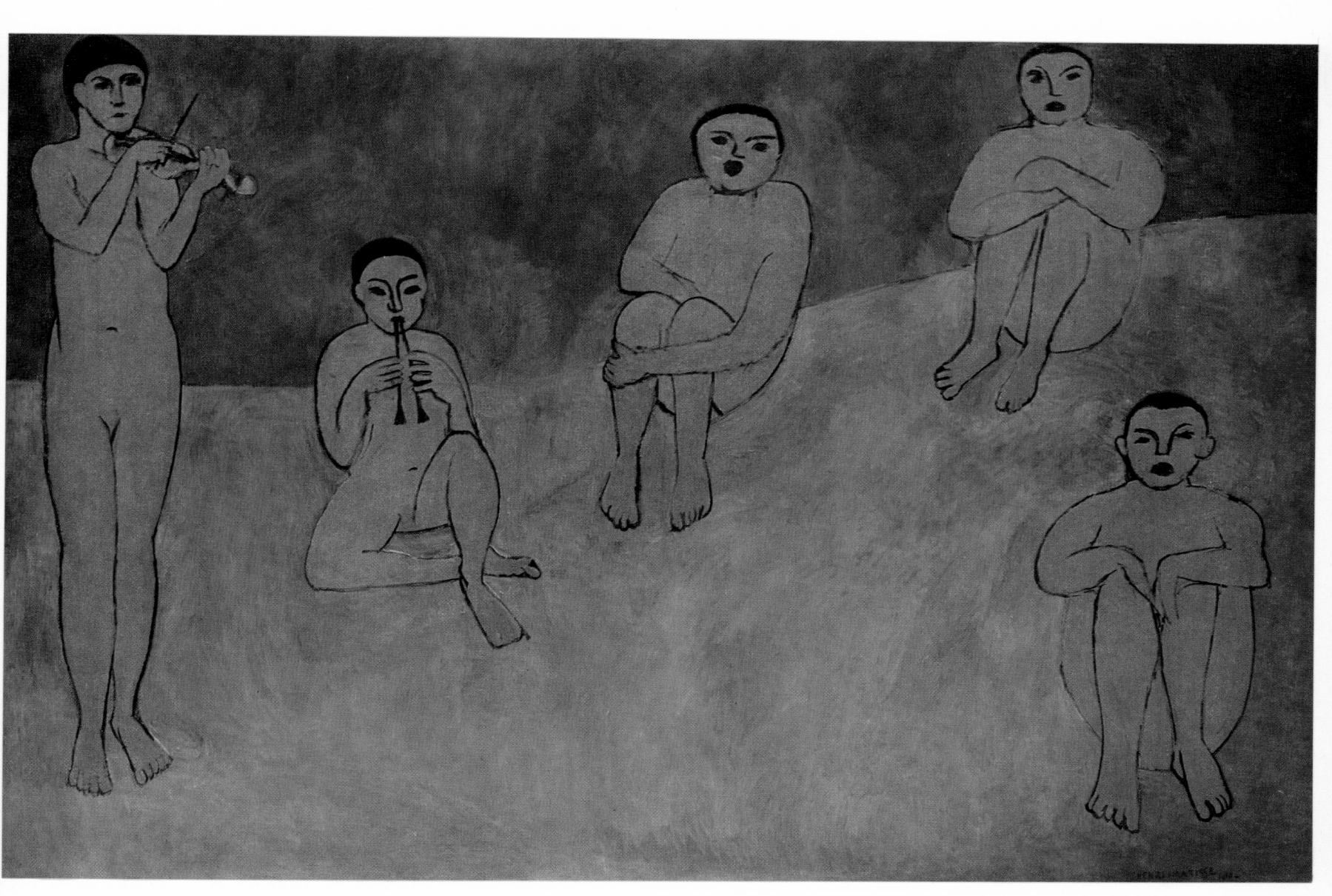

HENRI MATISSE (1869–1954)

Painted in 1911
Joaquina
Oil on canvas, 21 5/8 × 15 1/8″
National Gallery, Prague

Matisse long had his wife pose for him, and later his daughter or the models who came to Manguin's studio, his own Academy, or elsewhere. As he himself admitted, he always needed—and continued to do so until the end of his life—the presence of beings or objects to generate sensations and thereby stimulate his creative faculties. He is never concerned with painting a portrait as such; rather, he presents silhouettes, human types whose particular characteristics he notes, not without a certain brutality.

In his *Notes d'un peintre* he defines his attitude as follows: "My chief interest lies neither in still lifes nor in landscapes, but in the figure. It is the figure that best enables me to express the almost religious feeling that I have for life. I don't try to depict in detail all the facial features, or render them one by one with anatomical precision. If I have an Italian model who at first sight suggests only the idea of a purely animal existence, I nonetheless discover certain essential features in her, I explore among the lines of her face those which reveal the lofty gravity that exists in every human being. A work must inwardly contain its whole meaning and convey it to the spectator before he even knows its subject."

These explanations make it easier to accept certain figures where the violent use of color or linear distortions may seem startling and in fact shocked even Matisse's friends, not to mention Vauxcelles, who described them as "Kanaka faces." Although this *Joaquina*, painted in Seville in 1911, shows a close kinship with the Expressionist movement, as Jean Leymarie and Jean Cassou have pointed out, Matisse nevertheless does not share its fundamental tenets. With serenity and scrupulous respect he notes the marked idiosyncrasies of these "expressive heads," as he calls them, but gives precedence to plastic problems in order better to transcend reality and preserve the nobility of his hymn to life.

The years pass, and age and sickness begin to weigh heavily on him, but he never renounces his passion for the human figure and draws from it endless variations in which elation and sublimation are always blended. Often the faces have even been replaced by a simple oval, but the evocative force persists through the radiant harmony of color and form, even when the latter is only a paper cutout.

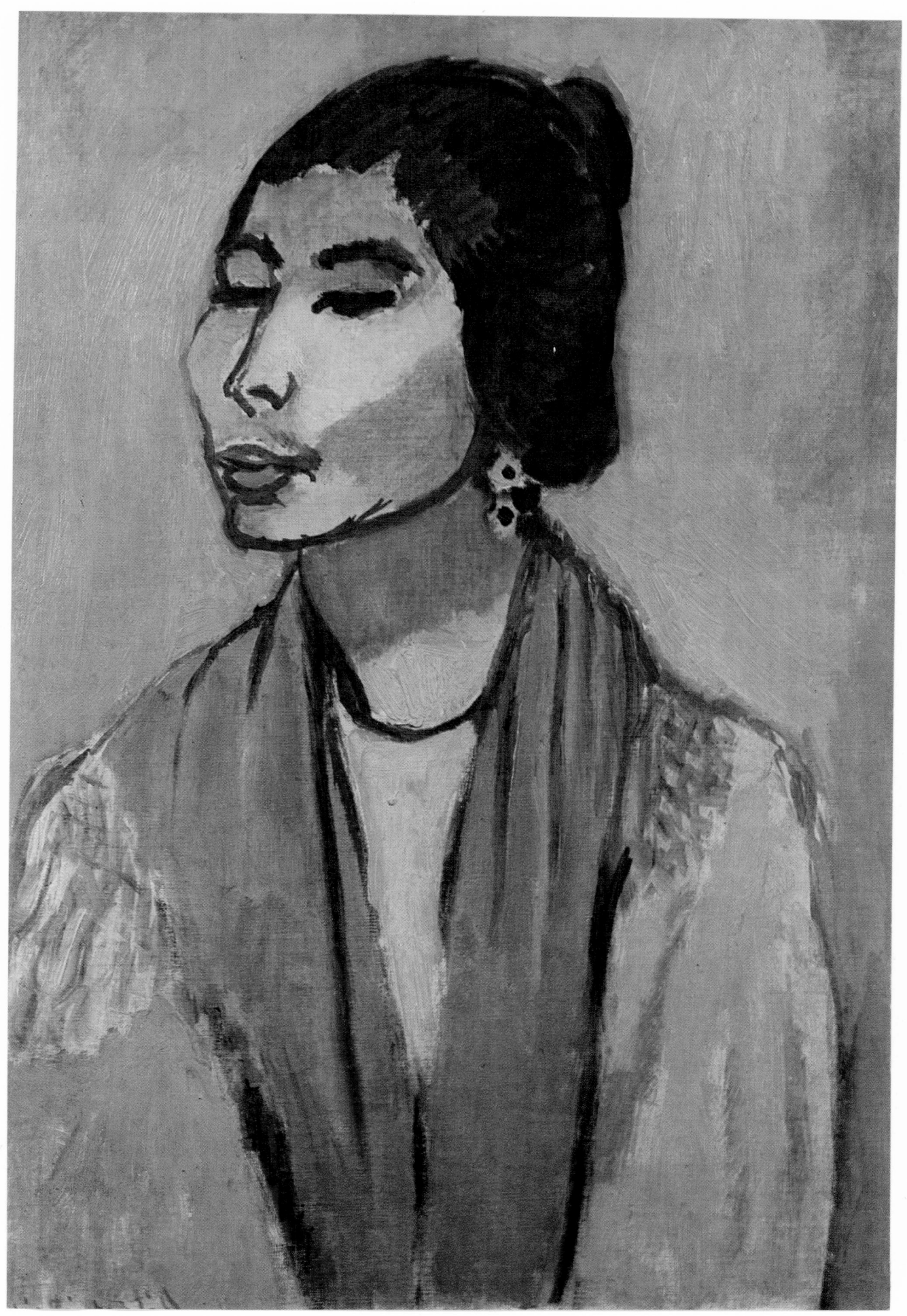

HENRI MANGUIN (1874–1949)

Painted in 1905
Model Resting
Oil on canvas, 31 7/8 × 25 5/8″
Collection Mme Lucie Martinais-Manguin, Paris

Manguin was born in Paris on March 23, 1874. After a period of preparation, he entered the Ecole des Beaux-Arts at the end of 1894 to study under Gustave Moreau, in whose studio he soon became close friends with Matisse, Marquet, Mathan, and others. Following his teacher's advice, he and his companions spent much time copying in the Louvre, and a number of his copies of Poussin, Titian, and Velázquez were to be bought by the State.

At the Pointe du Cotentin, where he goes with Mathan, he finds a landscape more in keeping with the Impressionist spirit and meets his future wife, Jeanne, whom he marries in 1899. Especially after the closing of the Académie Carrière, Matisse, Marquet, and Puy work from the model at the Manguins' house in the Rue Boursault and carry on long discussions, sometimes joined by writers and musicians, including Ravel, whose portrait Manguin paints in 1902. The same year he begins to exhibit at the Indépendants, and then in 1904 at Berthe Weill's and the Salon d'Automne.

At the 1904 Indépendants, half of his contribution consists of two pastels, a technique for which he has a predilection. The following year, however, he shows six canvases, of which one already belongs to Druet, and in his review Vauxcelles includes him among Matisse's followers and puts him at the head of the group of friends.

In the spring he goes to Saint-Tropez with the rest, but is one of the few to resist the lures of Neo-Impressionism. He enjoys the Mediterranean setting, however, and in the euphoric state in which he suddenly finds himself, plunges into intensive work. He feasts his eyes on the sights around him, the streets decked with flags (*The Fourteenth of July at Saint-Tropez*, fig. 11), the wealth of nature. The joy and enthusiasm that he experiences are reflected in the brilliant colors of the canvases which he sends to the Salon d'Automne and which are placed with his friends' works in the famous Room VII set aside for the Fauves.

When *The Siesta*, for which his wife had posed in the nude, was published in *L'Illustration*, it provoked a public outcry. Yet, judging by his *Model Resting*, no doubt painted on his return, the peaceful happiness that he extols has nothing scandalous about it. Manguin in fact already shows a highly personal style—even in his interiors—in his handling of dazzling color combinations, blending blues in the true Cézanne tradition with reds, oranges, and greens, which he used liberally but never harshly in faces. The excellent *Portrait of Jean Puy* (fig. 17), painted at this time, is sufficient proof of the quality of his observation, his self-restraint, and of the serious and irrevocable nature of his involvement.

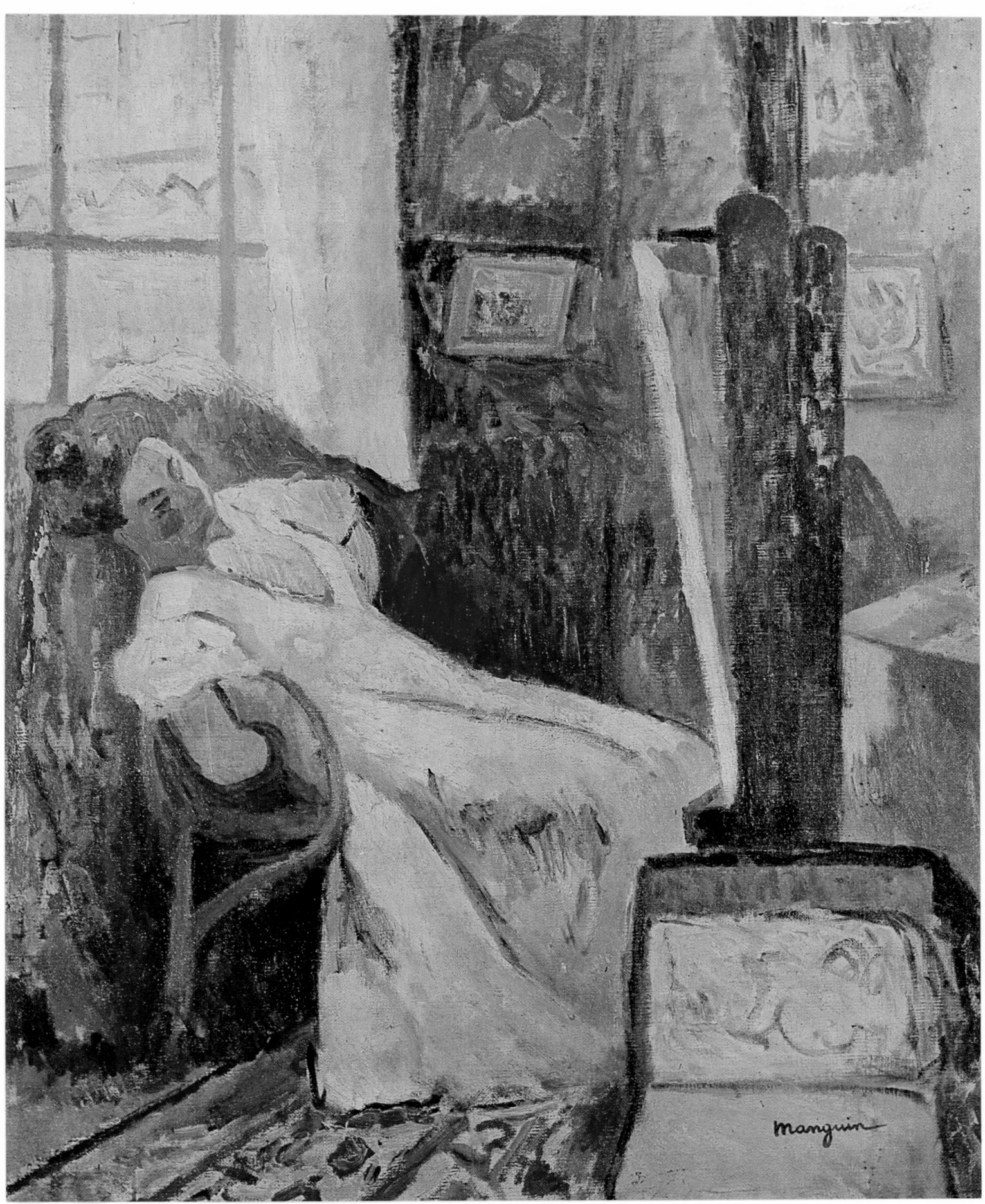

HENRI MANGUIN (1874–1949)

Painted in 1906
The Cork Oaks
Oil on canvas, 15 × 18 1/8"
Collection Mme Lucie Martinais-Manguin, Paris

As the spirit of his work suggests, Manguin at this time is a man blessed by destiny. His family life has so far been a happy one, and he has been relatively free from financial worries. Artistic success soon follows. At the end of 1905 he begins to take part in the Fauves' exhibitions at Berthe Weill's and at the Prath & Magnier Gallery. At the 1906 Indépendants eight of his canvases, most of them of Saint-Tropez, hang in Room VI, which Vauxcelles calls "the Salon Carré of the young school," and they earn him the critic's praises: "Freed from Cézanne's ascendancy, his talent is full of vigor . . . the vividness of warm colors." At the Salon d'Automne he is given a prominent place in Room III, reserved for the Fauves. Again Vauxcelles, although he finds his chromatic lyricism excessive, recognizes "the talent that he always shows . . . in his bold, full-formed nudes" in remarking on canvases which the artist had brought back from his stay at Cavalière.

Druet offers him his first one-man show and Vollard buys a hundred or so of his works in a single purchase. Collectors also begin to take an interest in him, not only the Frenchmen Saincère Rouveyre and Gasquet, but also the foreigners who are collecting Matisse's works, such as Leo Stein, and the Russians Shchukin, Morosov, and others, whose acquisitions now hang in The Hermitage.

In both his still lifes and such landscapes as *The Cork Oaks*, Manguin vividly expresses the enveloping heat and shimmering light of the South of France through strong contrasts, an incisive, vigorous touch, and a rich, vibrant use of color that strikingly sets off the purplish-blue tones against alternating greens and reddish browns.

Unaffected by the frenzied enthusiasm of some of his friends, he keeps a balanced, deliberate attitude. His transpositions are just as intense, if not more so, but they are always based on direct observation, and his color range is sufficiently wide and varied to produce a general effect of measured equilibrium. The delight in color that holds him in sway is in a way justified by an evident and natural sensuality that loses none of its distinction because of the tenderness that pervades and determines the work itself.

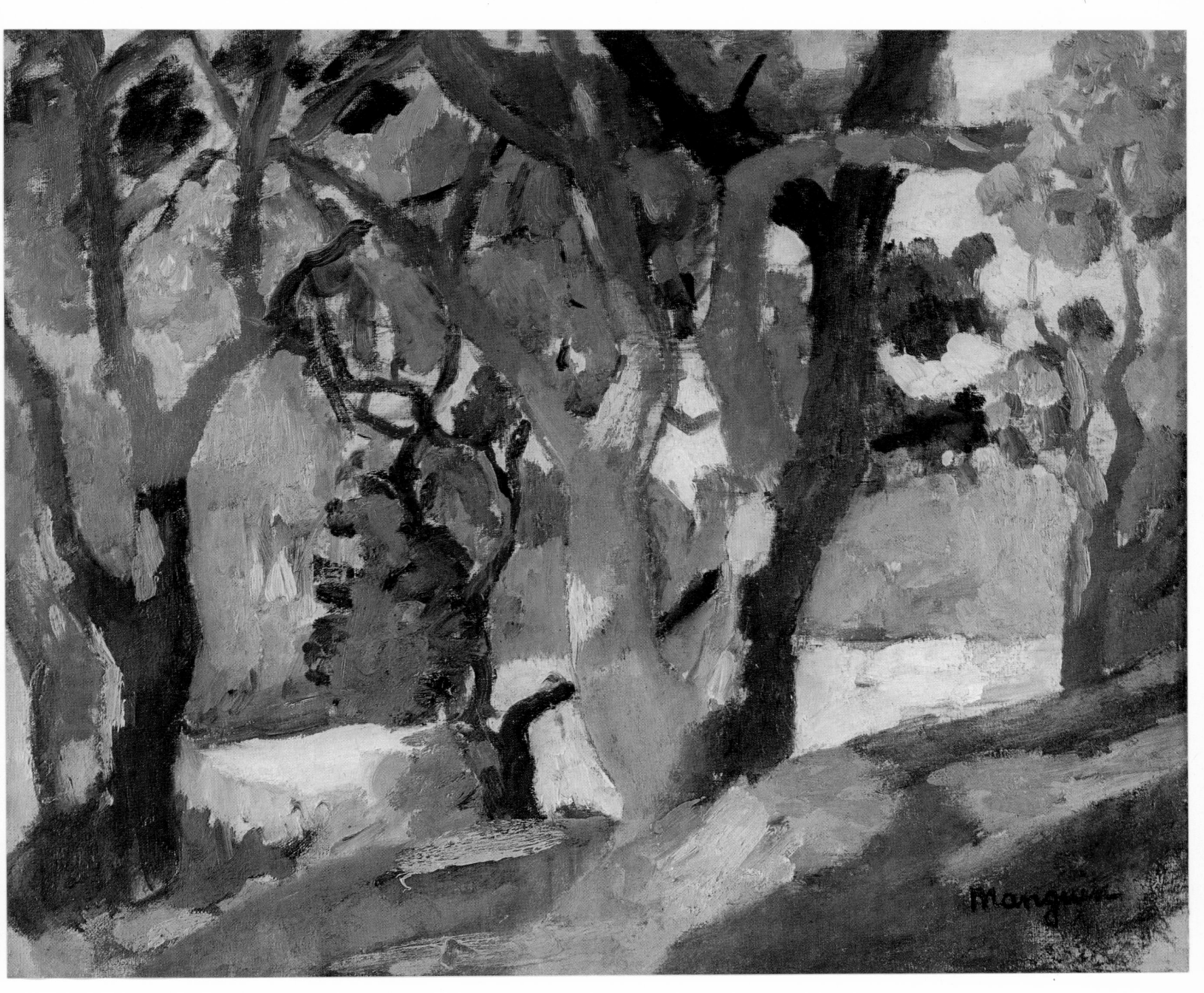

HENRI MANGUIN (1874–1949)

Painted in 1906
The Gypsy in the Studio
Oil on canvas, 18 1/8 × 21 5/8″
Collection Mme Lucie Martinais-Manguin, Paris

Manguin was not without a streak of violence, however, as can be seen from this painting, where he treats the model with neither kindness nor consideration. This may be due to his undeniably strong temperament or else simply to the proximity of Matisse, who is thought to have used the same gypsy as the model for the well-known figure so strongly imbued with bestiality (Musée de l'Annonciade, Saint-Tropez). The boldly accented outlines may well denote a similar influence or simply indicate the prevailing trend toward a more expressive idiom.

The more or less accidental origin of this picture, in which the overwhelming brilliance of the colors obscures the harsh nature of the line, is in fact of little importance. Manguin is a past master in this domain, as all his contemporaries readily acknowledge, beginning with Vauxcelles, who at the Indépendants of 1907 is already careful not to class Manguin any longer among the Fauves, whom he derides in order better to emphasize that the artist "is one of the most brilliant colorists of the Salon. He has the highest sense of color composition." At the next Salon d'Automne he again insists: "With steady tenacity Manguin is advancing . . . toward works that are decorative, well composed, and complete. The woman with a bunch of grapes is a fine painting."

Apart from his intrinsic qualities, the increasing restraint that he shows helps to win him warm praise from the critics. He is in fact returning to a traditional style that he had never wholly abandoned except for his use of an intense palette, to which he remains very attached. Showing his usual disregard for theories, he works frequently with Marquet in 1908 and travels with him to Italy in 1909.

For the rest of his life he continues to go his peaceful round of the flowering garden he had discovered in 1905. Apart from one or two stays on the Atlantic coast, he remains faithful to the Mediterranean and particularly to Saint-Tropez. Here, from 1920 on, he spends a part of the year at "L'Oustallet," never tiring of the warm light and festive interiors, which he always strives to "harmonize." This was a favorite expression of his, and was on his lips as he died.

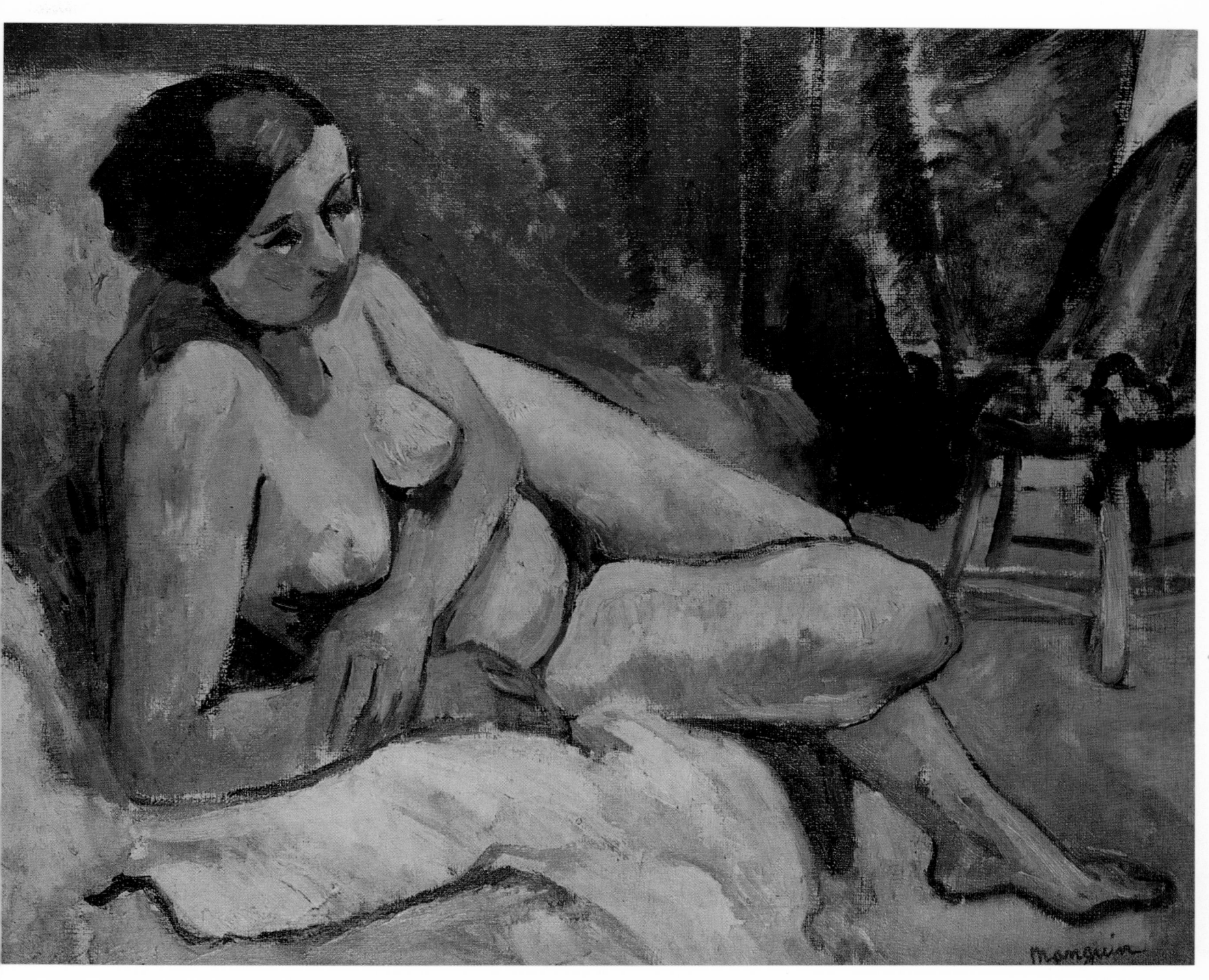

ALBERT MARQUET (1875–1947)

Painted in 1906

The Pont Neuf in the Sun

Oil on canvas, 28 3/4 × 36 1/4"

Boymans-van Beuningen Museum, Rotterdam

Born on March 26, 1875, in Bordeaux of a modest family—his father was employed by the railroad—Marquet was fortunate in having a mother who understood and encouraged his early artistic tendencies. At the cost of considerable sacrifice, she sent her son to study first at the Ecole des Arts Décoratifs, where he met Matisse, and then to the Beaux-Arts, where he studied under Cormon, Morot, and finally Gustave Moreau. But to the confined atmosphere of the studio, as well as of the Académie Carrière, the young man was often to prefer the spectacle of the streets.

Hard-working and obstinate, he at first expresses an inner violence in his brushwork and palette, but this soon gives way to a stern objectivity. He observes, explores, transposes the urban landscape that he discovers around him with a constant pleasure sometimes tinged with melancholy. The simple, familiar universe in which he buries himself becomes a refuge and a defense against the vicissitudes of an existence that seems to fill him with apprehension, for he is timid by nature besides being nearsighted and lame. It is only natural that he should consider art as a means of taking his revenge—a revenge without acrimony—and asserting himself. And in fact success arrives swiftly, but he refuses to exploit it, preferring always a quiet, secluded life with frequent trips, even after his marriage to Marcelle Martinet in 1923.

It was no doubt his Bordeaux childhood that gave him his predilection for the fluid, hazy images of riverbank and seashore that he was to paint throughout his life, emphasizing the luminous contrasts of land and water. The banks of the Seine are one of his favorite themes, and early in his career, in Matisse's company, he paints the Pont Saint-Michel and Notre Dame from his friend's studio and from the Quai de la Tournelle.

After moving to 25 Quai des Grands-Augustins in 1905, he paints a closely related series of pictures: *Quai des Grands-Augustins* (Musée National d'Art Moderne, Paris), *The Sun Through the Trees, View of the Louvre* (Pushkin Museum, Moscow), *Quai du Louvre and Pont Neuf* (The Hermitage, Leningrad), *The Pont Neuf* (National Gallery of Art, Washington, D.C.), and this canvas, which was exhibited at the Salon d'Automne of 1906.

With a downward perspective such as Pissarro used on the same spot, Marquet renders the panorama with sensitivity and admirable restraint. His gradations of greens and purples, which still keep the intensity of an already tempered Fauvism, will later become more muted and original, but his humble delight at the sight of this familiar yet perpetually fresh landscape remains unchanged.

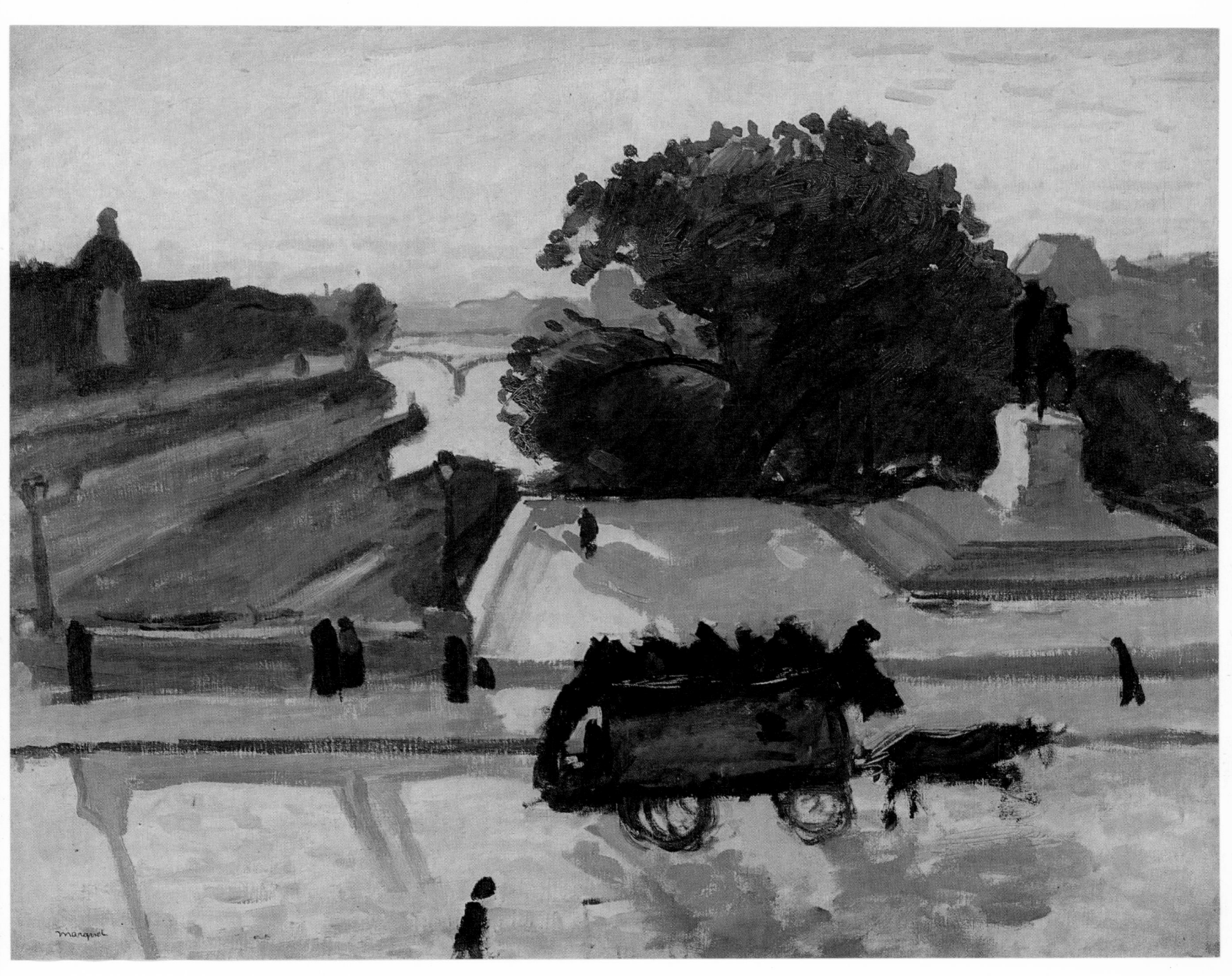

ALBERT MARQUET (1875–1947)

Painted in 1906
Sainte-Adresse
Oil on canvas, 25 1/4 × 31 1/8″
Collection B. J. Fize, Paris

Marquet could have been a worthy successor to Van Gogh or Lautrec as a portraitist. He shows the same ability in his forceful renderings of nudes, which stand out clearly in shadow or light. But most of his time was to be devoted to landscape, an urban landscape where, as Jules Romains declared, one can feel the human pulsation of the city expressed in the evocative form of a swarm of tiny black figures that suggest the teeming crowd.

In the summer of 1906, however, Marquet departs from his habits for a time in order to work with Dufy on the Normandy beaches. The satisfaction of having signed a contract with Druet several months before, the growing success of a movement that was to be fully represented at the next Salon d'Automne, and no doubt still more his companion's infectious vitality induce in him an overflowing enthusiasm rather alien to him, and which is revealed both in his technique and in his palette. For once he forces color and appearance in the manner of the other Fauves, returns to the bright tones of his early work that he had already rediscovered the year before at Anthéor and Treyas, and above all accentuates the joyous aspect of the scenes he depicts. In this summer season everything smiles on him, everything breathes happiness under the bright sunshine, and the two friends, setting their easels side by side, deliberately choose motifs where the range of colors is most heightened: a street hung with tricolors and streamers for the 14th of July celebrations at Le Havre, a paling covered with multicolored posters at Trouville, and the beach at Sainte-Adresse that Dufy knows so well. If their theme is identical, each treats it in his own way, from a different angle and using separate harmonies. There is more sprightliness, chromatic brilliance, and venturesome boldness in Dufy, a newcomer to Fauvism who will join the movement officially in October, and a steadier balance in Marquet.

Whereas in his *Beach at Sainte-Adresse* (Collection Harry Lynde Bradley, Milwaukee) Dufy gives a prominent place to brightly colored figures, Marquet in his painting leaves a broad strip almost empty in the foreground where the earth colors and light beiges set off the spots of yellow and orange and subtly harmonize with the pink tones in the background. He indulges in a mischievous poke at his friend, however, by introducing in his turn the little red and white parasols of which Dufy is so fond at this time. Discretion prevails once more when, alone, he paints *Beach at Fécamp* (Musée National d'Art Moderne, Paris).

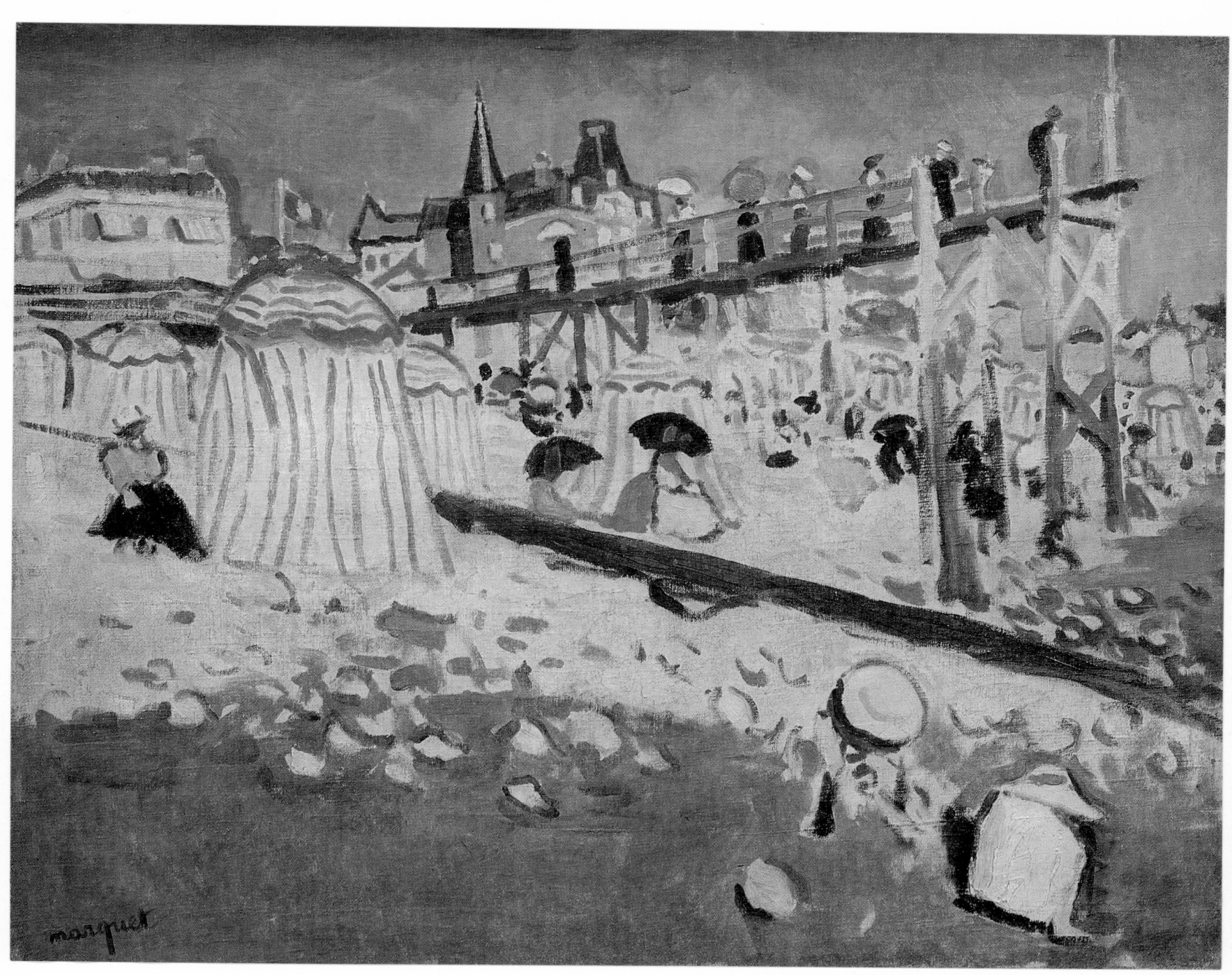

MAURICE DE VLAMINCK (1876–1958)

Painted in 1905
Under the Bridge at Chatou
Oil on canvas, 8 3/8 × 10″
Perls Galleries, New York City

Born on April 4, 1876, in Paris, Vlaminck inherited from his Flemish ancestry on his father's side a natural truculence and need for independence, and from his mother the Lorrainese characteristics of laborious determination and a practical approach to life, these last traits being much more pronounced in him than might at first appear. He was also stamped by the memories of his early childhood in the Halles quarter and especially of his adolescence at Le Vésinet, where he was left largely to his own devices, his parents being rather bohemian musicians who were obliged to give private piano lessons and had little time to devote to his upbringing. He learned to play the violin, however, and, like his parents, earned his living chiefly through his musical abilities.

Married in 1894, and soon the father of a family, he is obliged to become a jack-of-all-trades; taking advantage of his athletic build, he even becomes a racing cyclist for a time. His passionate interest in painting is fostered by the advice of Robichon, a member of the Artistes Français, and of Henri Rigal, a naïf painter and saddler at Le Vésinet, but he is chiefly attracted by the Impressionist exhibitions in Paris. His three years of military service from 1898 to 1900 are a sore trial to him, and it is during one of his last leaves, in June, 1900, as a result of a minor train accident that obliges him to walk back to Chatou, that he meets Derain. Differing in character but physically alike in their powerful build, the two young men become close friends and decide to work together. For ten francs a month, they rent an old abandoned restaurant, the Maison Levanneur, whose windows overlook the Seine, close by the bridge at Chatou and not far from the Fournaise restaurant, once frequented by the Impressionists, who depicted it in many famous paintings. And so the School of Chatou, as Vlaminck grandly christened it, was born, and in his books he was to describe even the most trivial episodes of its existence in order to emphasize its historical significance.

The Van Gogh retrospective organized by the Bernheim Gallery in 1901 enables him to meet Matisse, who comes to see his work, encourages him to continue, and will later invite him to the Indépendants of 1905. Above all, his discovery of Van Gogh's work leads him to abandon the rather somber and naive technique of his early paintings.

His colors, at first restrained, grow more intense, mingle in splashes and whirlpools, spread out in vibrant clusters, with the brushstroke passing progressively from comma-shape or whiplash to open division. Vlaminck specifies what for him is the chief problem in painting: "By using pure colors straight from the tube, to achieve chromatic orchestration; by interpreting life, to impart the atmosphere of its brilliant and powerful harmonies to a canvas. Fauvism was not an invention, an attitude, but a way of being, acting, thinking, and breathing."

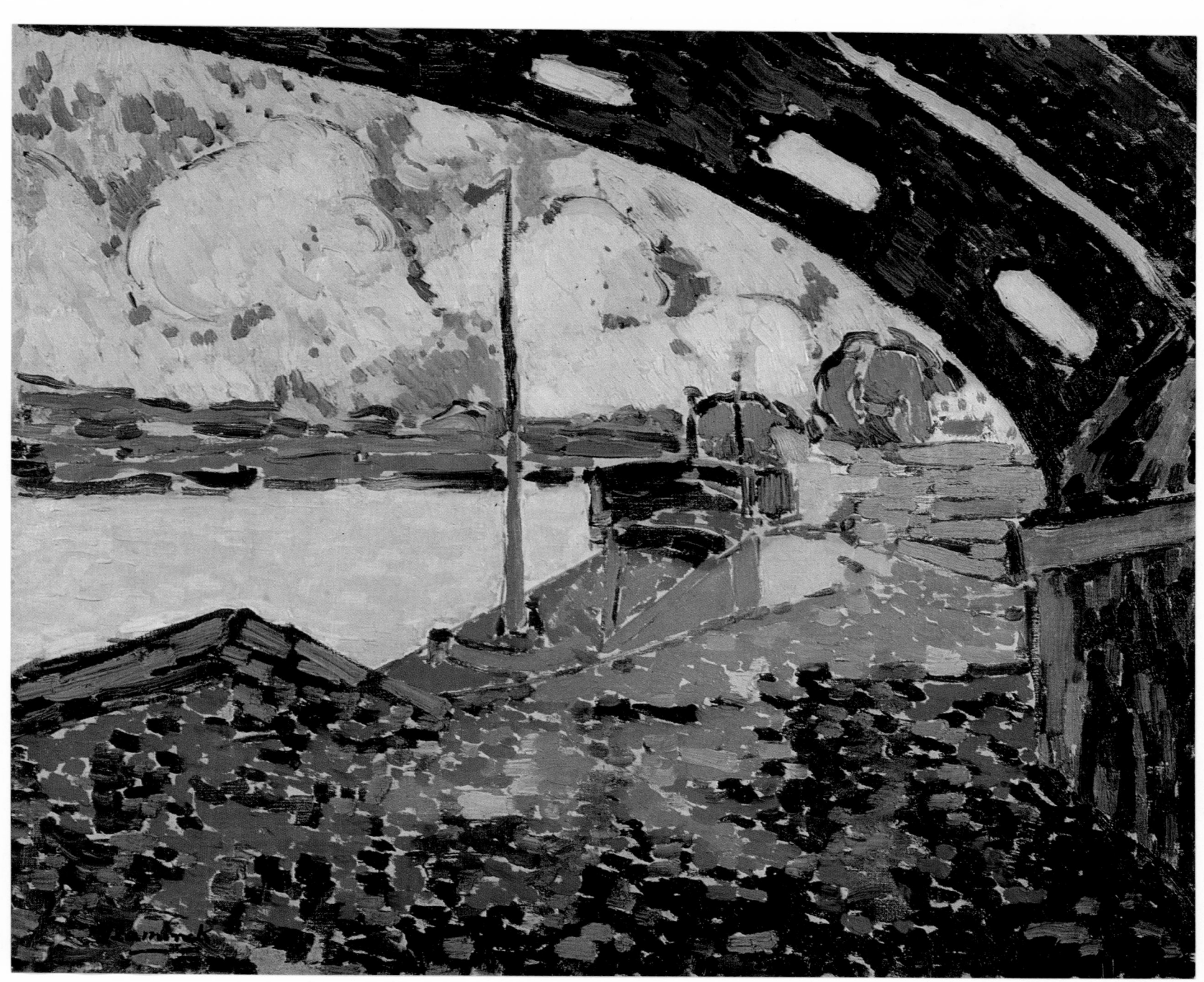

MAURICE DE VLAMINCK (1876–1958)
Painted in 1905
Reclining Nude
Oil on canvas, 10 5/8 × 16 1/8"
Collection David Josefowitz, Geneva

Use of the studio at the bridge of Chatou was to last only a few months, for—as Vlaminck humorously relates—the landlord soon put a stop to the pillaging of the furniture, which ended up in the stove, and to the overly familiar relations that had developed between his daughter and the two artists.

With Derain in his turn doing his military service at Commercy from 1901 to 1904, Vlaminck, still under the emotional impact of the Van Gogh exhibition, announces his new projects to him in a letter dated 1902: "I wanted to paint portraits, a series of portraits of the people, portraits of character, portraits as real as living landscapes, human landscapes, sad or beautiful, with all their defects, their poverty-stricken and squalid appeal."

This is no temporary excursion into vague sentimentalism, for like Van Gogh, Vlaminck always strives to stay in communion with people, with the earth, with the simplest of things, and examines them with passionate interest. A self-taught artist, his curiosity is ever on the alert, and he feels an almost frantic need to express himself by all possible means. He has already been writing for some time as a substitute for painting, and in 1900 he produces a novel with Fernand Sernada, *Graines au vent*, the title being changed to the more suggestive *D'Un Lit dans l'autre* by the publishers, the brothers Offenstadt. It carried a preface by Champsaur and twenty illustrations by Derain.

As Vlaminck himself explains: "Penniless and unable to buy paints and canvases, I continued to scribble. I tried to express reality with words in a tome that would contain everything that Life teaches us. What I found intolerable was my inability to express myself in one way or another."

Yet at this time, stimulated by Derain's return, introduced to the Indépendants in 1905, installed in the Fauves' room at the Salon d'Automne of the same year, he is finally able to satisfy his chief vocation, painting. He shows a rare violence and a spirited directness in the suburban landscapes that he sends in large numbers to both exhibitions. The only portrait, *My Neighbor's Daughter*, will be bought by Vollard, who a few months later decides to sign a contract with the artist, thus enabling him to work in the future without financial worries.

Vlaminck remains cautious, however, and apart from *Portrait of a Woman* (formerly Collection Adolphe A. Juviler), exhibited at the Indépendants in 1907, he does not send to the Salons the few portraits and nudes which he paints at this time and which might well shock the public still further by their brutality.

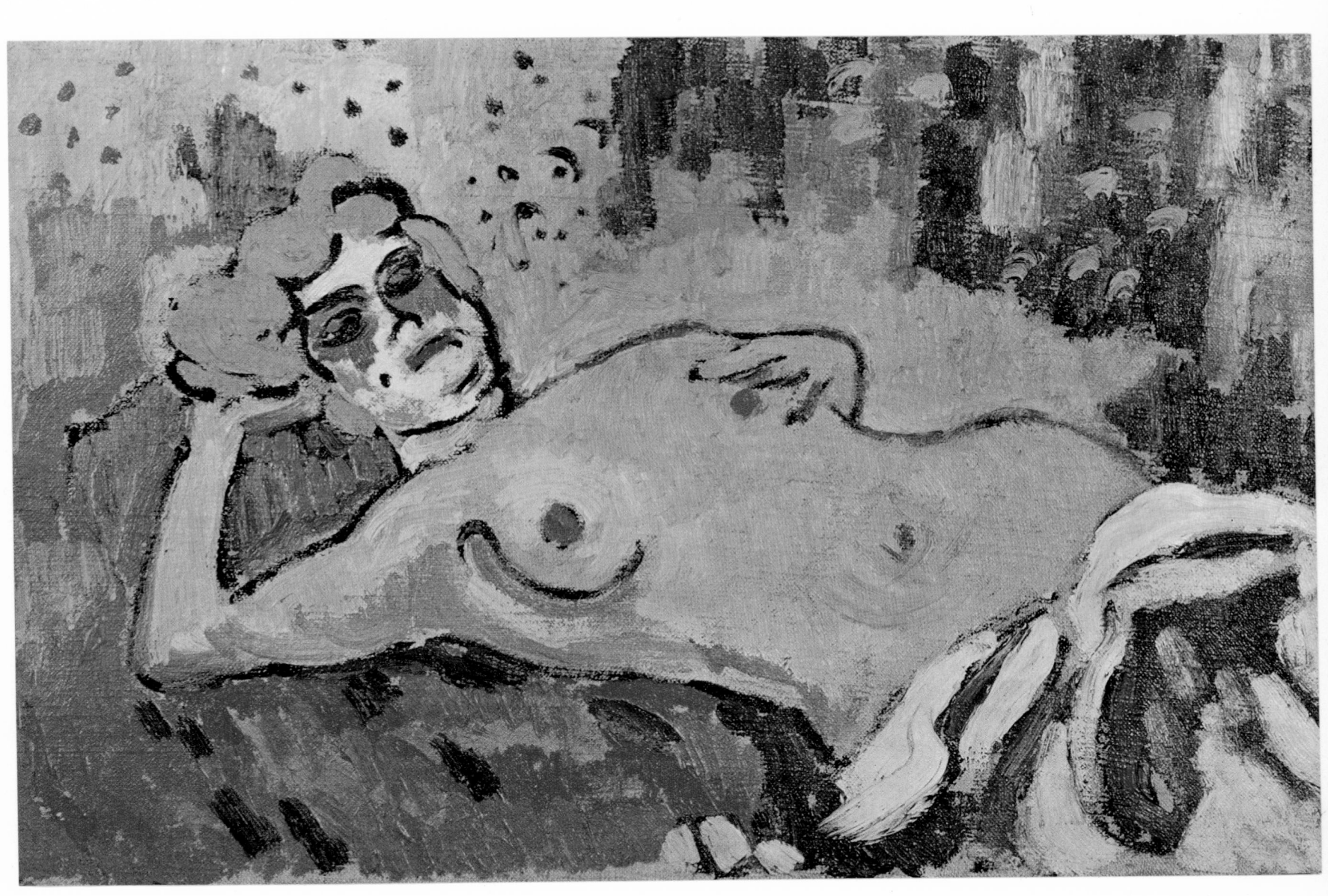

MAURICE DE VLAMINCK (1876–1958)

Painted in 1906
Landscape near Chatou
Oil on canvas, 23 7/8 × 29"
Stedelijk Museum, Amsterdam

Despite Vollard's contract, which he receives in 1906, Vlaminck in no way changes his way of life, continuing to live at Rueil, merely moving, soon after, from the Boulevard des Ornes to the Boulevard Victor Hugo. As he says in his memoirs: "The few hundred francs that Vollard paid me every month were enough to rid me of my worries: that was all I asked for! . . . Derain had rented a studio in the Rue Tourlaque. . . . I remained alone as I had always been, before and after the studio at Chatou. I worked at Bougival, Marly, Villesnes. I had no wish for a change of scene. All these places that I knew so well, the Seine with its strings of barges, the tugs with their plumes of smoke, the taverns in the suburbs, the color of the atmosphere, the sky with its great clouds and its patches of sun, these were what I liked to paint. . . . When I had spent a few days without thinking, without doing anything, I would feel a sudden urge to paint. Then I would set up my easel in full sunshine. . . . Vermilion alone could render the brilliant red of the tiles on the opposite slope. The orange of the soil, the harsh, crude colors of the walls and greenery, the ultramarine and cobalt of the sky achieved an extreme harmony that was sensually and musically ordered. Only the series of colors on the canvas with all their power and vibrancy could, in combination with each other, render the chromatic feeling of that landscape."

He has perhaps been too often accused of having, with unwarranted insistence, claimed the leadership of a movement that he boasts of having initiated. Although there is obviously some exaggeration on his part when, through many of his accounts, he tries to make us believe that Derain and Matisse, already fully fledged artists, owed him everything, it is nonetheless true that even in relation to them he played a role that fully deserves to be mentioned.

He in fact contributes something very special that none of the others possesses—not even Van Dongen despite his affinities—something unique in that he draws from popular sources and, driven by the anxiety of a self-taught artist, preserves a kind of marveling naiveté mingled with bold cunning before the mysteries of nature that attract him. He likewise practices an almost aggressive nonconformism, avoids every form of instruction and influence and abides exclusively by the resources of his instinct, sharpened by a rich temperament. Finally, he expresses himself with a savage violence and voluble eloquence that are his alone.

This sturdy vigor, this sometimes inflamed dynamism, this almost barbaric note that his work reveals could not fail to exercise some influence, direct or indirect, on his companions. When he mingles with these characteristics a disillusioned and demanding note, a feeling of anxiety in the face of these desolate suburban landscapes, he unwittingly comes close to the German Expressionists, whose spiritual anguish he seems, for all his pretended nonchalance, to share.

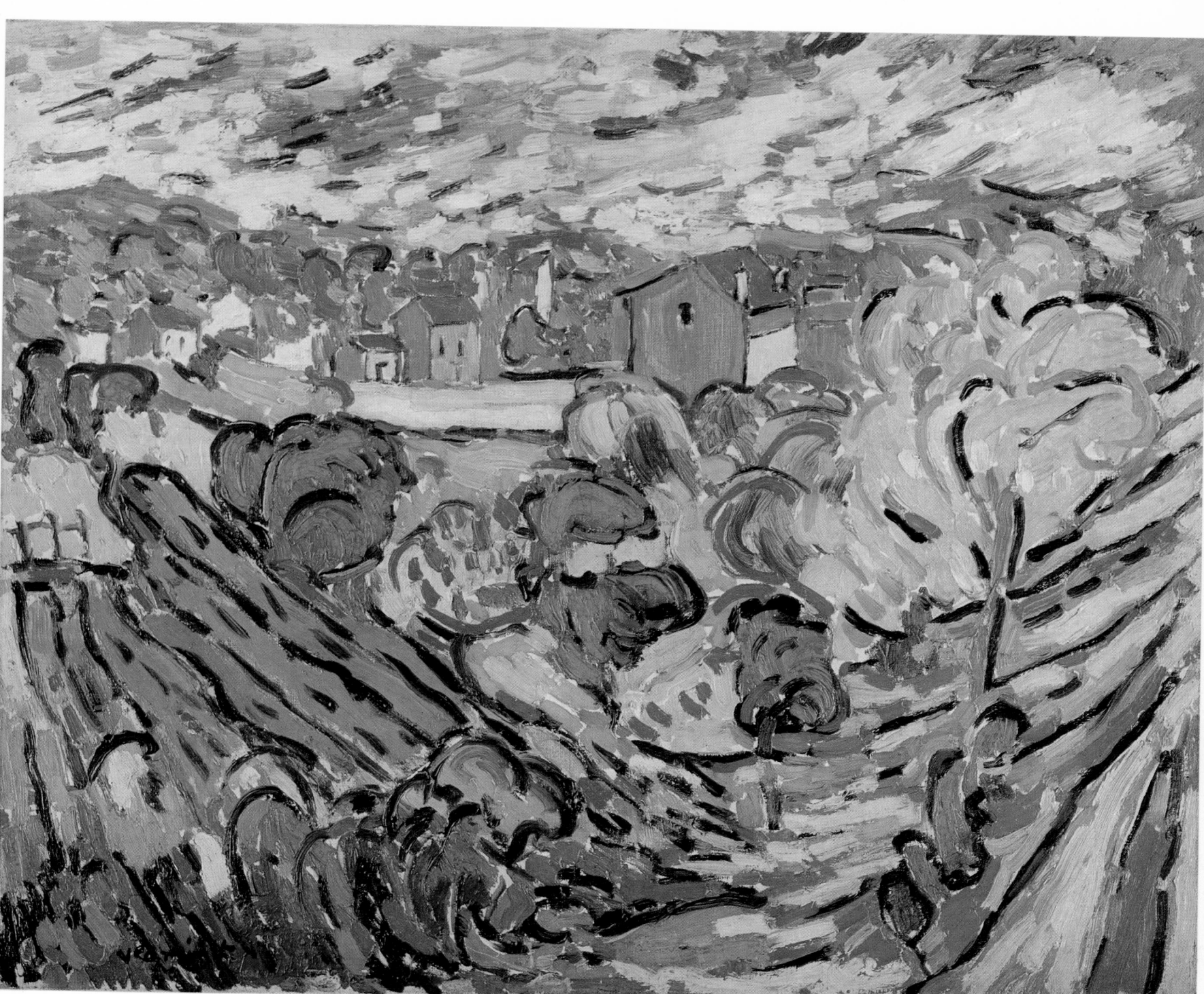

MAURICE DE VLAMINCK (1876–1958)

Painted in 1907
Landscape at Chatou
Oil on canvas, 23 5/8 × 31 7/8″
Collection Pierre Lévy, Troyes

Vlaminck had rapidly broadened his circle of friends, and from time to time frequented the Butte Montmartre, where, in the Azon restaurant, he would find not only Apollinaire, an old Chatou acquaintance, but also the whole Bateau Lavoir band: Picasso, Max Jacob, Van Dongen, Salmon. Vollard occasionally invites him to look at some of the masterpieces piled up at random in his shop, and it is perhaps the sight of these works, or that of the Gauguin retrospective at the Salon d'Automne in 1906, that leads to his effort to introduce more active rhythms, as in his painting *The Red Trees* (fig. 29).

He is shrewd enough to realize that with the elementary means he is using, he runs the risk of soon reaching a dead end and repeating himself. Yet as he wrote: "I doggedly stuck to my guns and refused to give in to the objections that Derain leveled at me in the course of our endless discussions. 'If you rely exclusively on the radiance of color that comes *straight from the tube,*' Derain argued, 'you'll never get anywhere. That's a dyers' theory! You'll never be able to get a redder red or a bluer blue than those produced by the paint manufacturer!' "

In fact, as this painting shows, in 1907 he already begins to mute his tones, introducing a little more lightness and gentleness into the sky, a little more tranquility into the landscape. Before long Vauxcelles will be able to predict that he will be one of the first to want to "defect."

He rebels against Cézanne's example and then submits to it more ardently than the rest. But he keeps his distrust of theories and resists the charms of Provence. "In his letters Derain extolled its beauty and its gentleness," he records for the year 1908. "One day I let myself be tempted and went to join him at Les Martigues. When I came back, I had little to show for it. Everything was foreign to me there: landscape, people, and sky."

Thus he never moved outside the charmed circle of the riverbanks. After Rueil he settles in Bougival, then in 1918 in Valmondois, which he leaves two years later for Auvers-sur-Oise. In 1925 he settles permanently at La Tourillière, but he finds it very difficult to adapt himself to this new landscape, the monotony of which becomes an obsession.

Thirty years later he told me: "I turned naturally to painting in order to express myself completely and without reservations. . . . By using pure color to the utmost, I wanted to destroy old conventions, to *disobey*, so as to re-create a tangible, living, and liberated world. For me painting must be emotive, tender and savage, as natural as Life. I used only seven colors, almost without intermediaries. Then I decided to widen the range by using black and white once more. And soon I felt more and more an intense need for human expression. Today, after so many years, when I look at it all I'm sometimes tormented by the things that happened, but at least I'm sure that I devoted myself entirely to painting with no thought for anything else."

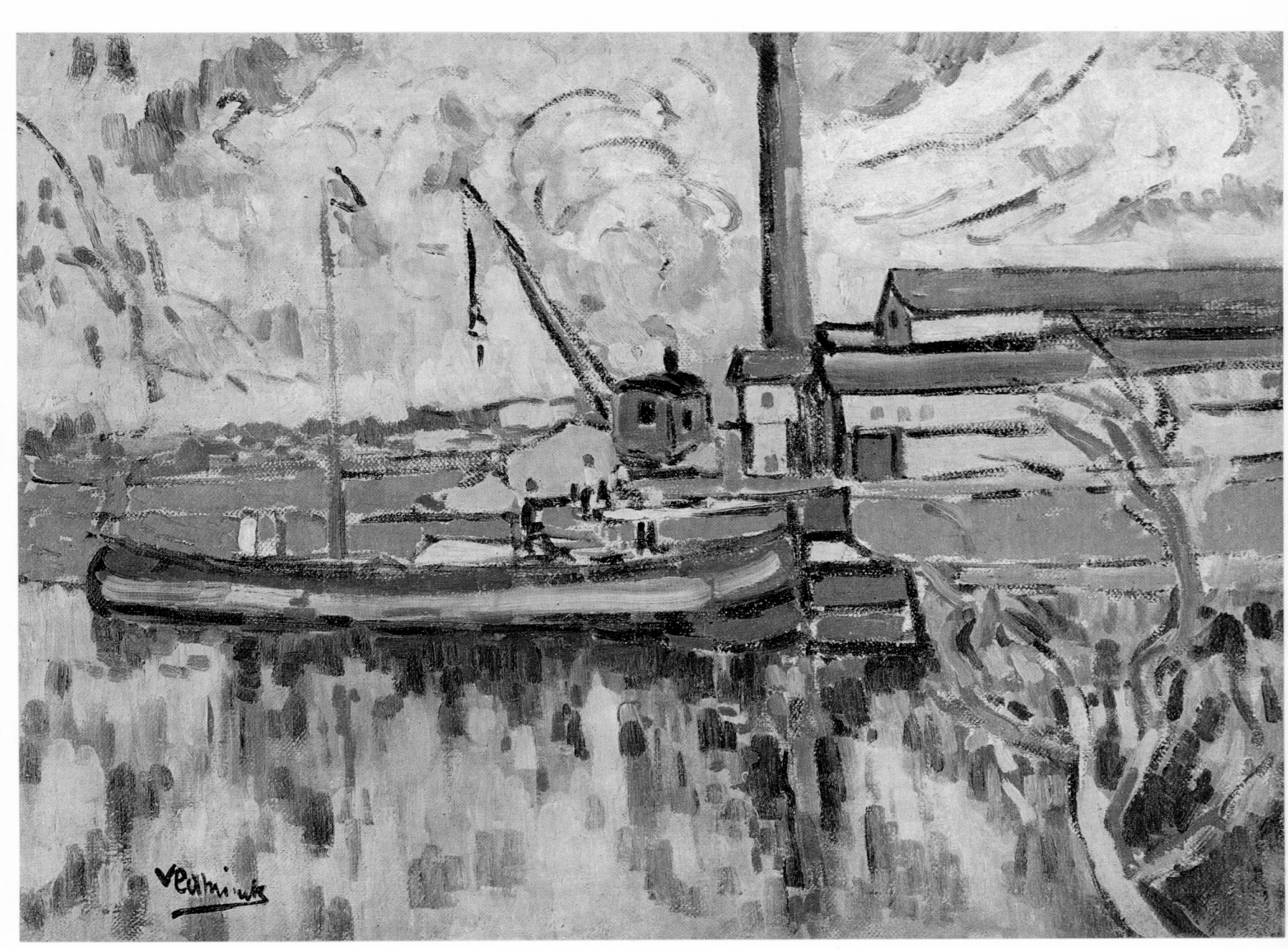

KEES VAN DONGEN (1877–1968)

Painted in 1905
The Shirt
Oil on canvas, 18 1/8 × 21 5/8"
Private collection, Paris

Born in Rotterdam on January 26, 1877, the second of four children of a family that owned two malt-houses, Van Dongen finished his secondary studies before entering the city's Academy of Fine Arts in 1894. Far from objecting to his vocation, his parents even allowed him to set up a studio in the attic of the house, where he painted his first portraits.

After a stay of several months in Paris with his compatriot Ten Cate in 1897, he returns to the Academy to attend the courses of Striening and Heyberg, and here meets Augusta Preitinger, whom he rejoins in Paris in 1899 and marries in 1901. Although permanently settled in Paris, he remains very attached to his native country, returning there almost every year to spend his holidays with his family.

As he had already done in Rotterdam and following the example of several of his friends in Montmartre, where he lives in the Impasse Girardon, he earns a partial living by selling brilliantly satirical sketches of popular life to the humorous newspapers.

Meanwhile he continues to paint and soon has enough canvases to make a conspicuous artistic debut in 1904, sending six paintings to the Indépendants and two to the Salon d'Automne. He also has a show at Vollard's, prefaced by Fénéon and consisting of 105 oil paintings and twenty watercolors and drawings. As is usual with him, half the works exhibited are of Dutch subjects, the other half of Paris and Normandy.

Encouraged by his success, he immediately makes an enterprising reappearance the following year and becomes one of the first to attract the attention of both the public and the galleries. By January he has several paintings on display at Berthe Weill's. He submits six canvases and two watercolors to the Indépendants, and his two oils at the Salon d'Automne are hung in the Fauves' room. He also takes part in the group exhibit at the Prath & Magnier Gallery, while Druet shows a small collection of his work. The unusual speed with which he has established himself in the Paris art world arouses strong animosities against him, to which he pays no heed.

Fortunately his painting reflects no such excessive self-assurance. Like his companions, he experiments for a time with Pointillism, but in his watercolors of 1904, and then in two paintings exhibited at the 1905 Indépendants, he seeks to free his impulse, using a firm, vigorous touch with which his technical skill enables him to achieve a play of colors, as in this canvas exhibited at the Salon d'Automne. The ill-disguised violence that it reveals is in keeping with his profoundly sensual temperament, which is not yet capable of combining an emotional and already lyrical perception of reality with his passionate need for a fine surface of paint.

Halfway on his course and still hesitant, Van Dongen here nonetheless gives proof of his gifts and the eloquent vehemence that led him to his first striking artistic statements.

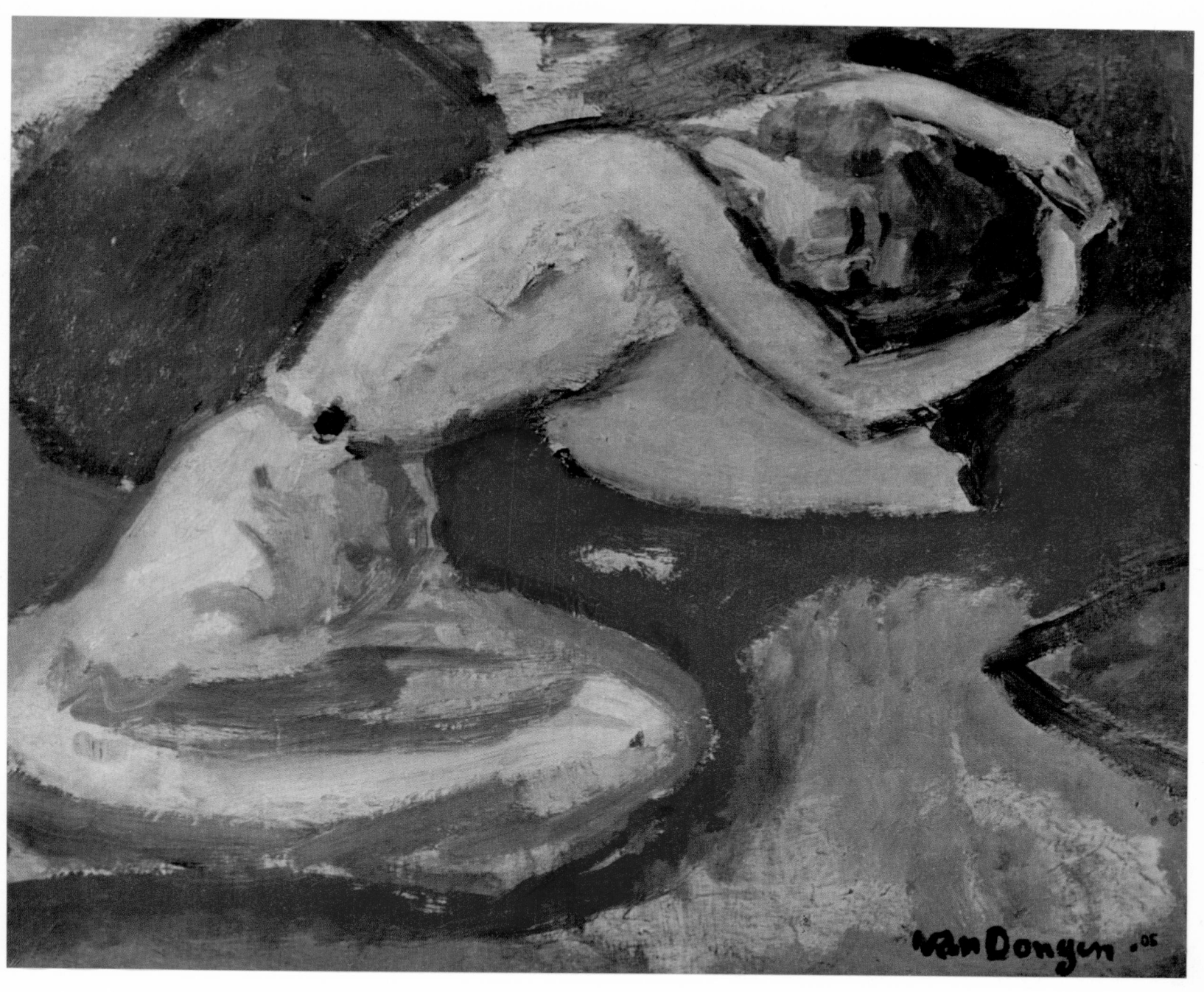

KEES VAN DONGEN (1877–1968)

Painted in 1906
Liverpool Night House
Oil on canvas, 39 3/8 × 31 7/8"
Collection David Josefowitz, Geneva

With his customary bantering air and ambiguous smile, Van Dongen told me, many years later, about this period of his life: "At that time I didn't really think of myself as a Fauve but rather as a distinguished gentleman. We were all young, with more illusions and enthusiasm than money in our pockets. We sang, we shouted, we rebelled thanks to color, we were all mad about it. Fortunately you could live on practically nothing in those days, particularly in Montmartre, a real artists' village where anybody could get credit and at any hour. To me it made no difference what I did to scrape up a living: furniture removing, house painting, and without a loan from *père* Luce I would never have been able to raise the twenty-five francs for the hanging at the Indépendants."

Actually, after his highly successful entry on the Parisian art scene in 1904 and 1905, Van Dongen was probably the most launched on his career of any member of the group, and his *Self-Portrait* (fig. 8) reveals his confidence and determination. At the Indépendants of 1906 his canvases are naturally hung in Room VI, and in his review Vauxcelles describes Van Dongen's entries at length and stresses his exceptional gifts. His reaction will be the same at the Salon d'Automne, where he remarks on the artist's "strange sketches depicting the girls at the Moulin de la Galette, chlorotic clownesses in flesh-colored tights."

Van Dongen had maintained his links with his native country. In Paris he again meets Van Rees, and especially Toorop, and Sluyters, who in his turn will depict the Parisian dance halls. He exhibits with them, as well as with Thorn Prikker, at the Rotterdam Art Circle in 1906, and then in Amsterdam in 1907. The memory of a journey to Le Havre with Dufy is still vivid in his mind in Holland during the summer of 1906, when he too paints a street decked with flags.

His truculence and vigor find full expression in paintings charged with color and texture. If he sends nothing to the Paris Salons of 1907 and only some old canvases to Toulouse for the exhibition held by the newspaper *Le Télégramme*, it is probably because Kahnweiler, with whom he has signed a contract, opposes the idea. He works with redoubled zeal, however, and this allows him to have a number of shows in 1908: one in Düsseldorf, another at Kahnweiler's in March, and a third in November at the Bernheim-Jeune Gallery, which now buys his works. His reputation is already so well established that he is the only one invited to exhibit with the Brücke artists, with whom he has unmistakable affinities.

In this picture, painted at the end of 1906 but exhibited at the Salon d'Automne only in 1908, he returns to a theme that he had already presented at the 1904 Indépendants, this time giving it more breadth and vigor. The setting and figures, boldly established with a few strokes, allow few illusions in a sordid universe immersed in an atmosphere of bitterness and disenchantment, but to which the magic of the color lends a little human warmth.

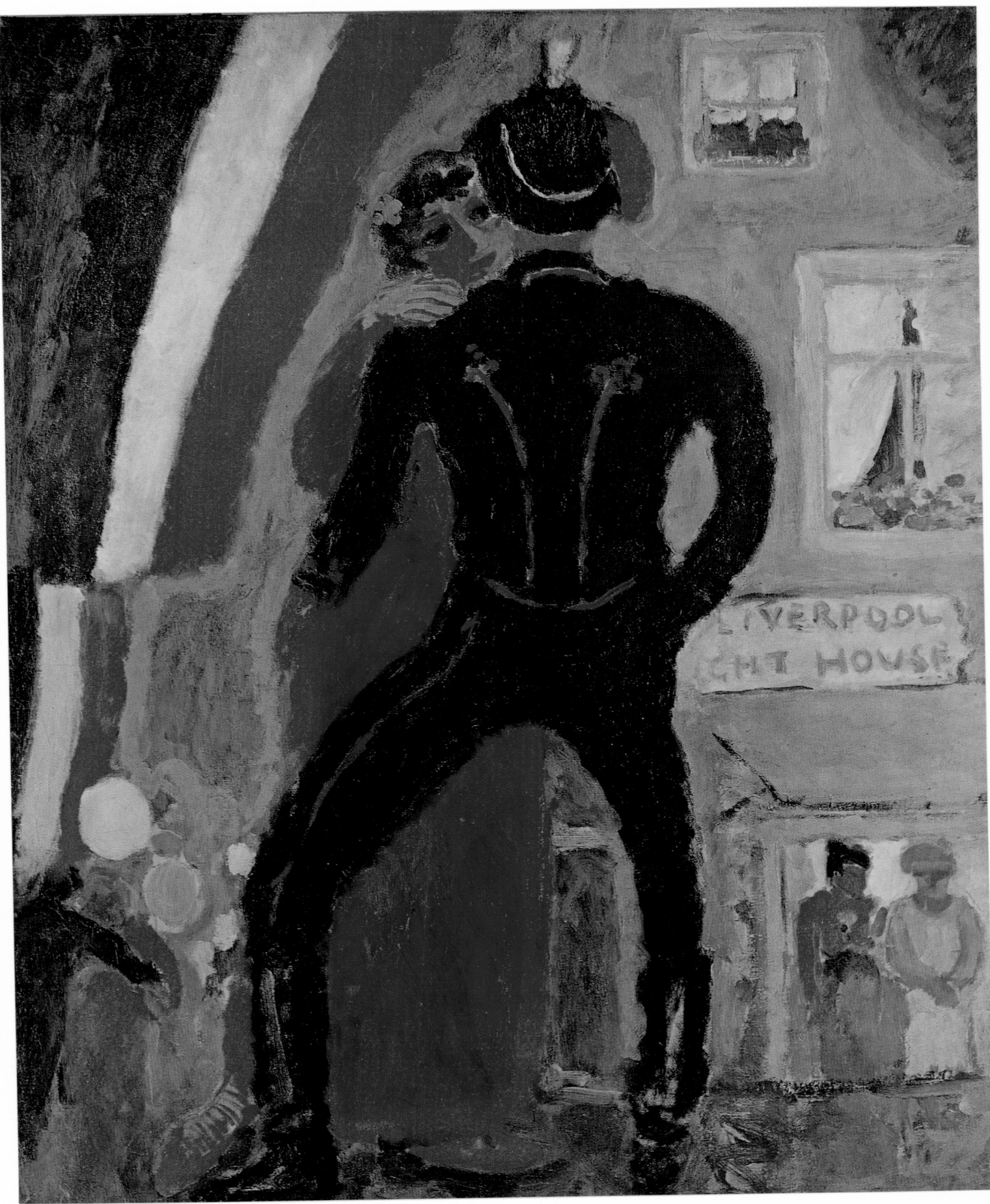

KEES VAN DONGEN (1877–1968)

Painted in 1907–8

Nude

Oil on canvas, 39 3/8 × 31 7/8″

Von der Heydt-Museum, Wuppertal

More and more Van Dongen tends to escape from the gloomy suburban world of his early career, where the atmosphere of dejection scarcely suits his appetite for pleasure. In 1908 he moves into the Rue Lamark so as to be closer to the Folies Bergères, where the nocturnal belles of the lounges, their escorts for the evening, and even the performers furnish him countless tempting models. These make up the bulk of the canvases submitted to the Indépendants and the Salon d'Automne in 1909.

If he likes to be a man about town and starts to paint an increasing number of portraits at this time, he nevertheless still pursues that personal vein where he gives free, almost ostentatious, expression to the sensuality that will always govern his life. Nudes invade his work at an early date: Anita the gypsy or Nini, a frequenter of the Folies Bergères, whose worn and sagging bodies still have about them a disturbing femininity, Fernande Olivier, and his own wife Guus, whom he also uses as a model with no more ceremony than reserve. This buxom display of naked flesh, embellished with lavish colors and often depicted in provocative attitudes, conveys an impression of such splendid bestiality that one almost forgets its immodesty.

In this painting, he accentuates the richness of contrast by the broad expanses of ultramarine that he begins to employ copiously at this time under the effect of the electric projectors by which he works at night.

For many years he continues to exalt what Elie Faure called this "sensual poem of the world," not without causing a certain amount of scandal at the opening of his Bernheim exhibition in January, 1913, or at the Salon d'Automne, but it earns him, in 1918, an enthusiastic preface by Apollinaire, who declares: "Today everything connected with sensual pleasure is surrounded by grandeur and silence. It survives among Van Dongen's immoderate figures."

Going far beyond the historical limits of Fauvism, Van Dongen is one of the few members of the group to preserve the impulse that carries him spontaneously toward what he himself calls "warm and ardent life." His nudes are not the only expression of this. At the slightest occasion everything—a charming scene, a graceful figure, a visit to Spain or Morocco during the winter of 1910–11, a stroll at Deauville, or a journey to Egypt—is a pretext for him to glorify the most commonplace aspects with his lively brush and glowing colors, which he skillfully mixes with grays, ochers, and blacks.

He indulges in the masquerades of the wild postwar period, indeed as one of its most active protagonists, until the day when, weary of being in the limelight, he succumbs to disillusionment and bitterness, and takes his revenge on this society by fiercely ridiculing it in his fashionable portraits.

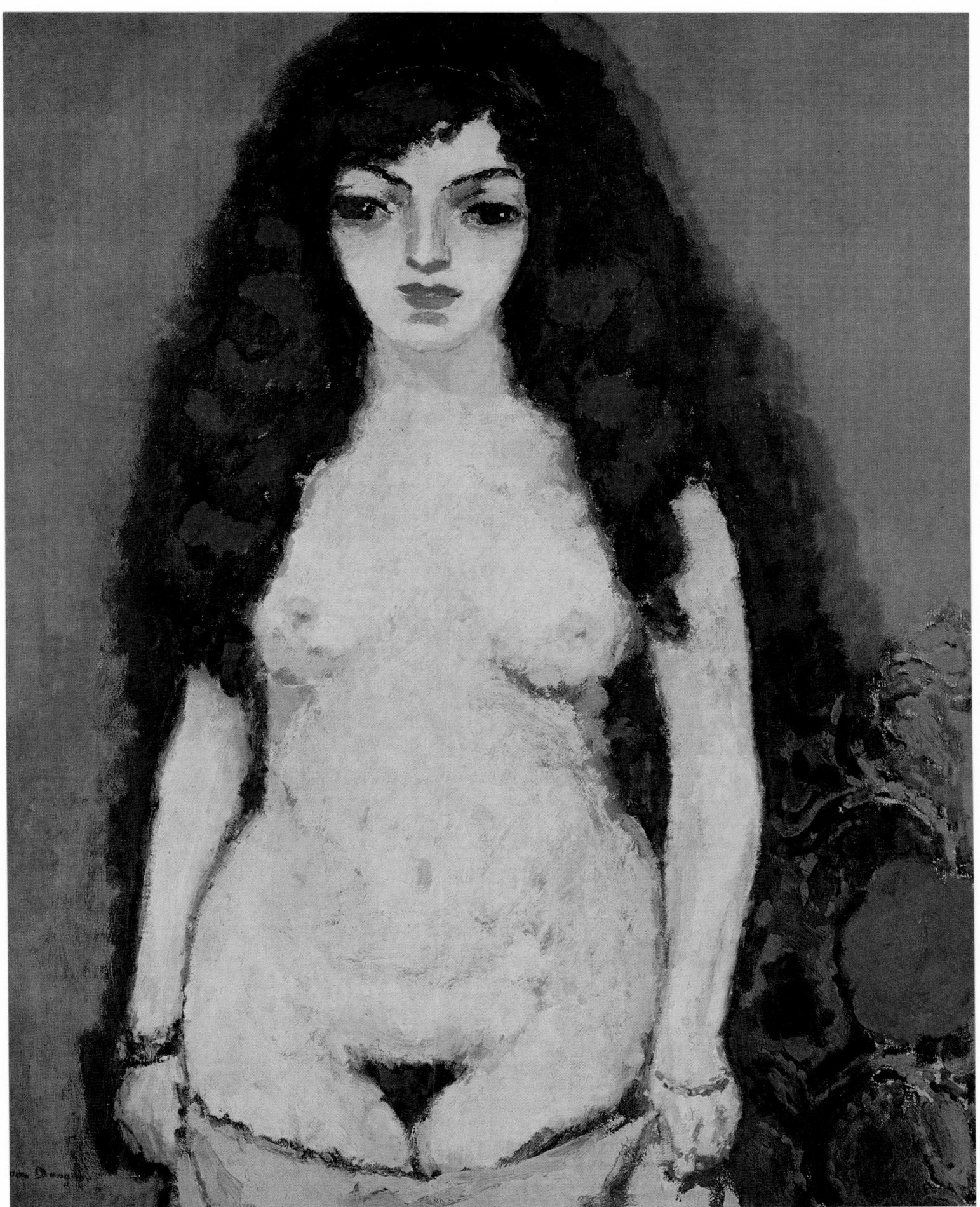

RAOUL DUFY (1877–1953)

Painted in 1906
The Posters at Trouville
Oil on canvas, 25 1/2 × 34 5/8"
Musée National d'Art Moderne, Paris

Born at Le Havre on June 3, 1877, Dufy, one of nine children in a family of very modest means, begins his career under difficult circumstances. At the age of fourteen he is obliged to abandon his studies and take an onerous job with a coffee importing firm, but his artistic gifts soon reveal themselves, and in 1892 he enrolls in evening classes at the Ecole Municipale des Beaux-Arts under the direction of Lhuillier. It is here that he later meets Friesz and Braque.

In 1900, after finishing his military service, he receives a scholarship from the municipality of Le Havre, which allows him to go to Paris and rejoin Friesz, who is already there, in Bonnat's studio at the Ecole des Beaux-Arts. They share lodgings in the Rue Cortot in Montmartre.

His admiration for the work of Boudin, which he has often seen at Le Havre, and his frequent visits to Paris galleries help him to escape from his academic background and to turn toward the examples of Manet and Pissarro. His works—both paintings and pastels— are pleasing, refined, and sensitive, and bring him a certain success. He comes to know Berthe Weill, who as early as January, 1903, includes him in several of her exhibitions, and in the same year he begins to exhibit at the Indépendants.

By 1904 he is using a light, dynamic touch and increasing the intensity of his colors. He soon falters, however, for these novelties scare away buyers and the Blot Gallery, which has been promoting his work, abandons him. It is not until 1906 that he resumes this vein, encouraged by the sight of Matisse's *Joy of Life* (fig. 25) at the Indépendants, and above all by his visits to Falaise with Friesz and with Marquet to Trouville. Forgetting his financial and sentimental worries, stimulated by the presence of his comrades, Dufy throws himself with youthful impetuosity into the use of bold colors, but never without seeking at the start some visual justification. When he exhibits at the Salon d'Automne for the first time in 1906, his seven canvases, one of them belonging to Maurice Denis, are placed in the Fauves' room, and Paul Jamot, in *Gazette des beaux-arts*, praises "the liveliness of his renderings of crowds in sunlight, fluttering flags, and walls covered with posters."

The last reference may apply to this painting, which Dufy executed boldly, while Marquet painted the scene with a more sober simplicity. Dufy's inborn fantasy leads him to exploit simultaneously the various elements that constitute his "particular reality," to use his own phrase. The motley crowd swarming along the boardwalk at Trouville is most skillfully evoked, and he adds to it the medley of colors of the Normandy houses which he will always use to great effect. Finally, the hoarding covered with multicolored posters provides a vibrant, kaleidoscopic background that stands out luminously against the sky. Without ever forcing the tone, Dufy fills his scene with a gentle gaiety.

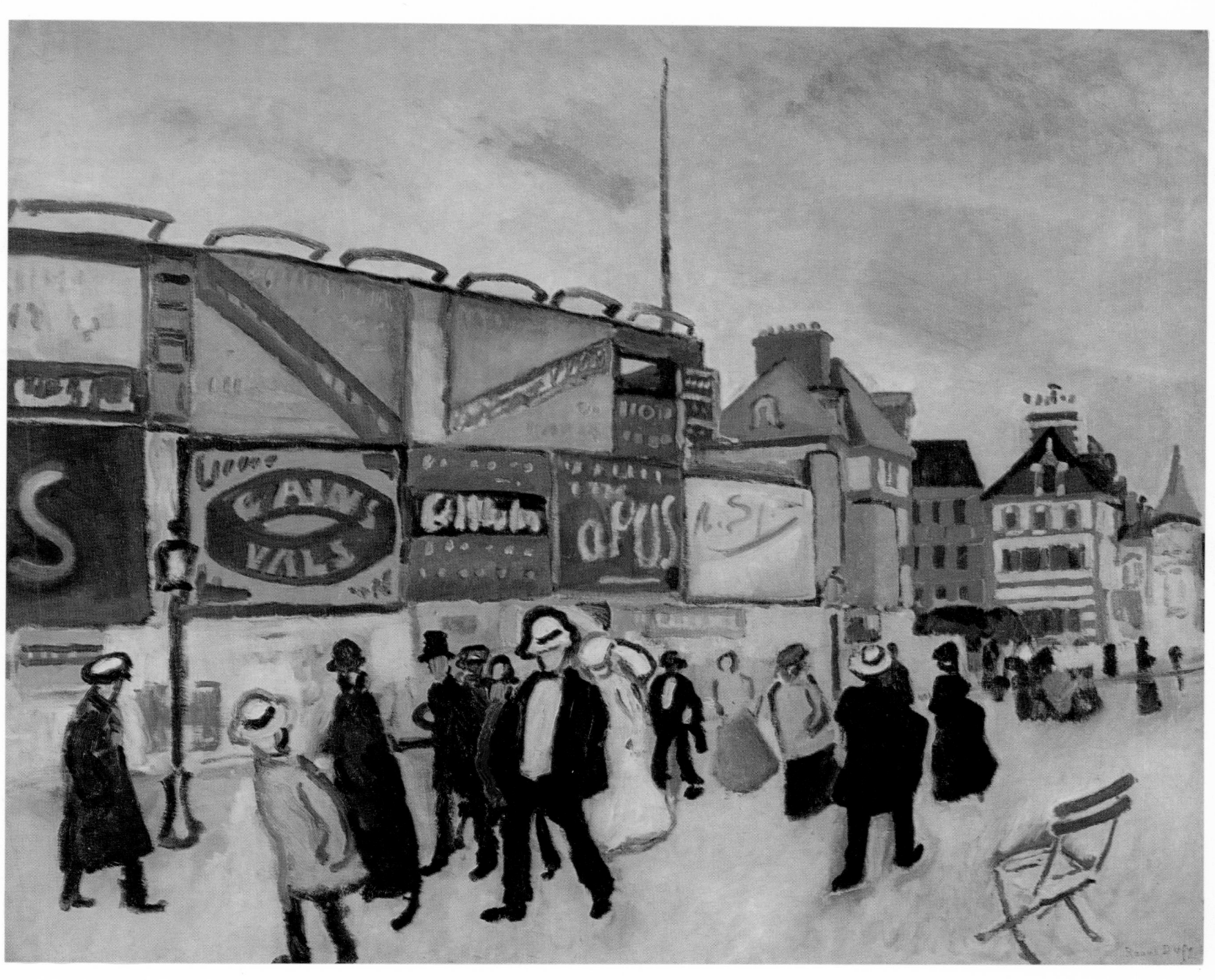

RAOUL DUFY (1877–1953)
Painted in 1906
Street Hung with Flags at Le Havre
Oil on canvas, 31 7/8 × 25 5/8"
Musée National d'Art Moderne, Paris

This picture was shown at the Salon d'Automne in 1906. Like his friend Marquet, Dufy often treats this theme—a favorite with the Impressionists, Van Gogh, and Ensor—and does different versions of it that are exhibited in 1906 and 1907.

His aim is to suggest simply and without exaggeration the holiday atmosphere and the movement of the crowd, while remaining attentive to reality. He makes full use of the flags and streamers, which fill the space with their festive note, and cleverly exploits the alternating colors of the facades, on which he throws a soft light in the foreground to avoid overly pronounced transpositions. He then merely sprinkles the ground and the far end of the street with a few distinct spots of green, blue, and mauve, sharing as he does with Braque a predilection for this last color.

It is easy to understand why the Fauves treated him with such reserve—Berthe Weill shows great indignation at this in her memoirs—and refused to accept him in their group in the exhibition at her gallery in October, 1905, thus forcing her to show him in a separate room. To indicate her vexation and help her protégé she will later organize Dufy's first one-man show in the Rue Victor Massé in October, 1906, just before the Salon d'Automne, where he is finally admitted to their ranks. Dufy, sure of the direction in which he is moving, bears them no grudge, and in a letter of October 20, 1907, to Berthe Weill he urges her to go on supporting his new colleagues: "Stand by us all, this whole crew that you've had. Do it with all your heart. . . . You can be sure that you have in Matisse, Vlaminck, Derain, Friesz, and a few others the boys of tomorrow and well beyond; this is clear enough from the Salon, isn't it?"

He does not spare his own efforts. At the end of the summer of 1906 he is in Durtal with Braque, the latter still full of enthusiasm after his visit in Antwerp with the painter Axilette, a temporary convert to Fauvism. Back in Paris, he settles on the Quai Conti to be closer to Marquet, but financial difficulties oblige him to return for a while to Le Havre. At the 1907 Indépendants Vauxcelles enrolls him officially among the Fauves, classing him, together with Friesz, immediately after Matisse and Derain. He spends a part of the summer in Marseilles with Friesz.

Thus, without making too many concessions, Dufy gradually joins the group and, with *Jeanne Among the Flowers* (fig. 34; Nouveau Musée des Beaux-Arts, Le Havre), even comes close to the experiments with form and space that Matisse is pursuing at this time.

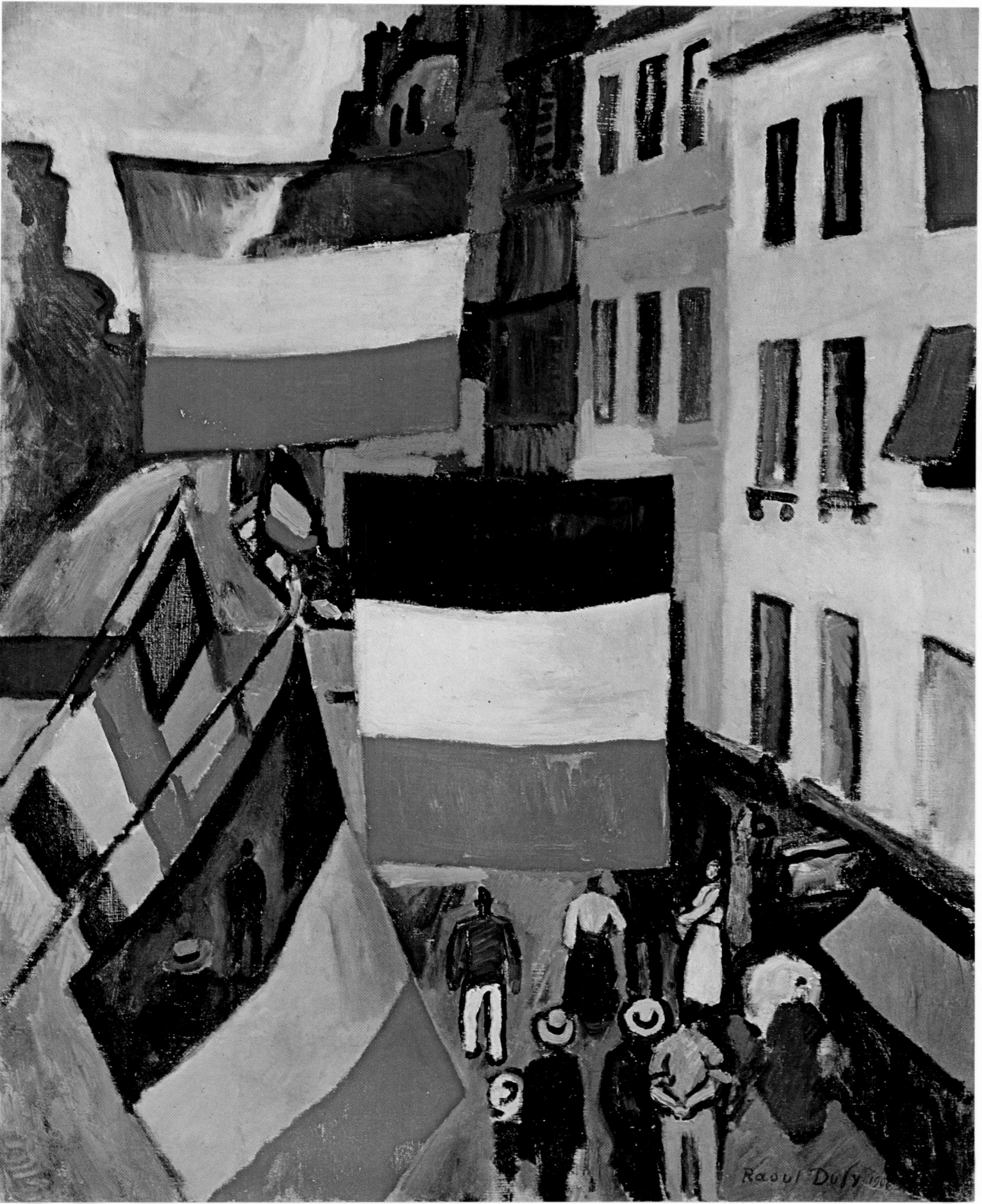

RAOUL DUFY (1877–1953)
Painted in 1906–7
Trouville
Oil on canvas, 21 1/4 × 25 5/8″
Collection David Josefowitz, Geneva

It will still take a while, however, for Dufy to feel at ease with this development, which he interprets in his own way with delicacy and lightness, with a smiling grace unequalled among his companions. In this canvas his chief concern would seem to be to reflect a happy, relaxed atmosphere. As he has already done earlier, he stresses only the architectural rhythms of the houses, which he observes minutely so as to extract from them the most fascinating tonal variations, like a melody where arpeggios of pink, light ocher, pale green, and mauve blend in harmonious counterpoint with the brick red of one of the facades, the dark green of the roofs, and the more sustained blue of the sky.

He is already master of a secret magic whose visual enchantment he will exploit to the full, after the war, at Saint-Cloud, Deauville, and Nice.

For the moment, the Constructivist tendencies that he already shows in the Trouville landscape grow stronger in 1908 under the influence of Braque, whom he has joined in the South of France. Hastily and without regrets, he moves away from Fauvism, the spirit of which he finally expresses with a roughness contrary to his nature in *Anglers at Sunset* (The Museum of Modern Art, New York City), or with rather disorderly rhythms in *The Apéritif* (Musée d'Art Moderne de la Ville de Paris).

The crisis that then confronts him is not immediately overcome. His trip to Munich with Friesz in 1909, and his visit to Orgeville with Lhote in 1910 carry him toward an involvement with Cubism in which he finds little satisfaction. One day, hard pressed for money, he has the idea of doing woodcuts to illustrate Apollinaire's *Le Bestiaire*, and soon after, in 1911, sets up a fabric design studio with the help of Paul Poiret. He works for Bianchini-Férier until the war, and again until 1930.

These decorative experiments, which he pursues, after the war, in ceramics as well as textiles, lead him rapidly to his salvation. Finally he gives free rein in his painting to his spontaneous and inventive spirit, which had worked such marvels in other fields. Under the influence of frequent visits to the Mediterranean, he once more intensifies his palette with brilliant colors, which stream generously over his canvases like a spring song.

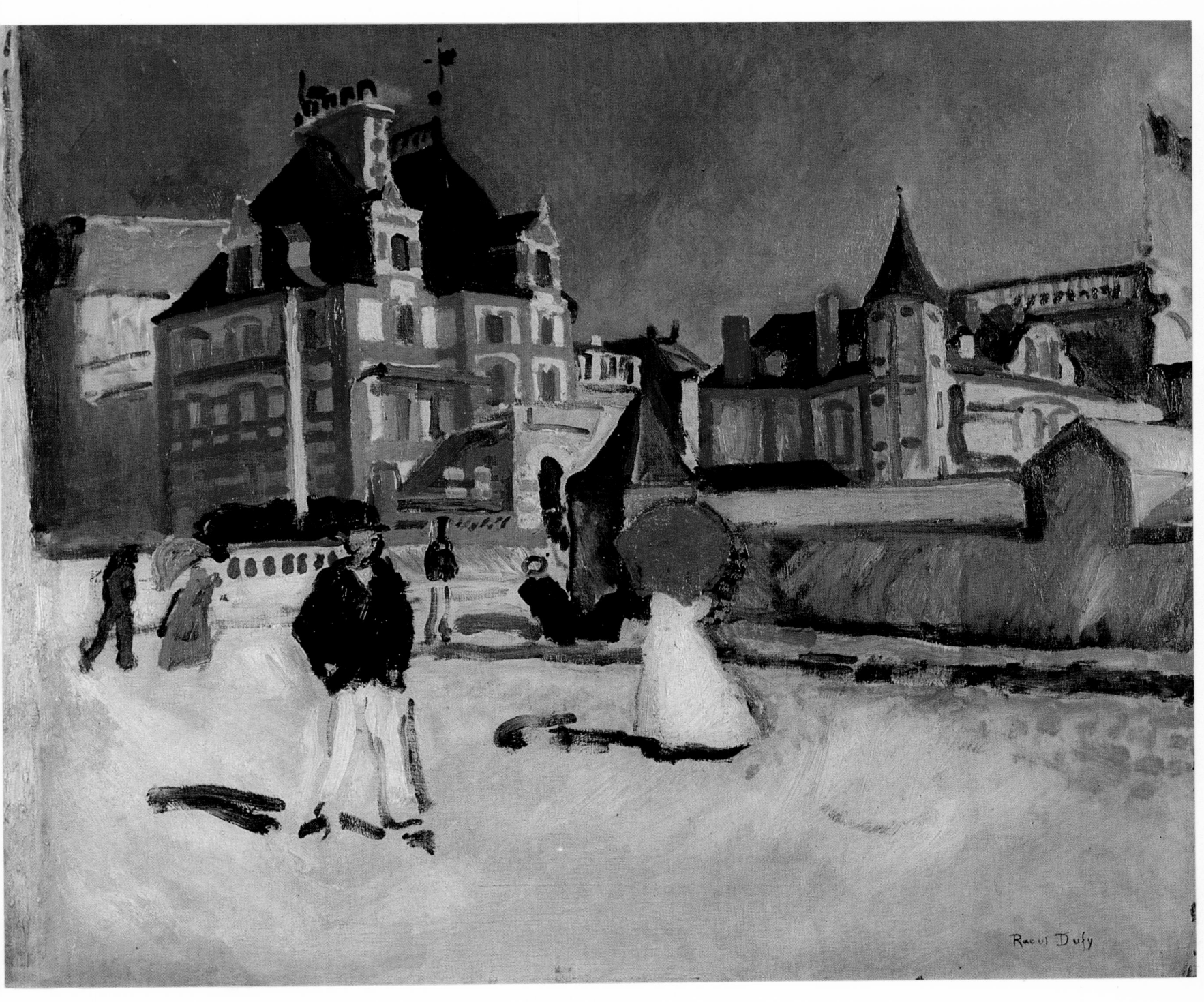

OTHON FRIESZ (1879–1949)
Painted in 1906
Antwerp Harbor
Oil on canvas, 21 1/4 × 25 5/8"
Musée des Beaux-Arts, Liège

Born at Le Havre on February 6, 1879, of a family of shipowners and master mariners, Friesz showed a precocious artistic bent and at the age of twelve, while still attending the lycée, began studying drawing and painting under Lhuillier at the Ecole des Beaux-Arts, where he was soon joined by Dufy and Braque. With a scholarship from the municipality of Le Havre, he goes to Paris in 1899 to study under Bonnat at the Ecole des Beaux-Arts, although he prefers to frequent the Louvre and still more the Impressionist exhibitions at Durand-Ruel.

After his military service, he participates actively at the Indépendants from 1903 and at the Salon d'Automne beginning in 1904, and has three successive one-man shows: at Soulié's and the Prath & Magnier Gallery in 1904, and at Berthe Weill's in May, 1905. His works are well received by the critics, with Vauxcelles emphasizing the progress he shows at each Salon, and praising "one of his landscapes bathed in fluid light," exhibited in Room VI at the Salon d'Automne in 1905, and "his broadly treated landscapes of Honfleur and Falaise" at the 1906 Indépendants.

Highly gifted and enterprising by nature, Friesz throws himself boldly into the use of pure color and frees his brushwork during a summer at Antwerp in 1906, sweeping along his friend Braque in this almost feverish outburst. The four Antwerp landscapes that he presents at the Salon d'Automne in the same year draw this comment from Vauxcelles: "Friesz has deliberately placed himself under the banner of Matisse and Manguin. He is broadening his style and brightening his canvases with fiery colors." Henceforth linked to the Fauves, he takes part in their exhibitions at the Salons and at Berthe Weill's, and in 1908 succeeds in organizing a group show in his native town, with a catalogue prefaced by Apollinaire. Druet buys his works by 1907 and gives him an exhibition, while Kahnweiler also shows interest in his work. That year, during his stay at La Ciotat with Braque and in his excellent portrait of his friend Fleuret (fig. 31), Friesz achieves full artistic expression. He has become friendly with Matisse and joins him in the Boulevard des Invalides in the late summer of 1908. As he would explain to me later: "We weren't opposed to Impressionism then, far from it, but we wanted to get away from the mediocrity of direct emotion, and get back to color. There was only one way to convey the equivalent of sunlight, and that was to do orchestrations of color. We began with the emotional response to nature to arrive at a passionate transposition. We did not achieve this all at once. Various truths and theories were established in the course of some intense and enthusiastic discussions."

Yet at the Salon d'Automne of 1907, which pays homage to Cézanne, Friesz's *Bathers* shows a strong influence of the old Aix master, and at the 1908 Indépendants Vauxcelles congratulates him for having abandoned his companions to return to the true tradition of the Le Nains and Millet. This moderating classicism was to have an increasing effect on his work, but his spirited brushwork continues and will be transmitted to all the pupils who later attend the classes that he conducts for many years.

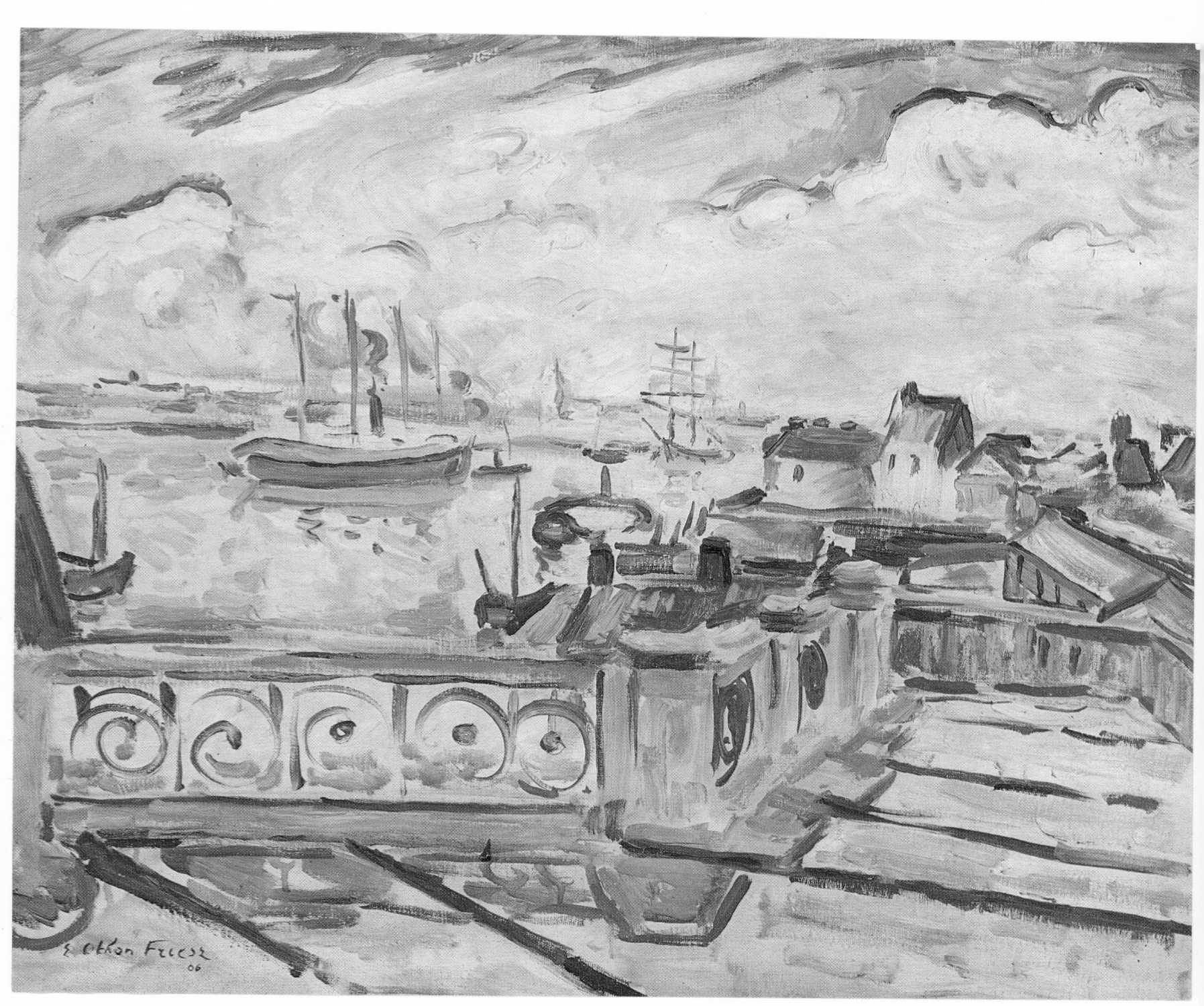

CHARLES CAMOIN (1879–1965)

Painted in 1904

The Pont des Arts Seen from the Pont Neuf

Oil on canvas, 13 × 16 1/8"

Collection Mme C. Camoin, Paris

Camoin was born in Marseilles on September 23, 1879. Thanks to an understanding mother, he was able to take courses at both the Ecole de Commerce and the Ecole des Beaux-Arts. In 1898 he went to Paris, entering Gustave Moreau's studio shortly before the latter's death and becoming a close friend of Marquet and Matisse. He frequented the Louvre but already preferred the sights of the street. Together with his friends, he abandoned himself as early as 1899 to the use of pure color.

During his three years of military service from 1900 to 1902 he continued to paint, and during the last three months, while stationed at Aix-en-Provence, he frequently saw Cézanne, with whom he was to keep up a correspondence until the old painter's death. Cézanne's influence is still visible in the fine portrait of Marquet (fig. 2), with its subtle modulation of blues within a rigorous composition, painted about 1904.

He exhibits with his friends at the Indépendants in 1903, at the Salon d'Automne in 1904, and also joins the group at Berthe Weill's. His carefree, exuberant Mediterranean temperament soon takes him to Naples and Capri, whence he returns with a series of paintings that attract much attention at the Salon d'Automne.

Working frequently with Marquet—in 1904 at Marseilles, during the summer of 1905 at Saint-Tropez, Agay, and Cassis—he expresses himself with growing eloquence and freedom, as can be seen from this exquisitely fresh rendering of one of his friend's favorite haunts in Paris. His joyful Mediterranean landscapes are entirely in keeping with the Fauves' room at the Salon d'Automne of 1905, and Vauxcelles discerningly notes that he "composes pictures overflowing with healthy, sturdy vigor," and achieves "bold, confident contrasts." He congratulates him again the following year at the Indépendants for his "bold rendering of the beautiful Japanese girl in the blue peignoir" and at the Salon d'Automne for his "four seascapes, which are in his best manner."

Camoin's work was to grow increasingly relaxed. From the beginning he had chosen moderation and an appreciation of the sweetness of life, even if he occasionally indulges in rather impetuous brushwork, or in an instinctive sensuality akin to that of Van Dongen. The balance that he shows, in contrast to the other Fauves, wins him the admiration of Vauxcelles, who describes his contribution at the Indépendants of 1907 as "one of the most coherent, the most balanced, and the most significant. His six paintings . . . [are] made very real by the fluidity of the sky and water, the tender quality of the green of the foliage, the scented freshness of the flowers, and painted in a truly decorative style." And in fact Camoin henceforth dissociates himself from the Fauves' experiments, which have grown too impassioned for his taste.

He in no way falls out with his friends, but he is more attracted by the peaceful pleasures of life than by plastic problems, as his admiration for Renoir shows. Only at the end of his life, under the stimulus of frequent visits to the South of France, does he revert to a very free use of warm colors.

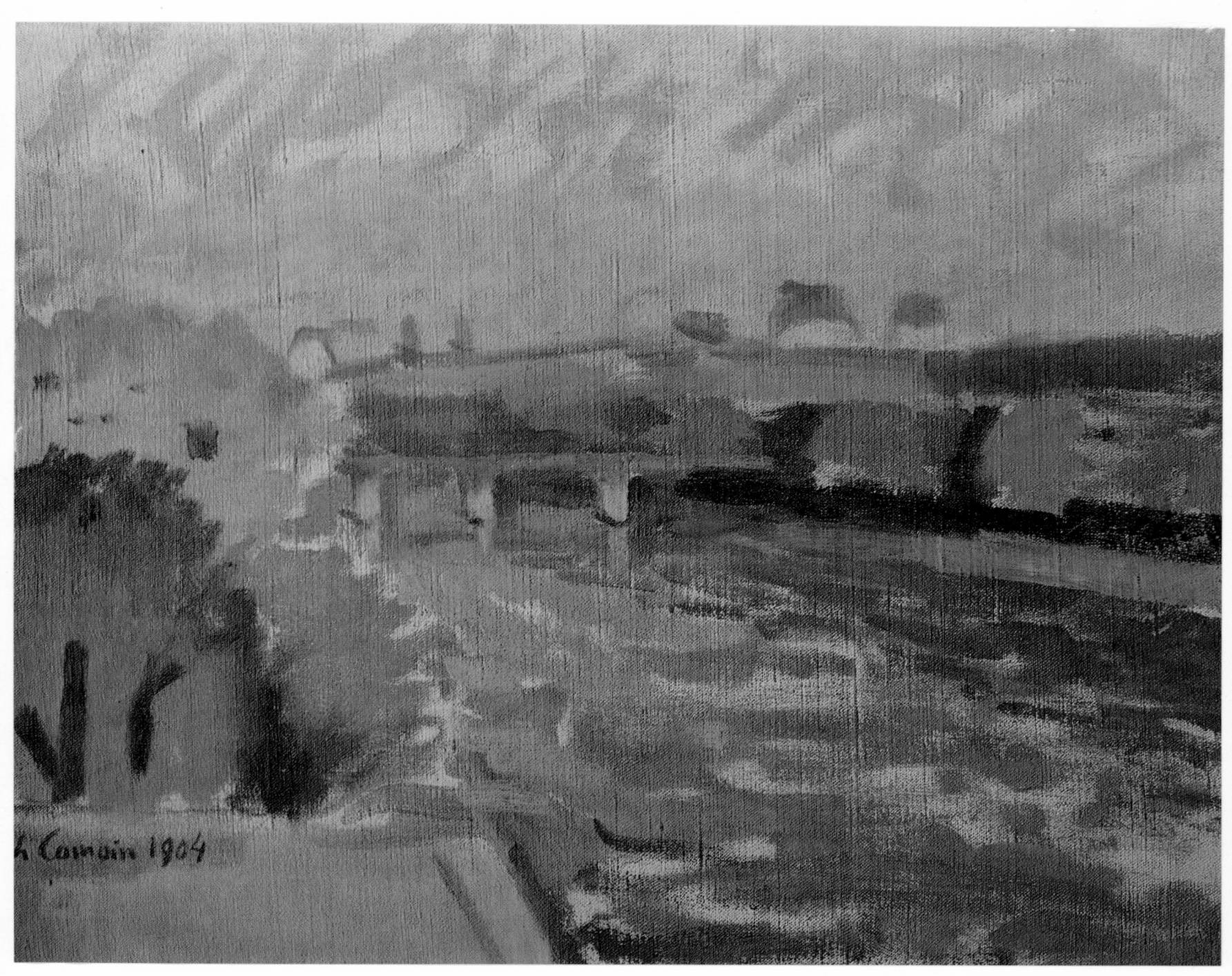

ANDRÉ DERAIN (1880–1954)

Painted in 1905
The Dance
Oil on canvas, 72 7/8 × 90 1/2″
Collection David Josefowitz, Geneva

Born at Chatou on June 10, 1880, Derain showed a precocious artistic bent. He did not finish school, leaving in 1895 to prepare for the entrance examination to the Ecole des Beaux-Arts, but as he told me later: "I hardly worked and soon began to stand on my own feet. . . . I spent my days in the Louvre and then in the country, where, between bicycling and canoeing expeditions, I would happily paint the landscape with *père* Jacomin—an old friend of Cézanne's—and his sons. But I was obsessed with the Louvre, and never let a day pass without going there. One day . . . I was amazed to see a copyist working on Uccello's *Battle* in the Primitives' room . . . it was my friend Linaret. . . . One might say that he was transposing. . . . The horses were Veronese green, the standards black, the men pure vermilion. . . . We immediately exchanged our ideas about painting and found that they had much in common. . . . Soon after, I met Matisse at the Académie Camillo in the Rue de Rennes."

Thus from the outset Derain was faced with the dilemma that was to confront him for the rest of his life. His athletic temperament encouraged him to break with the rules of a tradition to which in other ways he felt deeply attracted. His desire for emancipation was fostered at this time by his recent friendship with Vlaminck, another inhabitant of Chatou. In October, 1900, they began working together frequently in a ramshackle building, a former restaurant, which they had rented near the bridge. They had long discussions, visited exhibitions, made plans both literary and artistic, and Derain illustrated his friend's books. He continued a voluminous correspondence with Vlaminck during the three frustrating years of his military service.

On his return, he started painting again with great zeal, turned to Cézanne and Neo-Impressionism, frequented the banks of the Seine with Vlaminck, and renewed his friendship with Matisse. He worked with such diligence that he was able to exhibit at the Indépendants for the first time in 1905. Vollard had already bought his works.

His zeal grows even more intense during his long summer stay at Collioure, where the landscape, the light, and the presence of Matisse fill him with such enthusiasm that his feverish brushwork at first seems reminiscent of Van Gogh. Soon, however, he strives for greater stability, relying more on the advice of his companion and, like him, being deeply influenced by the works of Gauguin.

He admits in his letters to Vlaminck: "Everything I've done so far strikes me as senseless. . . . Just today I'm starting on the right track. . . . I'll come back with some real ideas about color and light. . . . I'll have done thirty or so studies by then. . . . I've never done such complex work, and so different that it may well baffle the critics." Several of his canvases were in fact, because of their richness of color, to be among the most striking features of the Fauves' room at the 1905 Salon d'Automne.

He also told Vlaminck that he was thinking a great deal about decorations and planning several large canvases. After an attempt that was still Pointillist in technique and rather confused in its composition, he finished this *Dance*, a still more ambitious and more successful painting. It crowns his efforts to date. Although Gauguin's influence is still evident in both the harmonies and the symbolism, a general concern with decoration and a strong theatrical sense already foreshadow the artist's brilliant future.

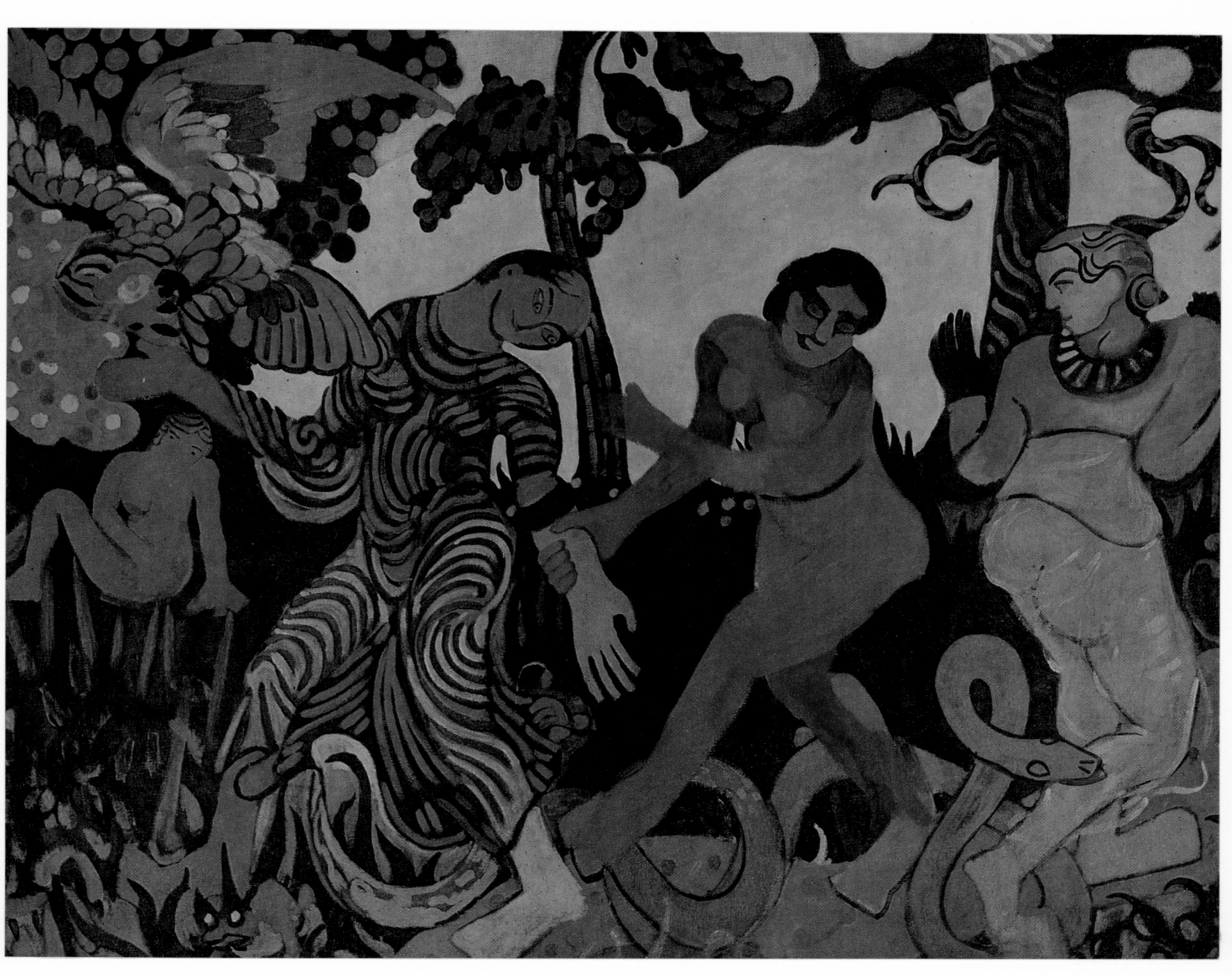

ANDRÉ DERAIN (1880–1954)

Painted in 1906
Big Ben
Oil on canvas, 31 1/8 × 33 7/8"
Collection Pierre Lévy, Troyes

At the beginning of 1906 Derain is a happy man, whose entry upon the artistic scene in the course of the previous year has been generously favored by destiny: a contract with Vollard, a good critical reception at the Indépendants, the formation of the Fauves group at the Salon d'Automne and its presentation by Berthe Weill in November. He is no doubt equally satisfied with the two large decorative canvases that he finished during the winter. He thus welcomes Vollard's suggestion that he go to London to try his hand at the themes that Monet has glorified just shortly before.

In a letter to Vlaminck written on his arrival in England early in March, he draws an almost philosophical conclusion from his experiences at Collioure with Matisse and, with his usual introspection, gives an excellent definition of the newborn Fauvist movement: "Our aim is happiness, which means a happiness of our own creation. There is a concrete form of happiness: this is serenity, certitude. . . . The main thing, then, is that I should keep my inner integrity, and my happiness is the birth of the universe that opens up to me."

With an amazing sense of inner fulfillment that was rather foreign to him, he takes an intense pleasure in everything that surrounds him. There is ample food here for his insatiable curiosity, and at twenty-six he is still filled with a ready enthusiasm that overflows in his correspondence with Vlaminck. On March 7 he writes: "A man all taken up with ordering his ideas is writing to you about painting, primarily in the conviction that we are on the right track. . . . I'm certain of this, I've seen Turner. . . . I'm rather moved by my sightseeing in London and my visits to the National Gallery, as well as the museum of Negro art. It's fantastic, wildly expressive. But there's a double reason for this surplus of expression: these are forms conceived in the open, in broad daylight, and they have to be seen in broad daylight. . . . The Thames is huge. . . ."

More vividly than in words, he expresses this feeling of euphoria, this passionate search for luminosity, this joyful quickening of his whole being, of his vitality, in a series of closely related paintings. Instinctively he reverts to the Pointillist technique which he had used so skillfully at Collioure, and which he had then tried to abandon, as he wrote to Vlaminck. But he introduces subtle variations, now using graduated colors with a play of different tones, now following Matisse's technique of violent contrasts to heighten the general harmony. This enables him to achieve astonishing light effects, such as the radiant sun whose reflections literally encompass the river in his *Sunset on the Water* (Musée de l'Annonciade, Saint-Tropez).

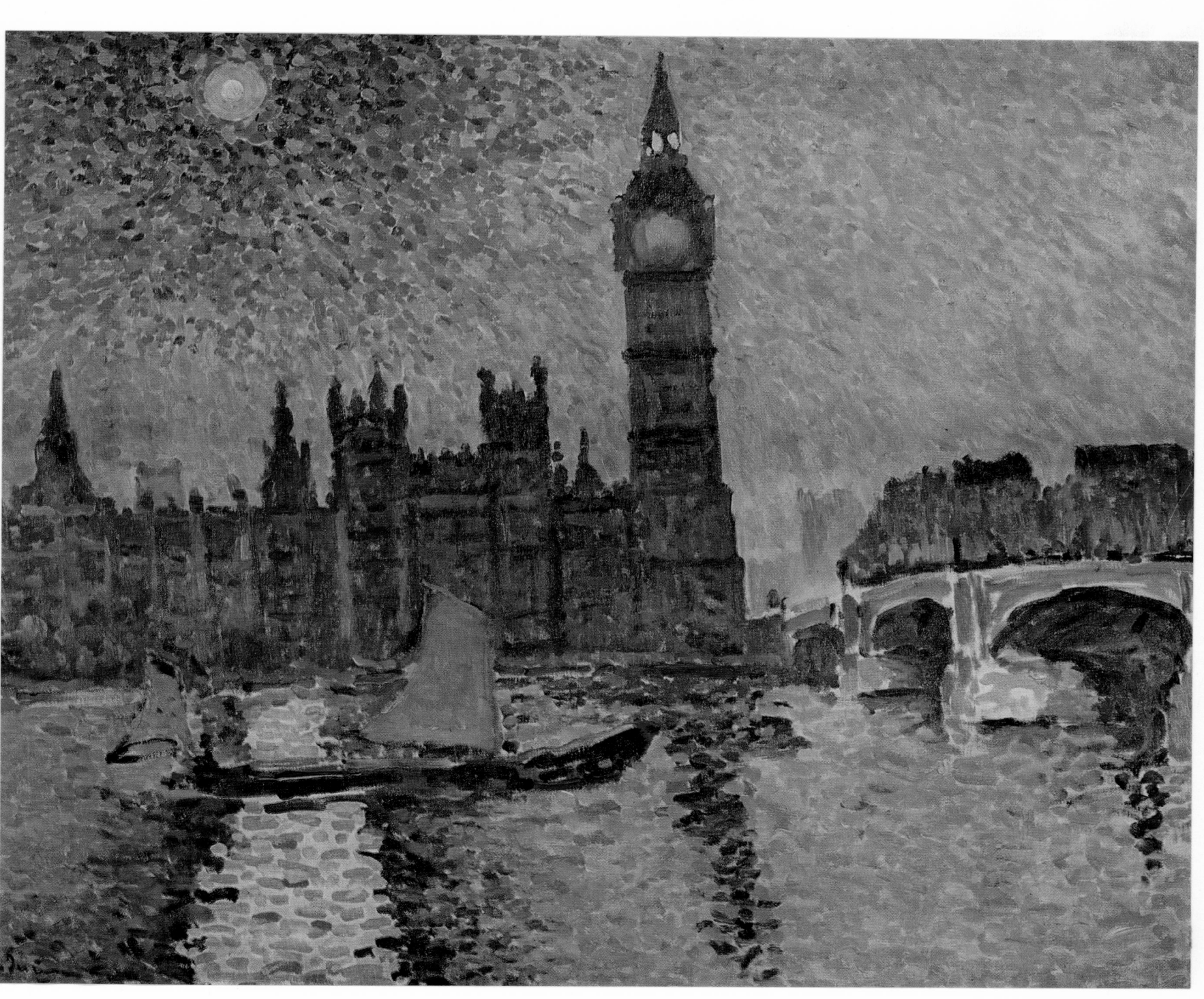

ANDRÉ DERAIN (1880–1954)

Painted in 1906
London Bridge
Oil on canvas, 26 × 39"
The Museum of Modern Art, New York City

Far from making use of his London experience as might be expected, Derain, constantly assailed by doubts, begins again to question his approach during his spring and summer stay at L'Estaque. As he confides to Vlaminck: "I'm quite at sea and I don't know what I'll be bringing back. . . . Yet I feel I'm moving toward something better, where the picturesque elements should be less important than last year. . . . Unless one's approach is a decorative one, the only possible course is increasingly to purify this transposition of nature. So far we have done this deliberately only for color. The same applies to design. . . . In short, I see a future only in composition. . . . I think the problem lies rather in grouping the forms in light and in harmonizing them at the same time with the paint."

Through a process of development similar to that which Matisse had followed earlier, and under the influence of the latter's famous *Joy of Life* (fig. 25), which had been exhibited at the Indépendants in 1906, Derain reached identical conclusions and paid increasing attention to the general composition. In the Provençal setting his thoughts turn to Cézanne and still more to Gauguin, whose memory has haunted him since Collioure. While preserving his happy, expansive lyricism, he subjects his landscapes to a severe construction that encloses and limits his usual vibrant colors. This is to be seen in a series of fine canvases, executed in almost the same spot, that he was to show at the next Salon d'Automne: *L'Estaque* (fig. 28), *Bridge over the Riou*, *The Three Big Trees*, and *The Jetty*.

The paintings that he did on his return to London at the end of the summer seem very different from his earlier pictures and share this new constructive and decorative spirit: *Westminster Bridge* (Collection Kaganovitch, Paris), which he exhibited at the Salon d'Automne beside his L'Estaque landscapes, *Hyde Park* (Collection Pierre Lévy, Troyes), *The Pool of London* (The Tate Gallery, London), and this *London Bridge*. The forms stand out boldly through the use of marked contrasts. Except for the surface of the water, where the divided brushstrokes evoke a luminous shimmer, the color is applied in strongly outlined areas in which broad curves contrast with powerful verticals.

This dense, vigorous, rather tense style, these more diversified ranges of color where the grays and earth colors are discreetly introduced, this expressive intensity, are to be found in other works subsequently painted in Paris, and show the direction in which Derain was about to move.

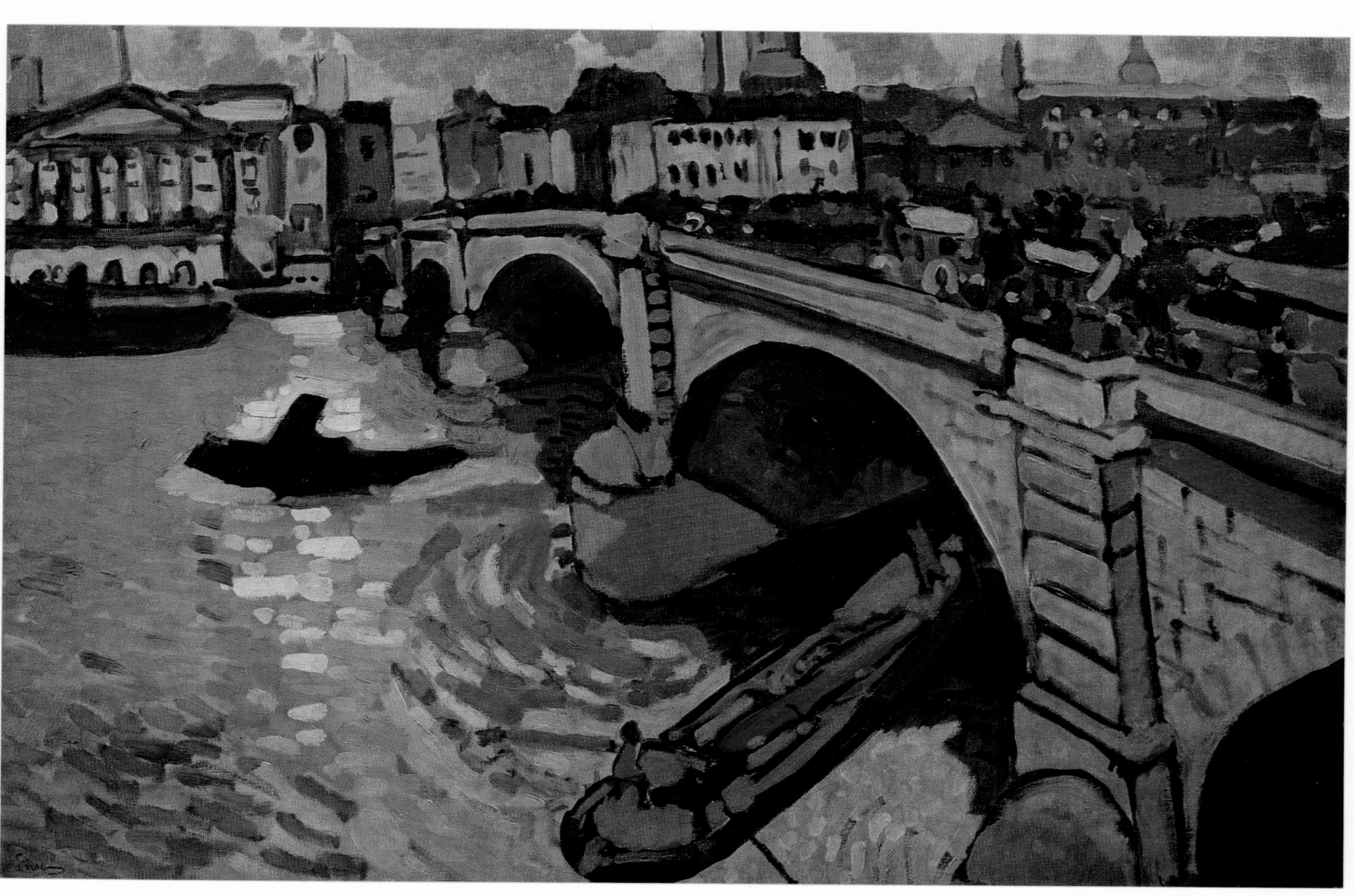

ANDRÉ DERAIN (1880–1954)

Painted in 1907
Seascape
Oil on canvas, 14 1/2 × 17 3/4″
Private collection, Brussels

The year 1907 is a crucial one for Derain, both in the profound changes that take place in his ideas and his work, and in the pioneering role he is now called on to play.

By showing a painting on the *Bathers* theme at the Indépendants and by taking it up again for his decorations executed with the ceramist André Metthey (fig. 65), he already anticipates the tribute paid to Cézanne at the next Salon d'Automne, where most of his friends first discover the old master's importance. Derain's inquiring spirit leads him still further, and as early as 1906 his desire for almost geometrical construction is apparent in a small *Provençal Landscape*, which for once he dates, and in other canvases painted during the winter.

It is not by chance that at this time he becomes involved with the Bateau Lavoir group, where similar experiments are being carried out by Picasso, with whom he spends the late summer in Avignon, or that Kahnweiler offers him a contract at his new gallery.

Although, when on the shores of the Mediterranean, he sometimes partially abandons the rigor that he prizes so much in favor of a rich, enameled flow of color whose vibration he heightens as he likes, as in this *Seascape*, he still turns increasingly toward serenity and the simplification of forms. While working at Cassis, he repeats in a letter to Vlaminck: "There's a lot to be done in painting by proceeding with design as we have done so far with color." He undoubtedly envies Matisse—who has come to spend a few days with him before and after his Italian journey—that natural tendency to happiness which seems to elude him. But he is already turning away from the very spirit of Fauvism and mocks at his colleagues Friesz and Braque for wishing to persevere in that direction: "They'll think better of it; there are other things to do than that."

This schematism that triumphs in his work, even in the woodcuts that he shows at the Salon d'Automne of 1907, and the austerity of his colors make him a true pioneer of Cubism. He becomes increasingly involved in the new movement, working at Carrières-Saint-Denis with Braque in 1909, and at Cadaquès with Picasso in 1910. His friends, headed by Apollinaire, classify him as a Cubist.

He abandons them before long, however, to return to the form of representation most stirring to his eyes, that of the Primitives, aspiring, as he says, "to what is fixed and eternal."

Only a few years before he died, to justify his volte-face toward the past, this early return to classicism, he explained to me: "You have to submit to the demands of your heritage . . . It is in museums that the mind is initiated. . . . Art is still and will always be the memory of generations."

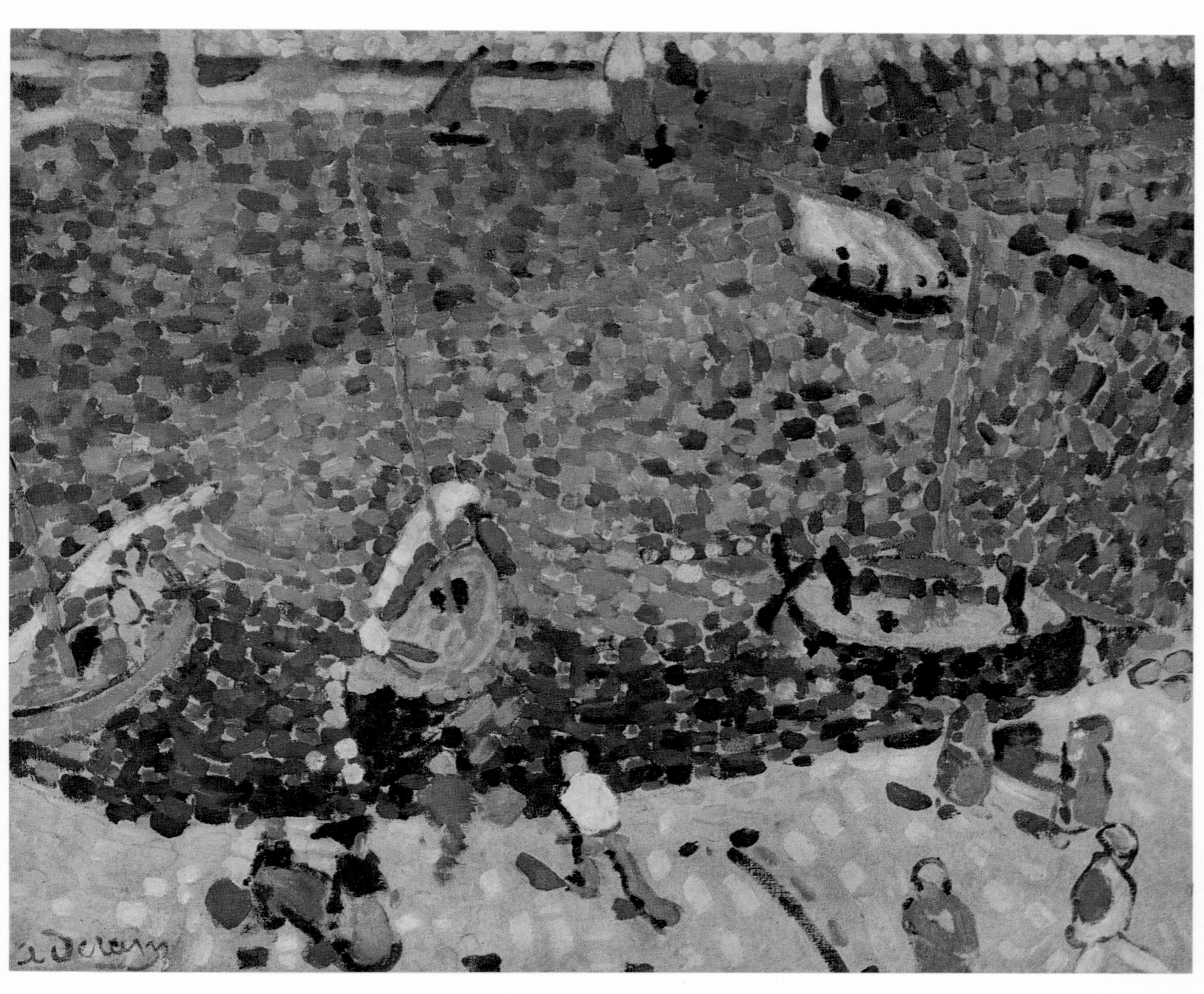

GEORGES BRAQUE (1882–1963)

Painted in 1906
Landscape at L'Estaque
Oil on canvas, 14 1/2 × 18 1/8"
Private collection, Paris

Braque was born at Argenteuil on May 13, 1882, and spent his boyhood at Le Havre, where his family settled in 1890. He left the lycée two years before finishing his studies in order to enroll at the Ecole des Beaux-Arts, where he met Friesz and Dufy, his seniors. His father, a building contractor and Sunday painter, encouraged him in his vocation, although he tried to persuade him to join him in his business in 1899. After a year's military service at Le Havre, he settled permanently in Paris in 1902, taking lodgings in Montmartre, attending the Batignolles evening classes, and then enrolling at the Beaux-Arts, in Bonnat's studio.

Here he has the companionship of his friends from Le Havre, but he nonetheless soon transfers to the Académie Humbert. He makes copies in the Louvre, is attracted by the Impressionists, whose exhibitions he visits in the Rue de la Boétie, and begins to study the flute with Dufy's brother. In 1905 he moves into a proper studio in the Rue d'Orsel and makes the acquaintance of Apollinaire, Picasso, Max Jacob, and the Butte circle, while continuing to lead a calm, balanced, and rather secluded life.

In 1906 he exhibits a number of fresh, sensitive, but still rather conventional canvases at the Indépendants. Then, during a summer stay in Antwerp, where he and Friesz paint together in an old dilapidated building facing the Schelde River, his friend initiates him into the Fauvist manner. Delighted with this new technique, which allows him to express himself with joy and freedom, Braque, long haunted by the memory of Cézanne, goes to spend the autumn at L'Estaque.

Many years later he gave me a frank explanation of his attitude: "For me Fauvism was a momentary adventure in which I became involved because I was young. You see, willy-nilly, one belongs to one's time. There's no question of originality. I was freed from the studios, only twenty-four, and full of enthusiasm. I moved toward what for me represented novelty and joy, toward Fauvism. It was in the South of France that I first felt truly elated. Just think, I had only recently left the dark, dismal Paris studios where they still painted with pitch! What a joyful revelation I had there!"

His first paintings of L'Estaque, such as this one, are more successful than his Schelde canvases—for example, *Le Port d'Anvers* (Antwerp Harbor) in The National Gallery of Canada, Ottawa (fig. 7)—which are still diluted and timid despite their well-ordered compositions. The Estaque pictures give a lighthearted impression through the scattering of iridescent splashes of rainbow color which Braque borrowed from Pointillism and already applies with a consummate knowledge of tonal relationships and the play of the brush.

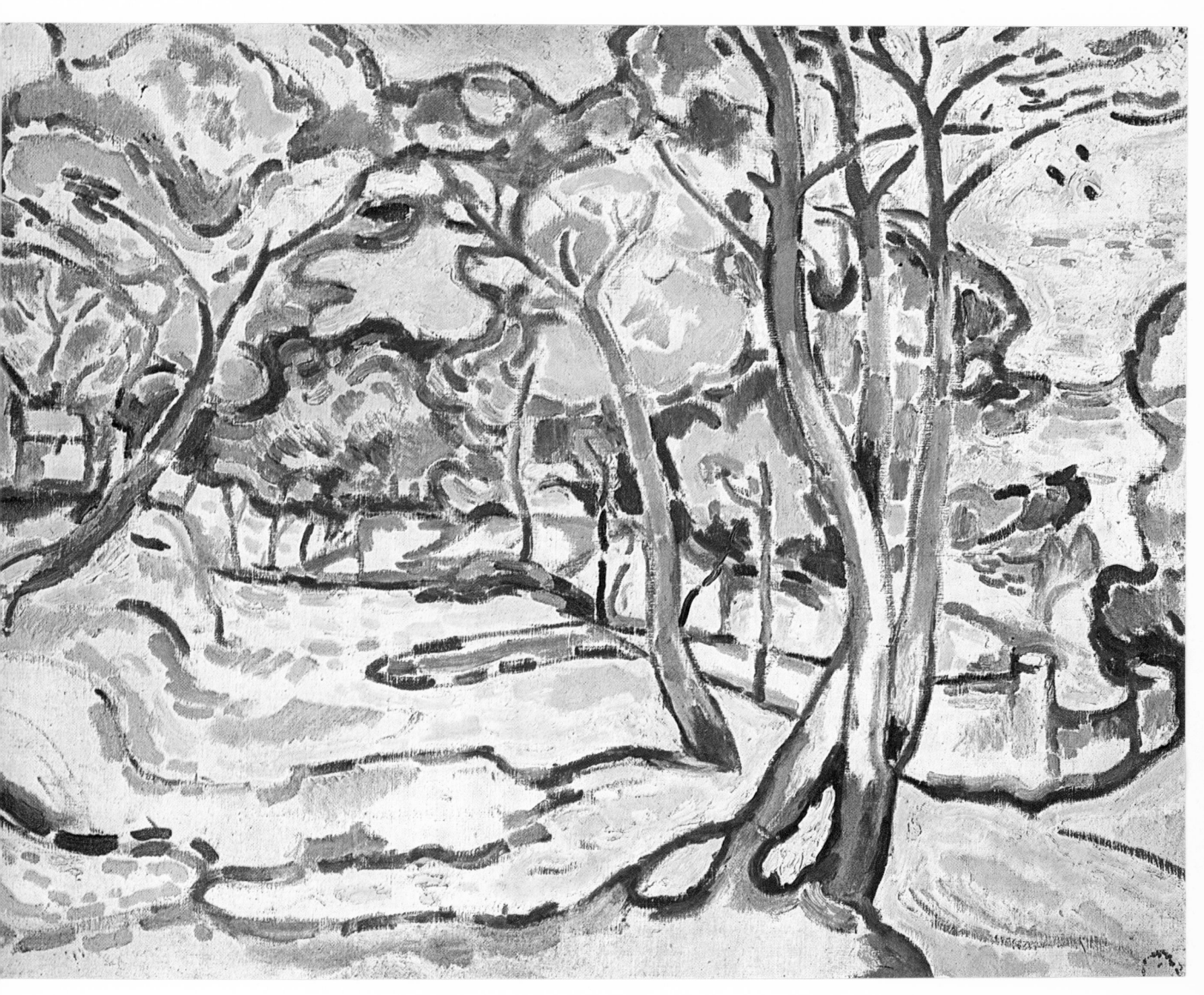

GEORGES BRAQUE (1882–1963)

Painted in 1907
Landscape at La Ciotat
Oil on canvas, 19 5/8 × 24"
Private collection, Paris

Fortified by his solitary work at L'Estaque and by the sense of delight that he experienced there, Braque returns to Paris in time to take part in the Indépendants of 1907, which affords him further satisfactions. First of all, it gives him the opportunity to meet Matisse, who strongly encourages him to continue on the course that he has adopted. Of the six paintings that he shows, only one evokes his visit to Antwerp. The others were painted in the South of France with the unexpected fervor that he felt at the sight of the landscape bathed in light and sun. The press, Vauxcelles in the lead, pays little attention to his contribution in the midst of the 5,406 works exhibited that year, but the discerning eye of the critic and dealer Wilhelm Uhde, interested at the time in Gauguin and the Fauves, immediately notices the unknown young artist's paintings. He buys five of them for the modest sum of 505 francs, as the receipt kept by Braque testifies. The sixth painting is bought by another painter, Axilette, who in his turn becomes a devotee of Fauvism.

Years later Braque recalled these events, which had given him such pleasure: "It was a great time," he told me, "so different from everything that came afterward. I've always had happy memories of it. You should have seen the spirit that reigned at the Indépendants then, it was quite unique, for all those who exhibited there couldn't show anywhere else. And yet they were all perfectly disinterested, without a trace of jealousy, and their only wish was to paint and to do what they wanted. Nothing daunted them!"

In the spring, full of impatient enthusiasm, his hopes for the future encouraged by his recent success, Braque sets out once more for the Mediterranean coast, where he decides to stay at La Ciotat. Far from letting himself be carried away, however, he remains true to his temperament by making a careful and deliberate study of the technical possibilities relating to the treatment and harmony of his pictures.

As can be seen from this landscape, he still retains the Pointillist manner while imparting to it a new breadth and flexibility. He diversifies his brushwork, sometimes lengthening it and spacing it out so as to take advantage of the white background of the canvas, at other times concentrating it in order to establish the foreground and the general shapes, which really constitute discreetly modulated flat areas.

His color undergoes a parallel development, being at times fluid and airy, at times almost oriental in its extreme richness and saturation, as in this picture. Yet it is always vibrant, varied, and almost pearly, to use Apollinaire's word, and invariably produces an enticing impression of carefree enchantment without ever falling into the least excess.

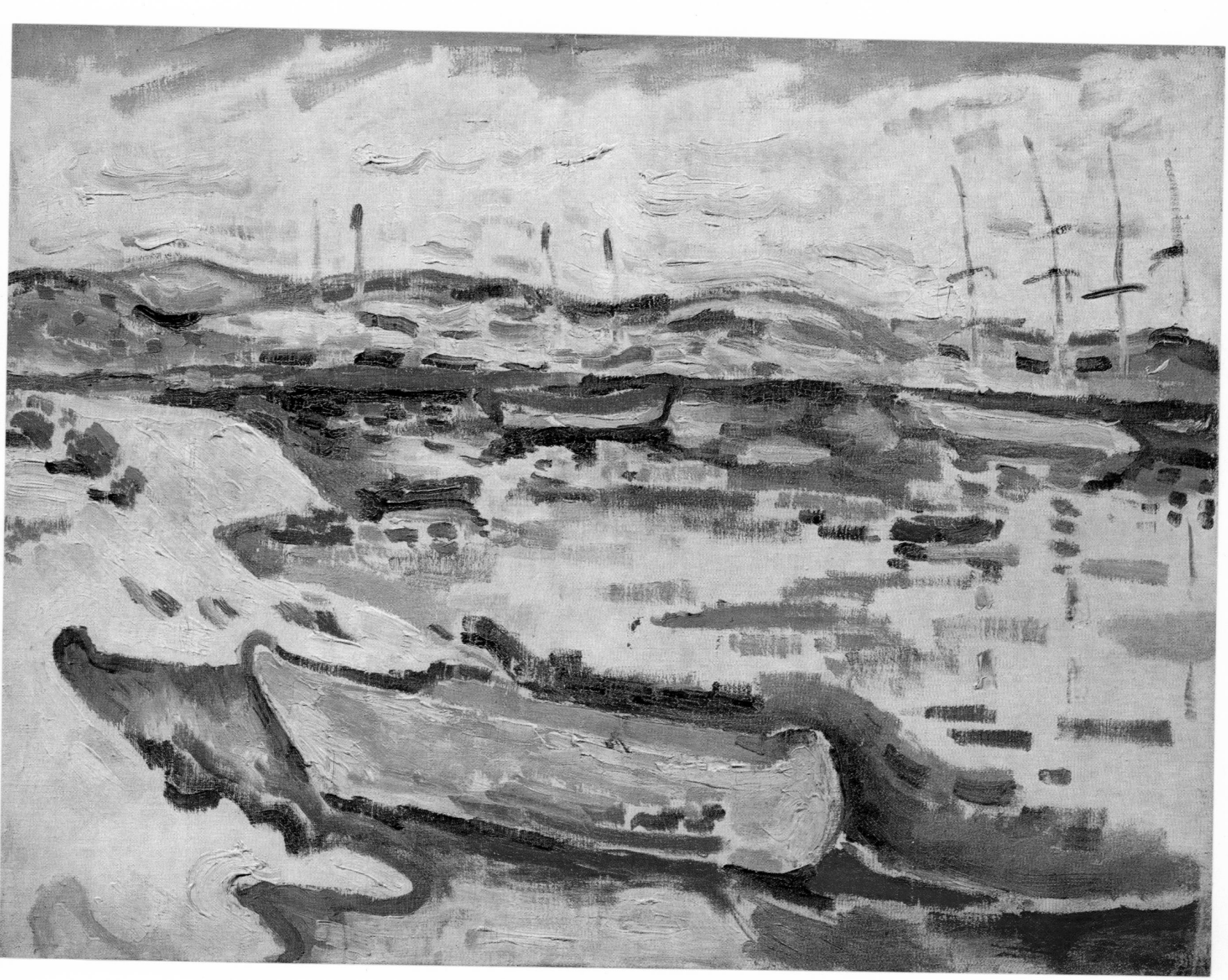

GEORGES BRAQUE (1882–1963)

Painted in 1907
Landscape at La Ciotat
Oil on canvas, 23 1/4 × 28 3/8"
Collection Mr. and Mrs. Leigh B. Block, Chicago

As he had done the year before, Friesz works with Braque during the summer of 1907. The two friends carry on a stimulating exchange of opinions, each trying to outdo the other in his enthusiasm.

Won over both by the majestic beauty of the landscape and by his companion's infectious eloquence, Braque is filled with a growing lyricism. He heightens his tonalities and rhythms, uses flat areas of color, accentuates his arabesques with colored outlines, and animates every surface with a magic iridescence. Yet, as this landscape shows, he retains his lucid self-control, seeking subtle harmonies through effective gradations of values and skillfully combining unusual, exquisitely delicate tones—mauves, light cadmiums, soft blues that are already highly individual—with the richest oranges and cobalts. The surge that lifts the whole composition is nonetheless a peaceful one, and to accentuate the effect of general balance, Braque is already careful to stress the ordering and distribution of the masses and the spacing of the architectural elements.

Although he now has his place among the Fauves and is on friendly terms with the whole group, he shows a certain reserve and sends only one painting to the 1907 Salon d'Automne, and four works—of which one, *The Small Valley*, already belongs to Kahnweiler—to the Indépendants of 1908. He takes no part in the shows at Berthe Weill's.

Deeply impressed by the Cézanne retrospective—an artist whom he had always admired —at the previous Salon d'Automne, he increasingly follows his natural bent for schematic and Constructivist composition, at the cost of sacrificing his most vibrant colors. This change is noted by Vauxcelles, who denounces him violently.

Thus he is hardly in the movement before being dismissed, and is fully aware of the discrepancies that have so quickly arisen. As he later explained: "I went back to La Ciotat, but I had changed. Painting is a perpetual adventure that, like life, can never stand still and cannot be judged in an attitude. This call, however passionate, no longer satisfied me. I was beginning to look more deeply. It was then—in 1908—that my four paintings were refused at the Salon d'Automne. Marquet tried to salvage one of them, but I decided to withdraw them all. I had left Fauvism for a more personal path. But that brings us to the history of Cubism."

And in fact the show, introduced by Apollinaire, that he was soon to present at the Kahnweiler Gallery inaugurates a new trend, initiated and headed by himself and Picasso. Yet here again his painful wartime experiences will cause him to abandon a position that might well have become too doctrinal. He instinctively returns to the path of free creation, which enables him to give masterly expression to his fervent appreciation of the humble spectacle of life, for the rest of his days.

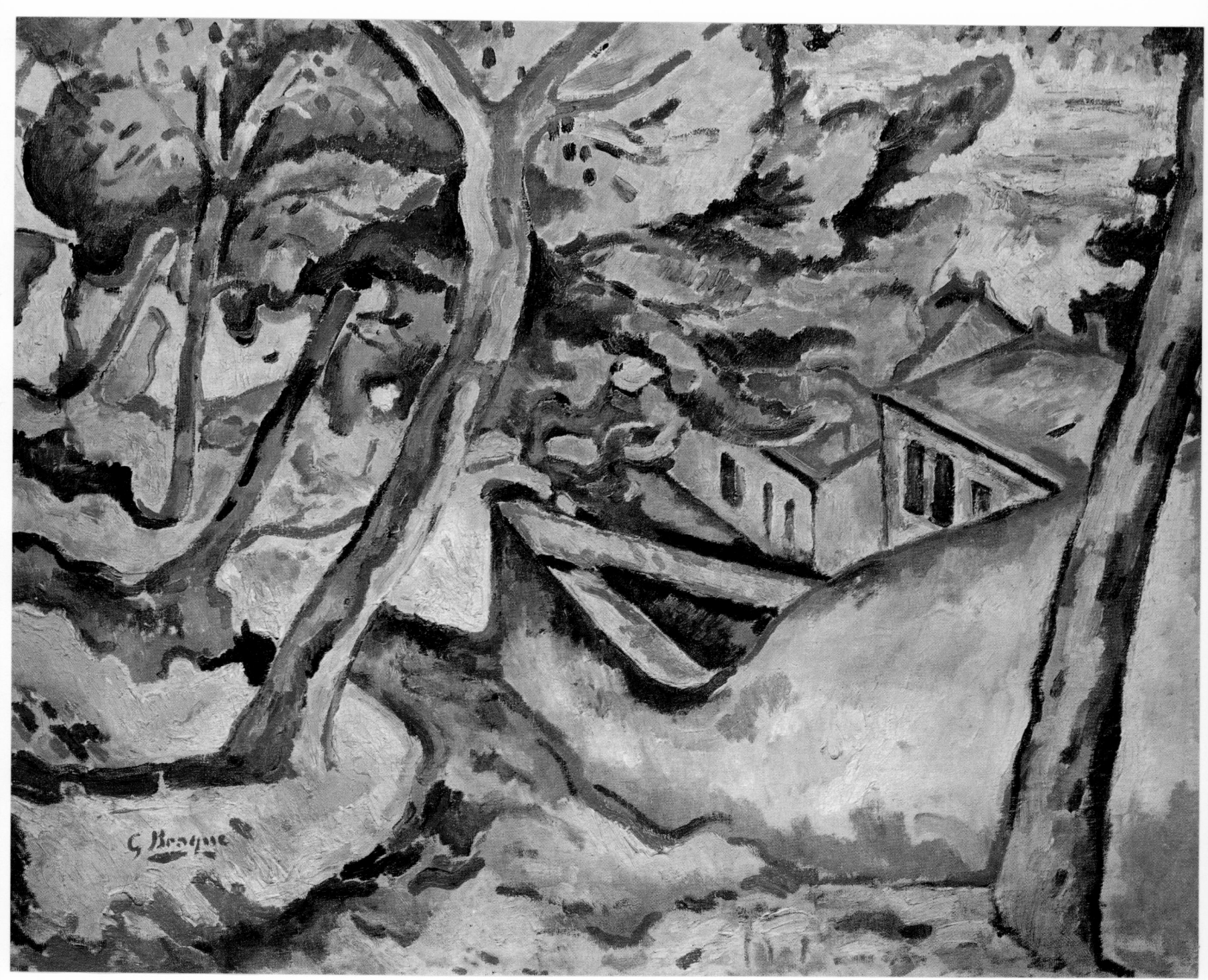

MAURICE MARINOT (1882–1959)

Painted in 1906
Interior
Oil on canvas, 36 5/8 × 28 3/4"
Collection Pierre Lévy, Troyes

Marinot was born in Troyes in 1882. On completing his studies, he went to Paris in 1901, and entered the Ecole des Beaux-Arts as a pupil of Cormon, but was soon dismissed as a "dangerous nonconformist." He finished his training by going to art galleries, where Gauguin and especially Cézanne aroused his enthusiasm.

In 1905 he begins to show his work, sending eight paintings to the Indépendants, including two female studies and two views of Notre Dame. His two canvases at the Salon d'Automne are hung in Room XV next to those of Valtat, Biette, Jawlensky, and Kandinsky; Vauxcelles, in his review, makes fun of the still life, noting that "the roundness of the apples is polyhedral."

As though in answer to this poor joke, Marinot's eight entries at the 1906 Indépendants include four still lifes, and he has the satisfaction of seeing the eight canvases that he submits to the Salon d'Automne—four interiors, three bouquets of flowers, and one still life —placed in Room III, where they are quite in keeping with the Fauves. Undaunted, Vauxcelles shoots another dart: "Wild flowers painted in genuine fashion in flat colors with all the crudeness of wallpaper but also a certain sincerity."

To be thus included officially among the Fauves, without having sought it and when the movement was at its peak, shows that his fellow artists were well aware of his merits. If we are to judge by this work, which figured prominently among his six canvases at the Indépendants in 1907, Marinot possessed all the necessary qualities, with his rich colors and luminous effects, the disciplined sobriety of his composition tempered here by the spots of color on the walls, and the bracing feeling that the picture conveys.

His *Woman's Head* (Musée des Beaux-Arts, Liège) of 1905, with its bold and vigorous accents, as well as his *Woman Nursing* (Musée National d'Art Moderne, Paris) of 1907, with its more detailed construction and interesting use of downward perspective, demonstrate that it was not an isolated experiment that he had undertaken, but deliberate and sustained work.

Unfortunately Marinot, living always in Troyes, in the Rue Bégaud, and rarely going to Paris, is unable to follow up his initial success. He remains isolated from his friends, confining himself rather too much to this no doubt favorite theme, which he repeats at every Salon.

When the group disbands, he turns to the technique of glass blowing, and from 1911 to 1938, when his glass-works at Bar-sur-Aube closes down, produces those masterpieces in the "incandescent medium" that were to make him famous. Returning once more to painting, he has the misfortune of seeing his studio in Troyes totally destroyed in 1944. But his participation in the Fauvist movement, short as it was, has since assumed its place in history, and this was to be his final satisfaction before his death.

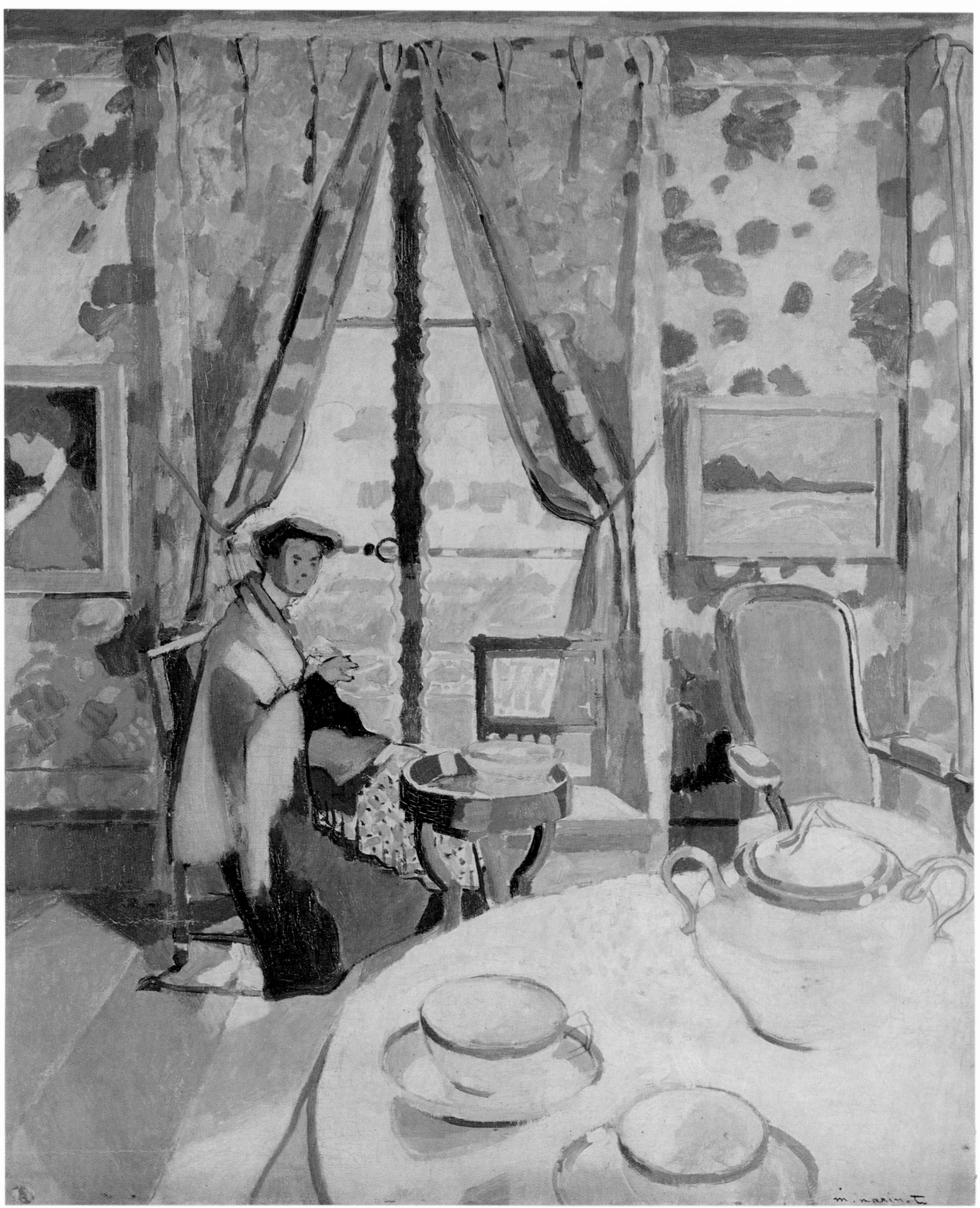

BÉLA CZÓBEL (b. 1883)

Painted in 1906
Man with a Straw Hat
Oil on canvas, 23 × 22 1/4"
Collection R. Stanley Johnson, Chicago

Czóbel was born on September 4, 1883, in Budapest of a well-to-do family. In 1901, immediately after graduating from high school, he entered the Nagybanya art school to study under Ivanyi-Grünwald, who imbued him with a spirit of innovation while allowing his personality to expand freely. The next year, following the established custom, he continues his studies at the Munich Academy under Herterich and Diez. Soon bored, he moves to Paris in the autumn of 1903 and enrolls at the Académie Julian. But he is chiefly absorbed by the Parisian atmosphere, where his exuberant vitality soon asserts itself.

Three of his paintings are accepted at the 1905 Salon d'Automne and immediately placed with the Fauves, and due to the confusion arising from his first name the critics speak of a female Van Gogh. He further establishes himself in 1906, exhibiting six paintings at the Indépendants and the same number at the Salon d'Automne. Vauxcelles hails his contribution in these terms: "What vehemence! This is Van Gogh, with careful proportions. A fine contralto with raucous tones."

This painting, dating from the same period, clearly reveals the high degree of maturity that he has reached despite his twenty-three years. The precision of its accents, skillfully distributed on face and background, conveys a joyful dynamism in a composition whose rigorous order is still more marked in *The Seated Man* (National Gallery, Budapest), with its emphasis on the floral designs of the carpet, in the manner of Matisse. The latter was in fact so impressed by the young artist's work that he had no difficulty in persuading Berthe Weill to organize a Czóbel exhibit in 1908, which thus established his eminent position in the Fauvist movement.

Every year Czóbel was in the habit of spending his holidays in Hungary. Already in the summer of 1906 his return caused a considerable stir among the artists of Nagybanya. Several of his seniors, as Istvan Reti reports, are shaken in their faith concerning *plein-air* naturalism. The younger artists are particularly enthusiastic about the new trends and decide to follow Czóbel to Paris.

Some of them will later constitute "The Eight" group, active in Budapest from 1909 onward and the pioneering element in Hungarian painting at the time.

Czóbel has continued until the present day to divide his time between his native country and Paris. Despite the severe damage inflicted on his works during the two world wars, the last living (and much neglected) patriarch of Fauvism still reveals, despite his age, a warm if slightly veiled lyricism that testifies to his fervent love of life and to the inexhaustible richness of his temperament.

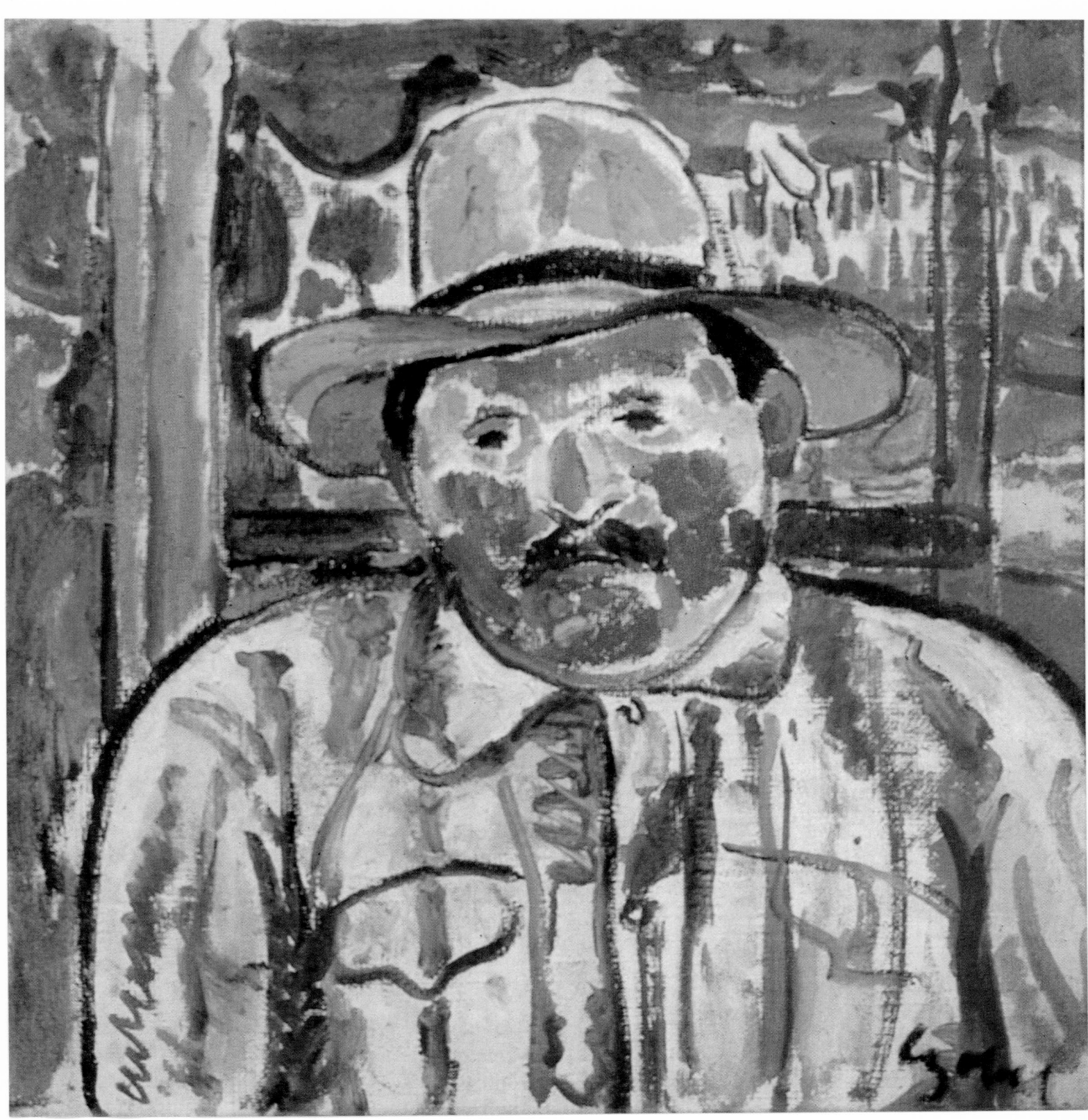

ROBERT DELAUNAY (1885–1941)

Painted in 1906
Self-Portrait
Oil on cardboard, 21 1/4 × 18 1/8"
Musée National d'Art Moderne, Paris

Because of the difference in age, it may seem arbitrary to include Delaunay in the Fauves' generation, yet he himself gave sufficient proof of his kinship to see his entry at the 1907 Indépendants placed in their room and to be incorporated forcibly into their ranks by Vauxcelles, grossly sarcastic about his extreme youth.

In 1904, at the age of nineteen, he begins to contribute regularly to the Indépendants, and in 1906 he is accepted at the Salon d'Automne, where at first he receives a cool welcome.

As this small picture shows, he lacks neither talent nor a deep determination, and this leads him, after some Pointillist experiments, to commit himself completely to a path that he will explore with passion. His series of self-portraits painted between 1905 and 1909 often resemble acts of faith in color, through which he achieves a play of luminous contrasts with almost intuitive skill. But parallel to his experiments on the decomposition of forms in space, which soon arrive at abstraction, he still continues for a long time to study the concentration of expression in faces through the vigorous alternation of complementary tones, as in his portraits of Massine, dated 1918, or those of Tzara of 1923, directly derived from the Fauve heritage.

More than his recourse to chromatic contrasts and modulated flat areas, the crusade that, through Orphism, he undertakes in favor of color, and which will have prolonged repercussions among his Blaue Reiter friends, reveals a spirit akin to many of the Fauves in the Dionysiac conception of his work and the radiant energy that he so admirably imparts to it.

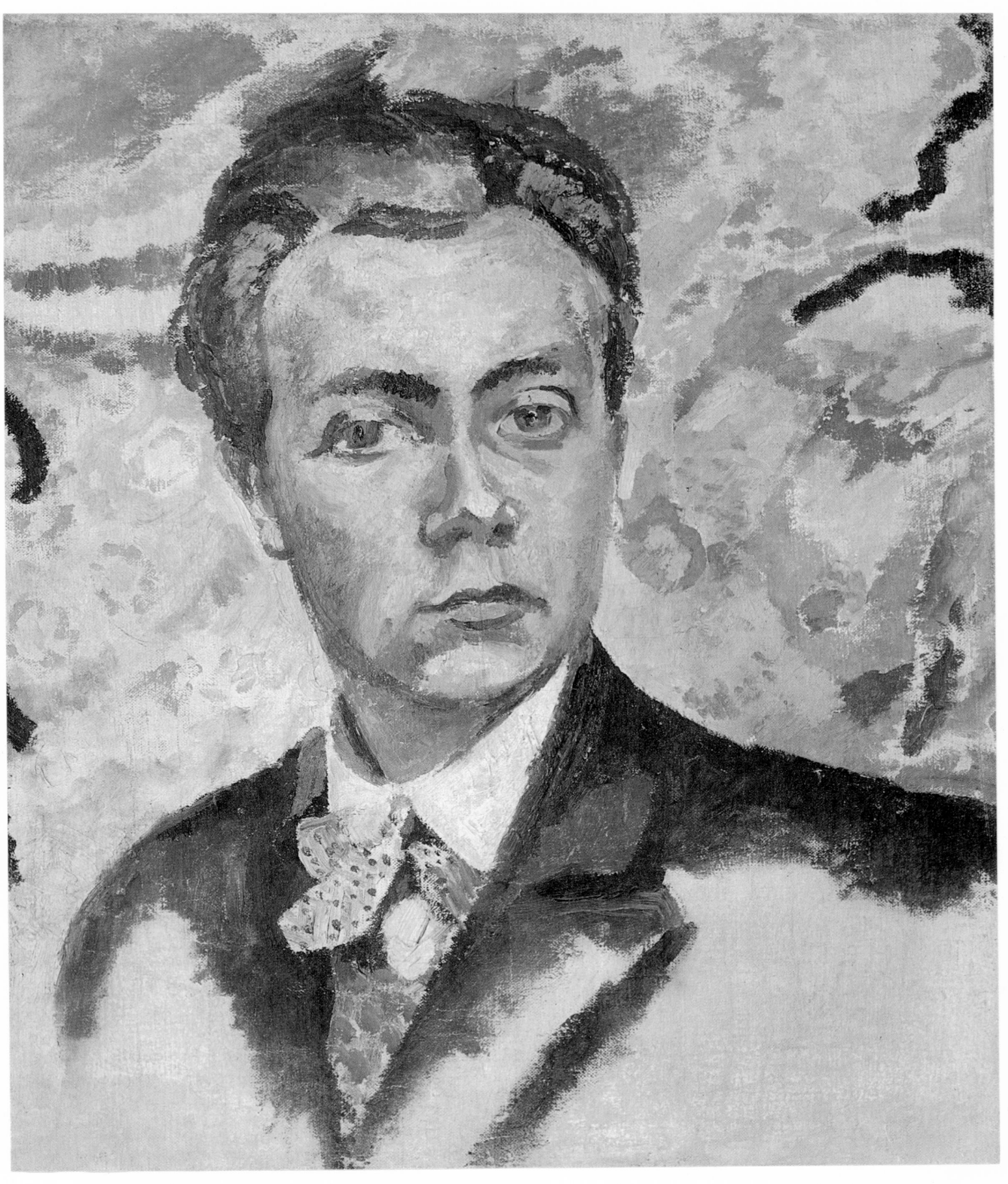

SONIA DELAUNAY-TERK (b. 1885)

Painted in 1907
Philomène
Oil on canvas, 36 1/4 × 21 1/4″
Collection the artist

Many factors justify the inclusion of Sonia Terk among the Fauves, even though at the time she never exhibited with the group at any of the Salons or galleries.

Very early in her career, during her two years of study at Karlsruhe and as soon as she arrives in Paris at the age of twenty—she was born in the Ukraine in 1885—she reveals a fervent admiration for Gauguin, which does not prevent her from asserting her own personality almost immediately. Through Wilhelm Uhde, who is to sponsor her first show and exhibits the Fauves in his gallery, she comes into contact with their work, from which she draws support for her own approach rather than direct inspiration.

The broad impastos that she is already using in 1905 soon extend to a series of powerful canvases partially inspired by a visit to Finland in 1906. The more numerous canvases painted in 1907 from different studies are particularly striking in their vigorous outlines, their simplification of form, and above all the density and variety of the flat areas of color. There is a remarkable tension linked to a knowledgeable chromatic register in which decorative effects are balanced and luminous contrasts heightened.

From this inner violence rises a solemn plainsong, majestic and ceremonial, that anticipates the triumphant burst of Simultaneism, with its remarkably ordered orchestrations of color, a few years later. Sonia Terk married Delaunay in 1910, and while her presence was to provide fruitful inspiration for him in his experiments, it never stopped her from enriching her own work by the simple lyrical magic of color.

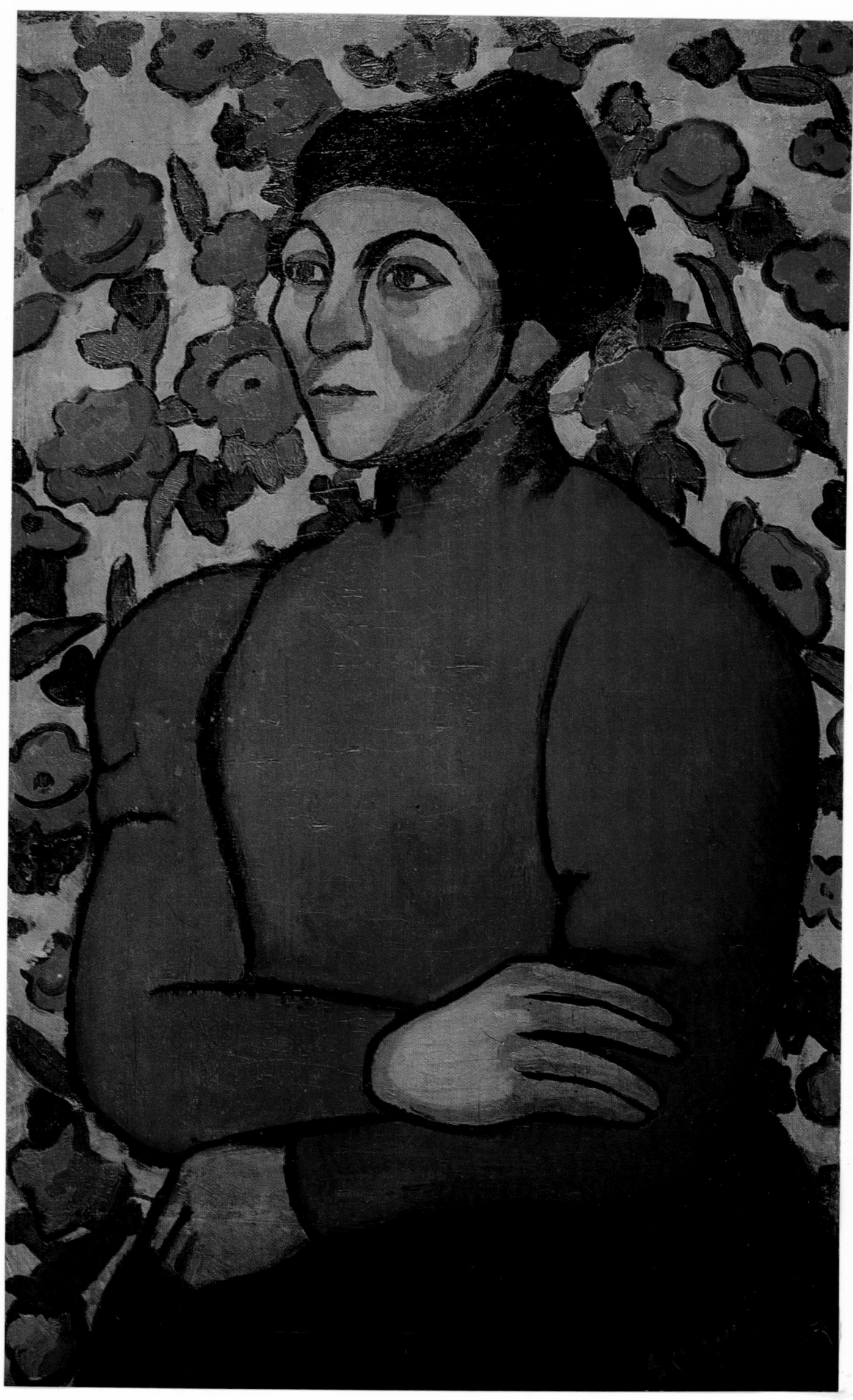

HANS PURRMANN (1880–1966)

Painted in 1912

Factory Landscape in Corsica

Oil on canvas, 19 5/8 × 23 1/2"

Wilhelm-Lehmbruck-Museum der Stadt, Duisburg

Purrmann must be placed in the front rank of the many artists who were the immediate and direct successors of Fauvism, for he was unquestionably Matisse's most assiduous and faithful disciple and friend.

Born at Speyer in 1880, he arrived in Paris in 1905 to continue the training begun and pursued at the Karlsruhe School of Fine Arts for two years and then in Munich under Hack and Stuck for a further five. He immediately joined a small group of former Munich inhabitants, including Walter Bondy and Rudolf Levy, who habitually gathered in Montparnasse at the Café du Dôme and so earned their historical appellation of the "Dômiers." At the end of the same year Will Howard, Weisgerber, and Pascin arrive, and as time goes on Ahlers-Hestermann, Nölken, Rosam, and Oskar and Greta Moll. Their ranks often include such writers and historians as Otto Ackermann, Klossowski, and Meier-Graefe, and art dealers such as Flechtheim and Uhde; Uhde at this time opens a gallery where he displays the works of Henri Rousseau and the Fauves. Most of the artists were already enthusiastic about the growth of Fauvism.

Through a fellow Dômier, the American Maurice Sterne, Purrmann had the good fortune to be introduced to the Steins in the Rue de Fleurus. They were collectors of Matisse's works, and through them he soon met the artist himself. To please Michael Stein's wife Sarah, who painted, Matisse agreed to give weekly advice in his studio to a small group of painters, including the Americans Patrick Bruce and Max Weber, the Swede Carl Palme, the Molls, and others. The news spread, and those who attended the Colarossi or La Grande Chaumière academies were eager to take advantage of Matisse's instruction. He had to leave the Rue de Sèvres for more spacious accommodations in the former convent of the Sacred Heart on the Boulevard des Invalides, and here, in October, 1908, he opened a real academy where Purrmann was at first the *massier*. Purrmann also accompanied his teacher on all his trips to Germany—to Munich and Nuremberg during the summer of 1908, to Berlin for his exhibition at Cassirer's during the winter of 1908–9, and to Munich with Weisgerber to visit the exhibition of Islamic art in 1910.

Unlike his companions, who do not hesitate to take part in the Salon d'Automne— Howard for the first time in 1907, Ahlers-Hestermann and Moll in 1908—Purrmann shows a cautious restraint and confines himself at this time to painting the portrait of the Academy model, Bibelacca. His real development begins in 1910, especially during his Mediterranean visit in 1912 to Collioure, Cassis, and Corsica with the Molls, as can be seen from this painting. Although still faithful to Matisse's teaching, he is able to introduce into his work a happy abandon, an all-pervading mellowness that he is never to lose. On many occasions after the war, both in his painting and his writings, he was to recall memories of this time, which had marked him and his friends so profoundly.

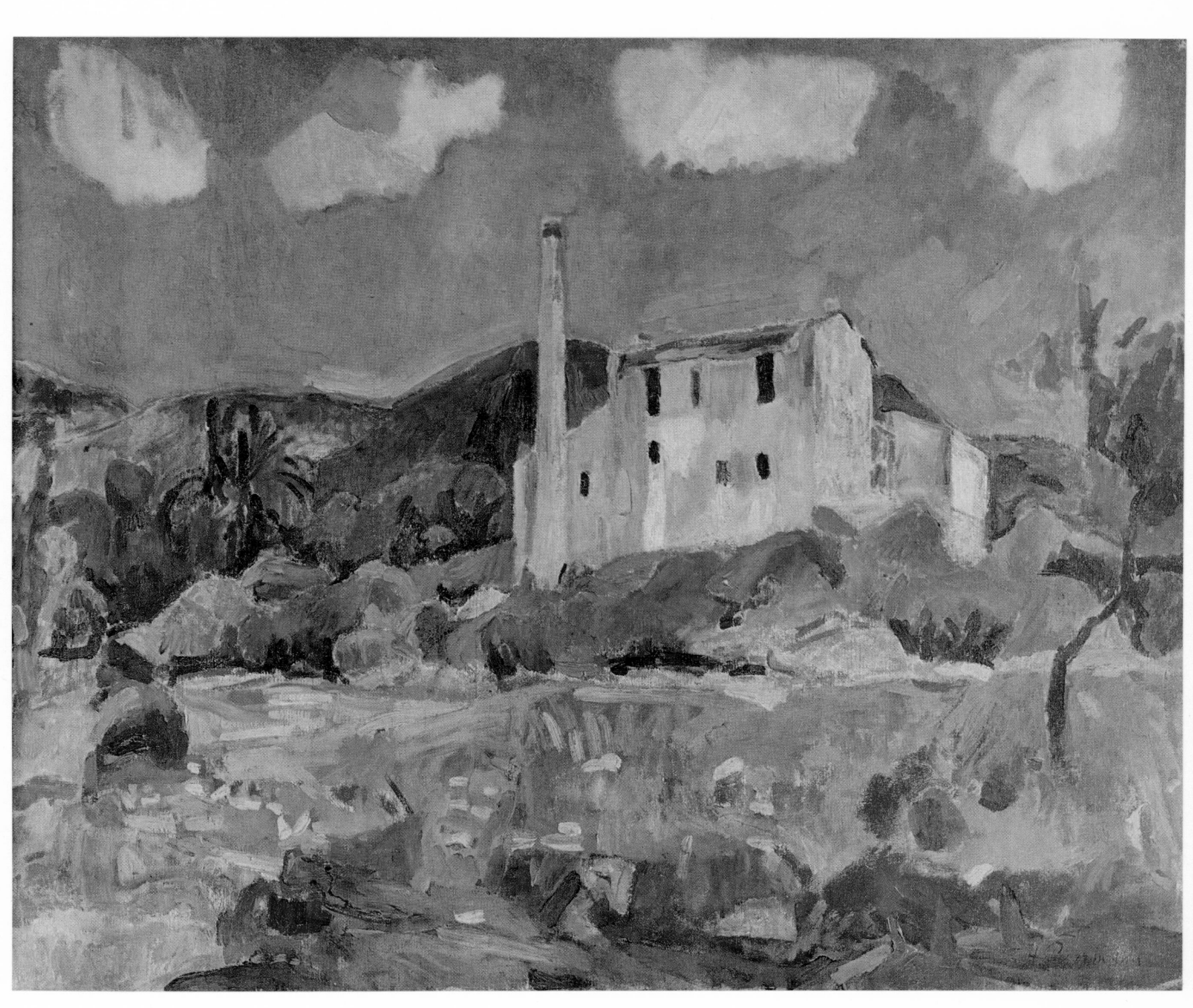

KARL SCHMIDT-ROTTLUFF (b. 1884)

Painted in 1910

The Doorway

Oil on canvas, 30 × 33″

Collection Dr. E. Schneider, Düsseldorf

The traditional antagonism that governed the relations between France and Germany before and after World War I long prevented any attempt at establishing contact between Fauvism and Expressionism, both parties professing ignorance of what was happening on the other side of the border despite the close and friendly relations that existed between many individual artists. Times have changed, and in recent years there have been many exhibitions in Munich and Paris offering the opportunity for comparisons.

Schmidt-Rottluff, born in 1884, still had a year of architectural studies to complete at the University Institute of Technology in Dresden when he joined Kirchner and Heckel to found Die Brücke in 1905. At first the young members of the group work in complete isolation, directing their instinctive revolt toward a return to medieval or primitive art sources, as shown by their first remarkable woodcuts, which follow the example of Munch. The addition of Emil Nolde and Cuno Amiet in 1906 was to bring them into contact with the outside world, while Max Pechstein, who has also joined them, eagerly sets out to visit Italy and France in 1907. Their exhibits at the Arnold Gallery, and their contacts with other artists, soon broaden their visions and conceptions, as the invitation extended to Van Dongen in 1908, to exhibit with them, bears witness.

Although he shares with his friends the same need for unrestrained subjectivity, the same almost painful elation, and the same cosmic feeling of existence, Schmidt-Rottluff is much less preoccupied by social and mystical problems, and being physically robust, he expresses himself outwardly with more directness. From his *Self-Portrait* of 1906, with its confused, feverish brushwork, to his well-composed and austere *Self-Portrait with a Monocle* of 1910, his rapid development leads to a relative equilibrium. His idiom, it is true, remains far removed from that of the Fauves because of its instinctive violence and strongly marked brutal accents, as we see by this painting. These differences of treatment are superficial, however, and he is often closer to them than it might seem. The intensity of color, too, gives his work a comforting human quality, a token of living communion with nature. The moment of fulfillment came for him especially after he settled in Berlin in 1911, when his works increasingly diverged from those of his friends, even if the ties between them persisted until the disbanding of the group in 1913 and well beyond.

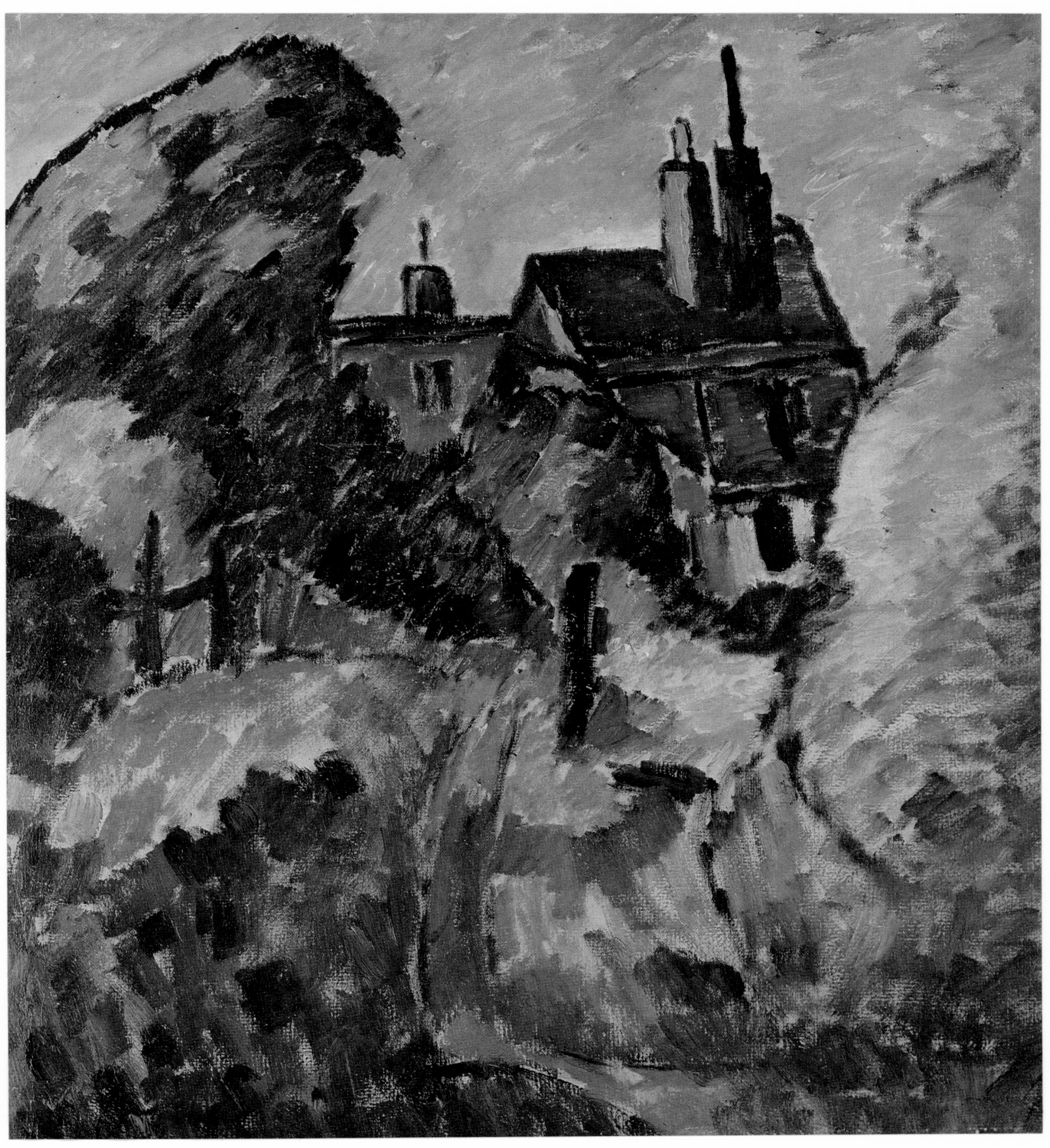

WASSILY KANDINSKY (1866–1944)

Painted in 1907
Landscape at Murnau
Oil on canvas, 26 3/8 × 37 3/8"
Collection Gustav Zumsteg, Zurich

The important role that Kandinsky was called upon to play after 1911 in the Blaue Reiter movement, especially in the birth and subsequent development of abstract art, has generally led scholars to minimize the significance of his temporary adherence to Fauvism, although it served as his point of departure. He himself was not sparing in his efforts in that direction, and always showed a particular interest in what was happening in France. After 1904 he began to exhibit regularly at the Salon d'Automne, and in 1907 intermittently at the Indépendants.

In that year he was able to witness the Fauves' success on the spot, living as he was in Sèvres, at 4 Petite Rue des Binelles, with Gabriele Münter, and submitting with his companion an impressive number of works to the Paris Salons: twenty to the 1906 Salon d'Automne, including nine paintings, four woodcuts, and some small decorative pieces, and six canvases to the Indépendants of 1907.

When he arrives in Paris, no longer in his first youth, he has scarcely embarked on his long career. Born in Moscow, at the age of thirty he had abandoned his profession as a lawyer and Russia itself in order to study painting in Munich with Azbe—through whom he was to meet Jawlensky—and then at the academy directed by Franz Stuck. Several of Monet's paintings exhibited in Munich influence his early efforts. Then, after directing an art school in 1902 and presiding over the group known as Die Phalanx, he visits Tunisia in 1903, Holland in 1904, and Italy in 1905. The memory of these journeys, especially of Tunis, is present in most of the oils and lithographs that he exhibits at the Salon d'Automne in 1905 and even in 1906. He experiences some difficulty in breaking away from his Impressionist technique of long strokes with the palette knife, which he still follows in his Parisian landscapes.

He is converted to Fauvism after the event, through a kind of romantic impulse, a need to dream that leads him to seek more freedom from the subject and greater expression and color. In the wilder setting of Murnau, where he spends the summer of 1907, his feelings of elation triumph, imposing their violent and simplifying rhythms, as can be seen from this painting. In the next couple of years, both in Munich and in Murnau, which he frequently revisits, a wave of joy invades his works, where the variegated colors are reminiscent of the peasant art motifs of his native country. These folk sources prove an inadequate source of inspiration, however, and in 1909 he abandons them for his *Improvisations*, which were in fact deeply thought out. Here he indulges freely in color fugues where, as in music, the half-glimpsed image serves as a pretext for a brilliant effusion, a true prelude to those visual incantations which will allow his creative spirit finally to impose itself and which will exercise a strong attraction on the painters assembled under his leadership in the Munich Neue Künstler Vereinigung.

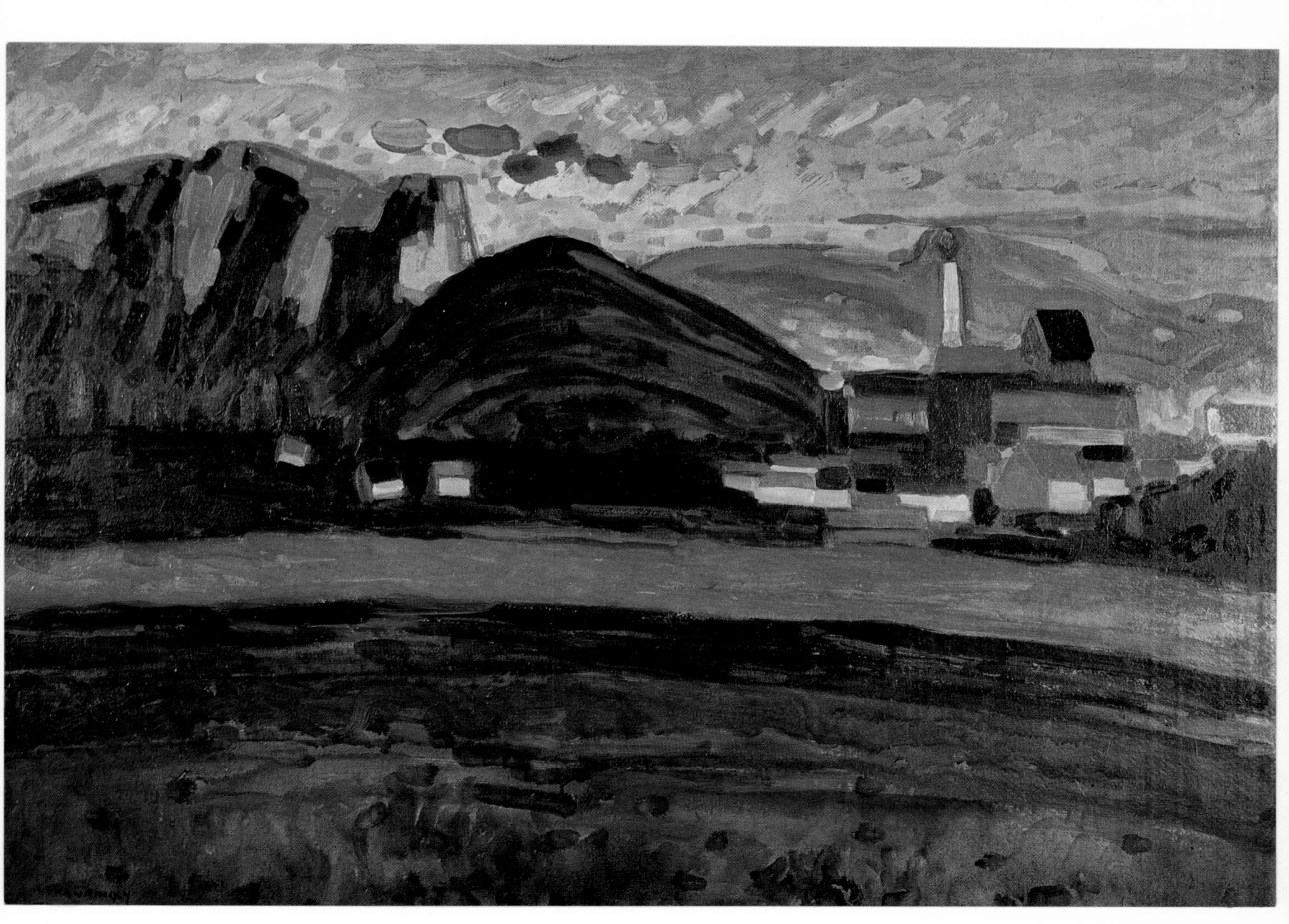

FRANTIŠEK KUPKA (1871–1957)

Painted in 1909
The Girl at Gallien
Oil on canvas, 41 1/2 × 39 3/8″
National Gallery, Prague

As in the case of Kandinsky, Kupka's subsequent development tends to make one forget the role, albeit marginal, that he played at the time of Fauvism. It is true that when he sends his first female figures, with their strong satirical note and their rather somber harmonies, to the Salon d'Automne of 1906, it never occurs to Vauxcelles to associate them in any way with the Fauves; noting Kupka's entries in Room XII, he exclaims with his usual irony: "Kupka has depicted three buxom gossips in a murky light, it could be Jordaens reworked by Jef Lombeaux!" If in his next experiments Kupka still clearly betrays his admiration for Toulouse-Lautrec and his penchant for caricature, which he has been practicing as a means of livelihood for several years, we can be sure that he does not set out on this path without serious reflection, since he pursues it until almost 1911, when he embarks with such assurance on abstraction.

Kupka was born in 1871 at Opocno in Bohemia, but settled in Paris in 1895, after studying at the School of Fine Arts in Prague and then in Vienna. He had taken an early interest in Impressionism, but so far had devoted himself to a kind of spiritual and intellectual quest, as well as to illustration work by turns scientific, poetic, and religious. Thus, painting comes in the beginning as rather a sideline that offers him a means of distraction from his somewhat esoteric preoccupations. This accounts for his outbursts of scathing humor and impetuous strokes, often taking on Expressionist characteristics.

Yet instead of following this course to the point of extreme distortion, Kupka quickly recovers himself, turning his attention more to problems of order and composition than to those of society. At the 1907 Salon d'Automne he presents a project for a mural.

He takes obvious pleasure in stressing the picturesqueness of street scenes and prostitutes, and continues to exploit these themes with increasing skill, as in this painting, bringing out the fullness of the well-defined forms and the variety of color in a way that is scarcely removed from Fauvism. These affinities grow even stronger in 1910 when he indulges in a mock simplicity, which he soon relinquishes, however, not being tempted by facile solutions. His approach nonetheless has a significant influence on his studio neighbor at Puteaux, Jacques Villon, and especially on the latter's brother Marcel Duchamp. By this time, however, Kupka has resolved to restore to both order and color their full spiritual power through the inspiration of music.

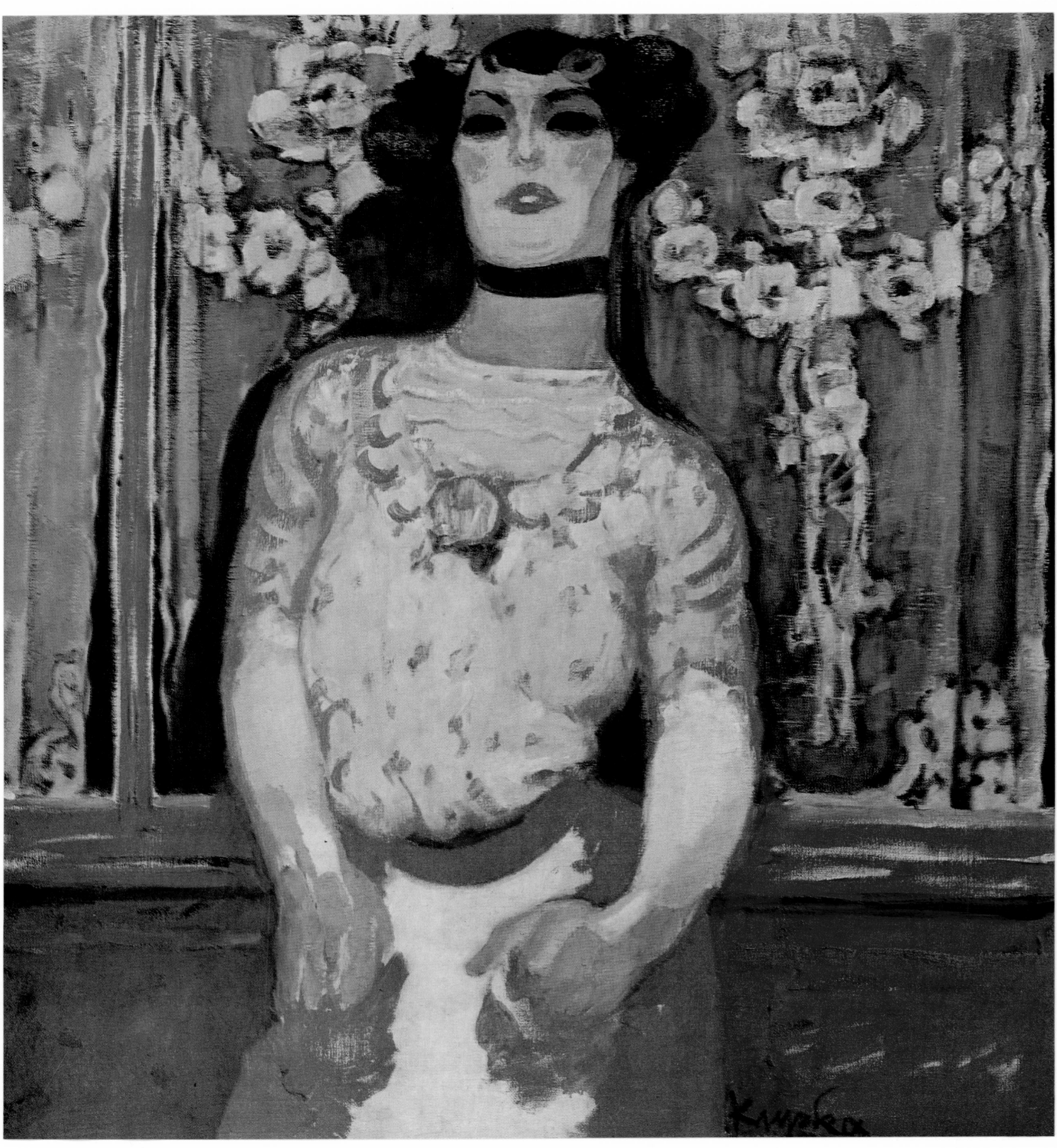

MATTHEW SMITH (1879–1959)

Painted in 1916
Nude, Fitzroy Street, No. 2
Oil on canvas, 41 3/4 × 30″
The Arts Council of Great Britain, London

Although Matthew Smith's affiliation with Fauvism was direct, it was more sentimental than real, since he arrived, so to speak, after the battle, and enrolled at the Académie Matisse just a month before it closed.

Smith was born in Halifax in 1879, and studied at the Manchester School of Art and the Slade School. For a long time his father, a collector of academic paintings, prevented him from going to France. When he finally obtained permission in 1908, it was with the strict proviso that he not go to Paris, and so the admiration that he already felt for Gauguin led him to work at Pont-Aven. When he was finally able to satisfy his desire at the end of 1910, it was too late. The general feeling in London was in fact hostile to French artistic movements, for it was not until 1905 that a large exhibition of Impressionist works had been held at the Grafton Galleries, which during the winter of 1910–11 was to present their successors under the general title of Post-Impressionists, while a nationalist reaction arose in the form of Vorticism.

Smith's vigorous temperament enabled him gradually to free himself from all impediments, and he received encouragement from Walter Sickert, a well-established exhibitor at the Salon d'Automne and frequenter of the Café du Dôme, who since 1911 had presided over the fate of the Camden Town Group, radically reorganized in 1913 to become the London Group, with Smith as one of its members. In 1914 Smith began to take up the Fauve legacy point by point, although he still kept a lingering taste for dark colors. As we can see in this painting, he was already a master of the art of connecting complementary colors and exploiting chromatic brilliance.

A patent sensuality ends by asserting itself in the texture as much as in the color. Electrifying reds reign supreme in works he painted by turns on both sides of the Channel, thus acting as a link between the two countries.

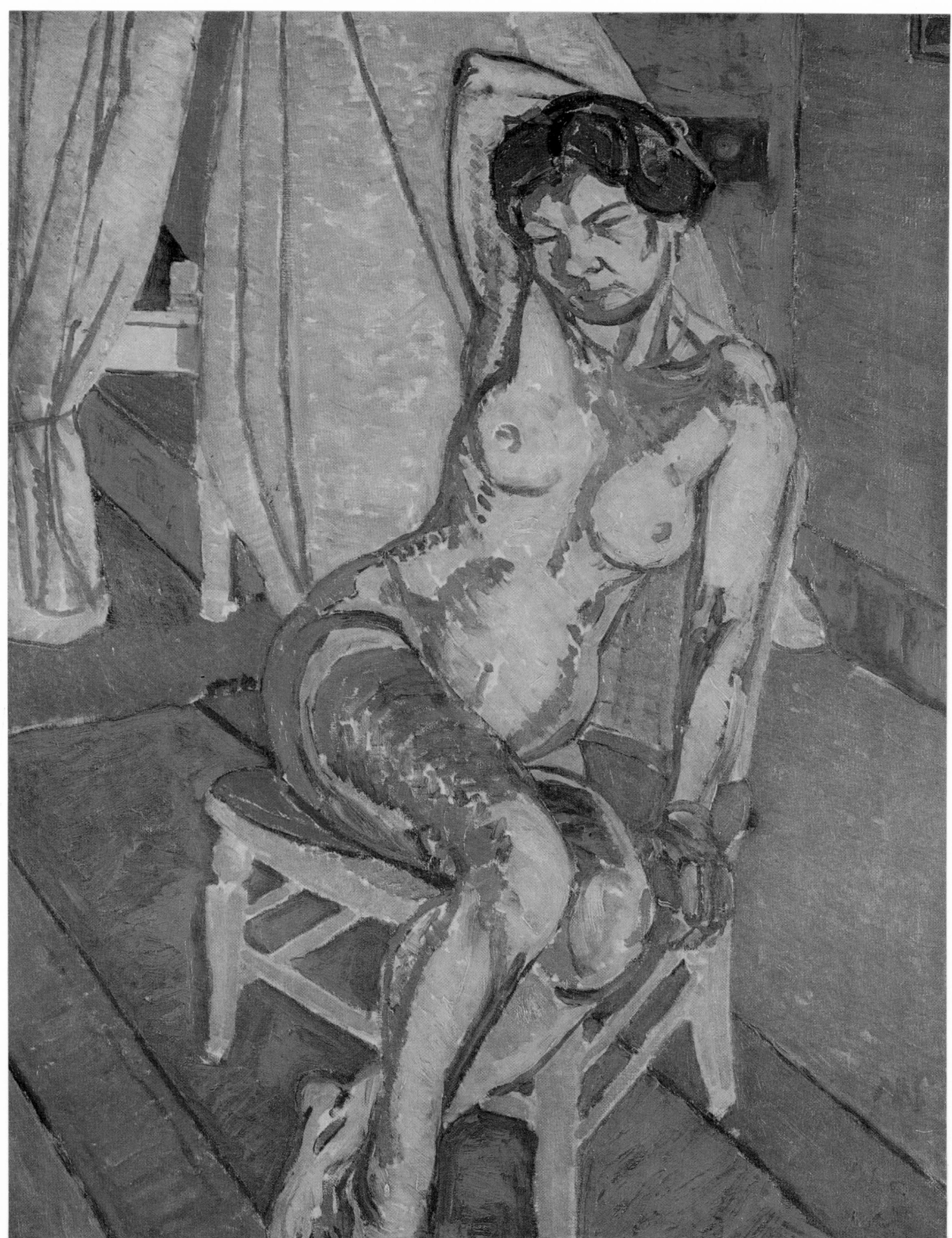

CUNO AMIET (1868–1961)

Painted in 1913
Autumn Sun
Oil on canvas, 28 3/4 × 23 5/8"
Kunstmuseum, Winterthur, Switzerland

When the Swiss painter Amiet renewed his relations with Paris by regularly taking part in the Salon des Indépendants from 1907 on—which perhaps gave him the opportunity to know the work of the Fauves—his past had already prepared him for the encounter. From a distance, on his farm at Oschwand where he was to live until his death, he easily kept abreast of them, sharing the same sentiments and technique, as many of his paintings, including this one, show.

Born at Soleure on March 28, 1868, and thus a year older than Matisse, he reaches maturity much more rapidly. He leaves school early, receives the advice of Frank Buchser, and then enrolls at the Munich Academy, where he makes friends with Giovanni Giacometti, whom he persuades to go with him to Paris the following year, where he enters the Académie Julian. From 1888 to 1892 he works closely with the Nabis, but, attracted by Gauguin's example, he finally decides to spend a year, from 1892 to 1893, at Pont-Aven, where he paints and holds discussions with Séguin and O'Connor.

When he returns to his native country, it takes him a long time to assimilate fully all that he has acquired, to fight against the often depressing solitude, and to free himself, through this invigorating contact with nature, from the profound imprint left by the Nabis, mannered stylization. His natural exuberance prevails and allows him, in the early years of the century, progressively to achieve a freer, more impetuous touch, a palette charged with pure colors, and a real quickening of his whole being that comes to fulfillment almost at the very moment of the birth of Fauvism.

This powerful current that henceforth carries him along is so manifest that, on the occasion of an exhibition at the Arnold Gallery in Dresden in 1906, he is officially accepted by the founders of Die Brücke. But his adherence to the group is only temporary, because of his wish to be independent, and because his approach to painting is fundamentally different. He has never aspired to anything but a paean of life, whose rich "enchantments"— to use a word with which he himself entitled one of his large panels—he rediscovers daily.

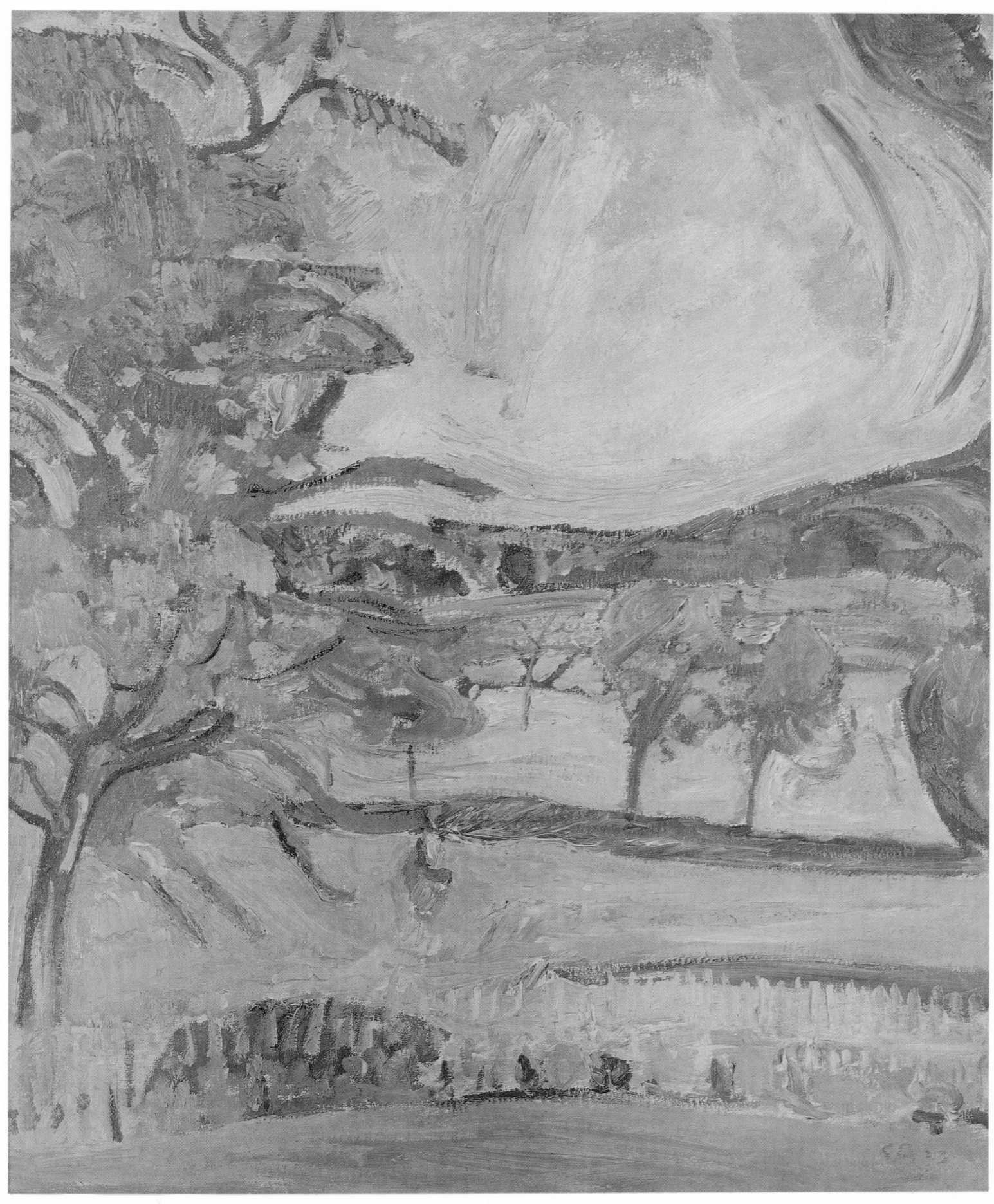

PIET MONDRIAN (1872–1944)

Painted about 1909
Portrait
Oil on canvas, 22 × 17″
Collection Hannema-De Stuers, Kasteel "Het Nyenhuis," Heino, The Netherlands

The mention of Fauvism in connection with Mondrian is not only interesting in terms of a chance phenomenon that demonstrates the almost immediate diffusion of the movement outside France, but it also recalls the importance of this stage in the artist's development before he embarked on his major creations.

Mondrian was born at Amersfoot in 1872, and began his career as a drawing teacher at Winterswijk, submitting himself, after completing five years of study at the Amsterdam Academy, to a traditional style of painting to which he finally was able to give greater flexibility. Toward 1904, in the midst of the rather monotonous and impecunious existence that he had quietly accepted, he first glimpsed the possibility of a more expressive use of color. As evidenced by *Evening Landscape*, saturated with blue and freely treated, here in Brabant where he is now working he seems to be thinking of Van Gogh, whose works he has recently admired at an exhibition in Amsterdam.

It is not until 1906, however, that he experiences a real awakening. In that year the enthusiastic talk of his friends Jan Toorop and particularly Jan Sluyters, just back from Paris, the Amsterdam exhibition of the works of Sluyters, who has already turned to Fauvism, and Van Dongen's paintings displayed in Rotterdam all combine to overthrow his habits and fire him with a desire for change, to which he yields in 1907 on seeing the new exhibition in Amsterdam of works by Van Dongen, Sluyters, and Van Rees, the last a resident of Paris since 1904.

Color progressively invades his canvases in long, bold sweeps that free him from his excessive concern with realism. A feeling of confidence and optimism begins to reign in his work, which he strives to deepen and refine.

More unusual in theme and restrained in color, this portrait shows the same deliberate attempt, but carried out with a rare vigor of touch to achieve a better distribution and balance of flat areas. It shortly precedes his first rhythmical experiments with surfaces, which he carries forward in 1910 in his *Dunes* series, and where, without letting himself be drawn into the Luminism professed by most of his friends, he achieves similar but more rigorous effects while concentrating on the need for condensation and simplicity that he already considers to be a cardinal artistic criterion.

The maturity he slowly acquires, partly through the example of the Fauves, will enable him, on his arrival in Paris in 1912, to commit himself fully to a more stringent course, beginning this time with the Cubist decomposition of apparent forms.

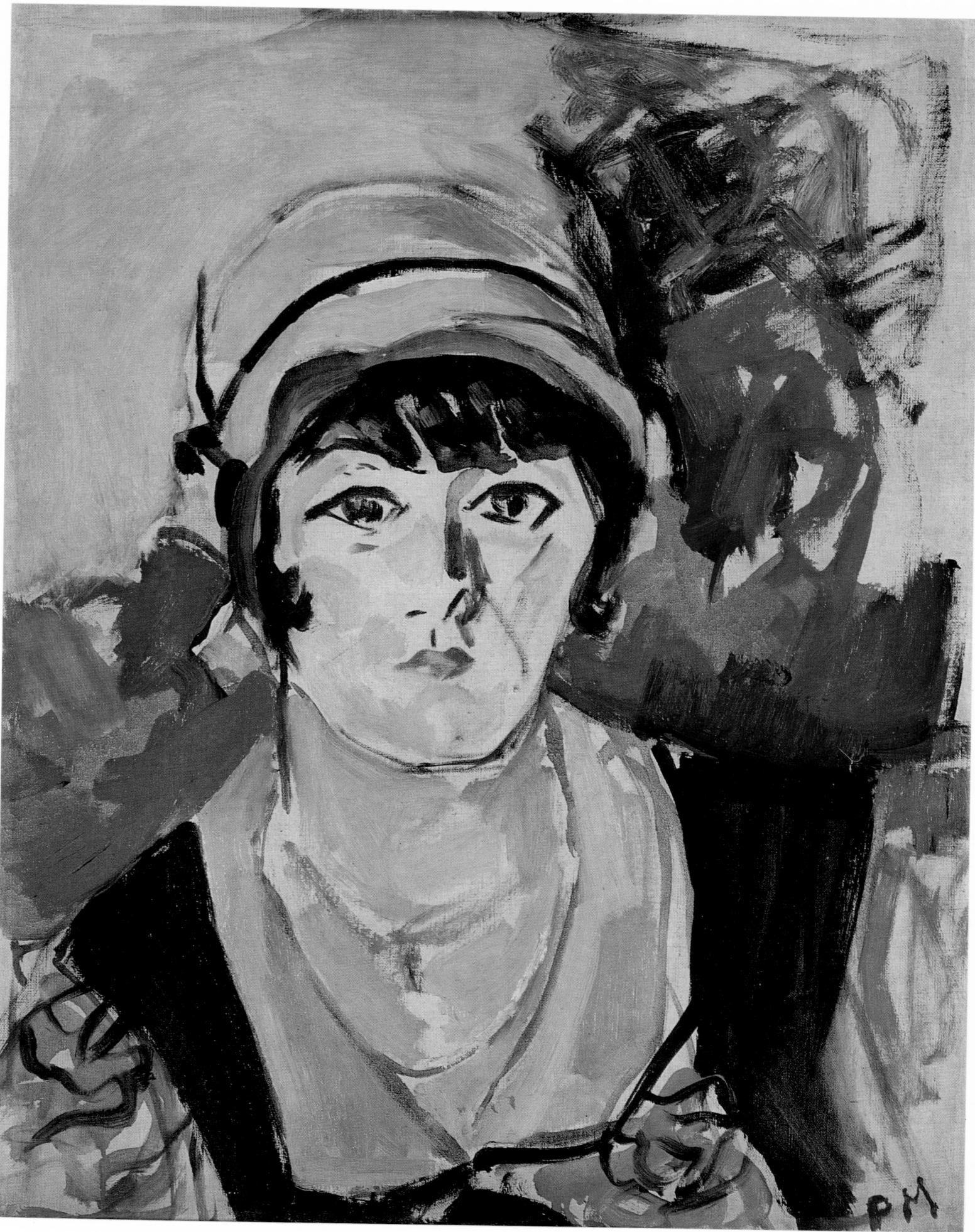

RAYNAL, MAURICE. *History of Modern Painting*. Geneva: Skira, 1950.

SALMON, ANDRÉ. *La Jeune Peinture française*. Paris: Société des Trente, 1912.

SCHMIDT, P. F. *Geschichte der modernen Malerei*. Stuttgart: W. Kohlhammer, 1961.

WILENSKI, R. H. *Modern French Painters*. New York: Harcourt Brace and World, 1963.

ZERVOS, CHRISTIAN. *Histoire de l'art contemporain*. Paris: Cahiers d'Art, 1938.

MONOGRAPHS

BRAQUE

GIEURE, MAURICE. *Georges Braque*. New York: Universe Books, 1956.

LEYMARIE, JEAN. *Braque: Biographical and Critical Study*. Geneva: Skira, 1961.

MULLINS, EDWIN. *The Art of Georges Braque*. New York: Abrams, 1968.

DERAIN

DIEHL, GASTON. *Derain*. New York: Crown, 1964.

HILAIRE, GEORGES. *Derain*. Geneva: P. Cailler, 1959.

SUTTON, DENYS. *André Derain*. London: Phaidon Press, 1959.

DUFY

COGNIAT, RAYMOND. *Raoul Dufy*. New York: Crown, 1962.

LASSAIGNE, JACQUES. *Dufy: Biographical and Critical Study*. Geneva: Skira, 1954.

WERNER, ALFRED. *Dufy*. New York: Abrams, 1970.

FRIESZ

GAUTHIER, MAXIMILIEN. *Othon Friesz*. Geneva: P. Cailler, 1957.

JAWLENSKY

WEILER, CLEMENS. *Alexej von Jawlensky*. Cologne: M. DuMont Schauberg, 1959.

KANDINSKY

GROHMANN, WILL. *Kandinsky: Life and Work*. New York: Abrams, 1958.

VOLBOUT, P. *Kandinsky*. Paris: F. Hazan, 1963.

MANGUIN

CABANNE, PIERRE. *Henri Manguin*. Neuchâtel: Editions Ides et Calendes, 1964.

MARQUET

DAULTE, F. and MARQUET, MARCELLE. *Marquet*. Lausanne: Editions Spes, 1953.

JOURDAIN, F. *Marquet*. Paris: Editions Cercle d'Art, 1959.

MATISSE

BARR, ALFRED H., JR. *Matisse: His Art and His Public*. New York: The Museum of Modern Art, 1951.

DIEHL, GASTON. *Henri Matisse*. Paris: P. Tisné, 1954.

ELSEN, ALBERT. *The Sculpture of Henri Matisse*. New York: Abrams, 1971.

GUICHARD-MEILI, JEAN. *Matisse*. New York: Praeger, 1967.

MONDRIAN

JAFFÉ, HANS L. C. *Mondrian*. New York: Abrams, 1970.

SEUPHOR, MICHEL. *Piet Mondrian: Life and Work*. New York: Abrams, 1956.

PURRMANN

GÖPEL, B. and E. *Leben und Meinungen des Malers Hans Purrmann*. Wiesbaden: Limes Verlag, 1961.

SCHMIDT-ROTTLUFF

GROHMANN, WILL. *Karl Schmidt-Rottluff*. Stuttgart: W. Kohlhammer, 1956.

SMITH

HALLIDAY, F., HENDY, P., and RUSSELL, J. *Matthew Smith*. London: G. Allen, 1962.

VALTAT

COGNIAT, RAYMOND. *Louis Valtat*. Neuchâtel: Editions Ides et Calendes, 1963.

VAN DONGEN

CHAUMEIL, LOUIS. *Van Dongen: L'Homme et l'artiste; la vie et l'oeuvre*. Geneva: P. Cailler, 1967.

DIEHL, GASTON. *Van Dongen*. New York: Crown, 1969.

VLAMINCK

SAUVAGE, MARCEL. *Vlaminck: Sa Vie et son message*. Geneva: P. Cailler, 1956.

SELZ, JEAN. *Vlaminck*. New York: Crown, 1963.

WOUTERS

AVERMAETE, ROGER. *Rik Wouters*. Brussels: Editions l'Arcade, 1962.

INDEX

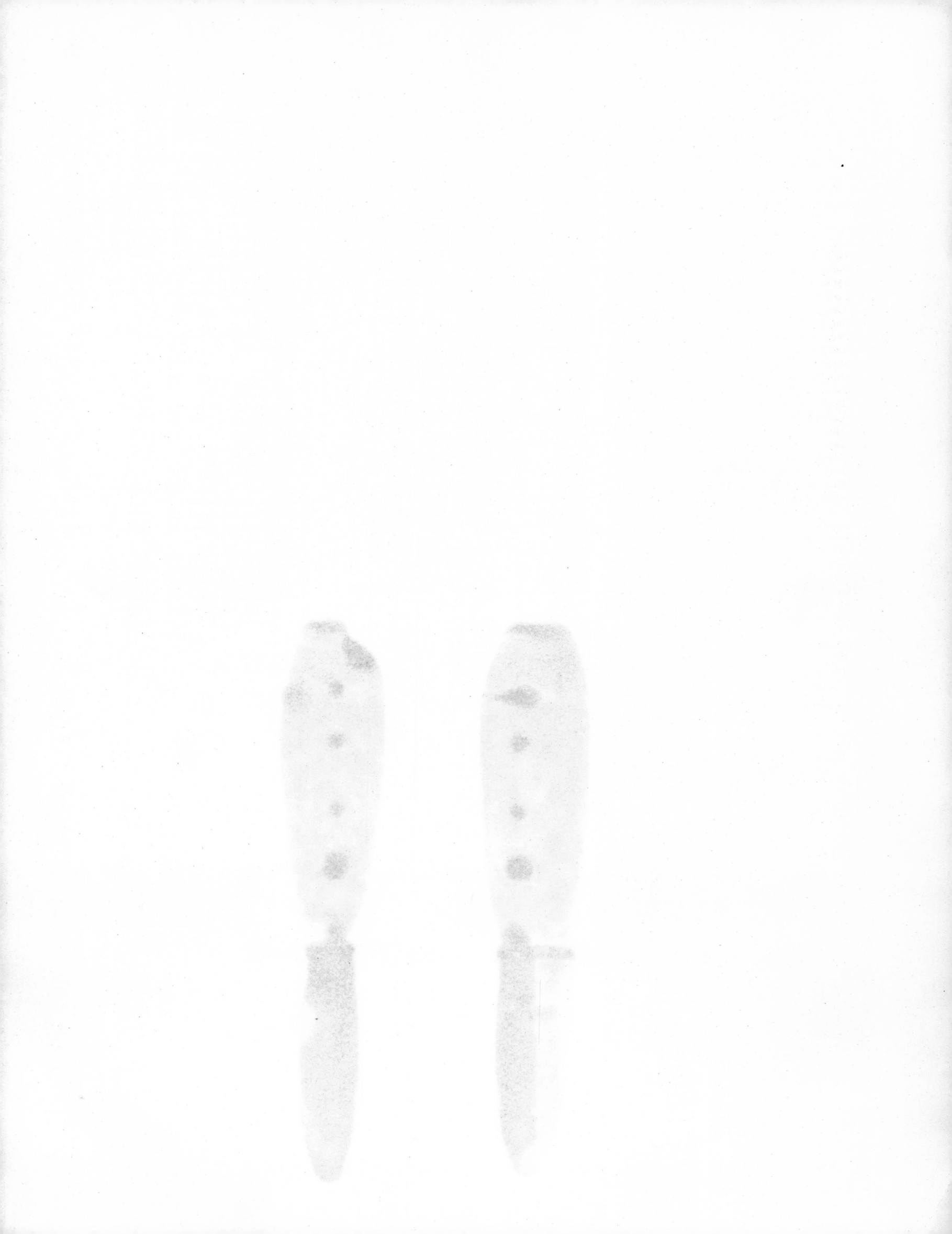